FRAGMENTATION
the Condition, the Cause, the

CURE

by
Craig Jensen

Published by
Executive Software International, Inc.
701 North Brand Boulevard
P.O. Box 29077
Glendale, California 91209-9077

Library of Congress Cataloging-in-Publication Data

Jensen, Craig
93-073968/Craig Jensen. – 1st ed.
p. cm.
1. Jensen, Craig. 2. Computers – disks – fragmentation

ISBN 0-9640049-0-9

Printed in the United States of America
March 1994
FIRST EDITION

Grateful acknowledgement is made to
L. Ron Hubbard Library for permission
to reproduce selections from the
copyrighted works of L. Ron Hubbard.

TABLE OF CONTENTS

TABLE OF DIAGRAMS

TABLE OF EXAMPLES

TABLE OF TABLES

TABLE OF GRAPHS

ACKNOWLEDGEMENTS

The author would like to thank the following people for their contributions to the creation of this book. The quality of the final product owes much to their assistance. Responsibility for any errors is mine alone.

Howard Butler
Rick Cadruvi
Derek De Vette
Mary Duran
John Eberhard
Peter Ford
Henning Heldt
Mary Heldt
Sally Jensen
Caroline Kleinschmidt
Vaughn McMillan
Gary Quan
Gary Stoermer
Keith Walls
Barry Watson
Mandy Wildman

DEDICATION

This book is dedicated to the VAX and Alpha AXP[1] System Managers of the world. I was a System Manager for many years and I know that the System Manager is in the difficult position of being fully responsible for much of an organization's most valuable, often irreplaceable information. At the same time, he or she often has relatively little authority to make the critical decisions that must be made to preserve and even to utilize those records.

I also realize that the System Manager's job is often a thankless one. While users and even management are quick to condemn a System Manager for computer problems, it is a rare day indeed when someone comes up to the System Manager and says, "Hey! The computer's performing pretty well today. Nice work!" (I know, dream on.)

I believe that System Managers are good people and well-intentioned. I believe that they really want to provide great service to their users and to management. I believe that they try their best to do their job within the limitations of too little budget and too little authority. And I believe that they really want to learn everything they can about their systems and be the best System Managers they can be. If they could dance their fingers over the keyboard and make that machine do magic, you can be very sure they would do so.

It is to these System Managers that this book is dedicated. I hope you like it. I hope you learn something from it that helps you achieve your goals.

---

[1] For the sake of brevity, when the term "System Manager" is used in this book, it will refer to a manager of either Digital's VAX or its Alpha AXP computer system.

DEDICATION

PREFACE

Who Should Read This Book?

This book is intended for managers of Digital's VAX and Alpha AXP computer systems. VAX is the brand name of a computer system made by Digital Equipment Corporation of Maynard, Massachusetts. The various models of the VAX computer range in capacity from a desktop workstation to a company-wide mainframe. Alpha AXP is the brand name of another computer system made by Digital which uses the same operating system as the VAX. A System Manager is the person who is in charge of or responsible for such a computer system - its maintenance, operation and management. Put bluntly, the System Manager is the person who gets in trouble when the computer goes down[2] or isn't working as well as it should.

Naturally, for this book to be of any use to you at all, you have to have a VAX or Alpha AXP computer system or at least be planning to have one in the future. That VAX or Alpha AXP has to have disks[3], since the problems we will discuss occur only on disks. The computer has to be turned on, not shut down for use as a doorstop somewhere, and it has to be at least occasionally used. If you don't use it, you won't get the fragmentation[4] disease and you wouldn't care if you did.

This computer of yours has to be running the VMS (or OpenVMS[5]) operating system. Other computers and other operating systems suffer from fragmentation too, but this book is specifically written with the OpenVMS system in mind. The fragmentation problem is so important, and so inherent in the OpenVMS system, it would be a mistake to try and generalize this discussion into something applicable to any computer or operating system.

VAX and Alpha AXP System Managers, this book is for you!

System Managers run into a lot of problems keeping their users happy with the performance of the computer system. One problem that haunts virtually every System Manager, and literally plagues those with more than a few disk drives[6] to care for, is *fragmentation. Fragmentation,* more fully defined in a later chapter, is a sort of disease that affects computer systems, causing them to slow down and perform badly, somewhat like an arthritic old man who these days just can't get around quite as well as he used to. The problem is so widespread and so damaging and, surprisingly, so poorly understood, that an entire book on the subject is warranted.

---

2 **goes down:** Computer industry slang for "stops running".

3 For a definition of **disk**, see page 1.

4 **fragmentation** is defined on page xvi.

5 **VMS,** or **VAX/VMS** is the name of the operating system most commonly used on VAX computers. However, in 1993 Digital officially changed the name to **OpenVMS**. The two names are synonymous, and for the purposes of this book, we will use the term "OpenVMS."

6 **disk drive:** This term is defined in Chapter 1, as are the other technical terms used in the preface and introduction. If you are unfamiliar with them, see the Glossary in the back of this book.

So, who should read this book?

Any VAX or Alpha AXP System Manager who is interested in fragmentation.

What This Book Can Do For You

- Help you recognize whether there is a fragmentation problem.
- Show you how to find fragmentation.
- Show you how to know it when you see it.
- Help you see where it's coming from.
- Help you understand it and what it is doing to your system.
- Make it easy and simple to understand and deal with.
- Help you handle it.
- Show you what changes have to be made to handle it and prevent it.
- Tell you what equipment and tools you must have to handle it.
- Help you predict fragmentation problems and solutions.
- Get you started.
- Get you handling fragmentation.
- Help you rid your system of fragmentation forever.
- Show you how to spot and correct errors in fragmentation handling.
- Give you the ability to deal with fragmentation routinely.
- Show you how to keep fragmentation handled all the time.
- Show you how to handle fragmentation without *doing* anything.
- Show you how to prevent fragmentation from ever coming back.
- Help you improve conditions in the VAX or Alpha AXP management area.

- Show you the way to a life without fragmentation.
- Help you be more in control of your computer system.

INTRODUCTION

To discuss fragmentation intelligently, it is first necessary to establish what we mean when we use the word *computer.* The simple definition of *computer* is:

> An electronic machine for making calculations, storing and analyzing information fed into it, and controlling machinery automatically.[7]

There is more to it than that, however. It is important to note as well that a computer does not think, that a computer has speed and power out of proportion to anything else in our day-to-day lives, and that a computer can be used to "enormously increase the production and income of an area." I really like the viewpoint expressed by this last quotation, as it tends to perk up the ears and interest people in the real potential of this marvelous machine. The quote is from an essay entitled *What is a Computer?* by L. Ron Hubbard, which is included in full in Appendix A.

The computers with which we are specifically concerned are those which run on the OpenVMS operating system, namely the VAX and the Alpha AXP.

VAX is defined as:

> A computer made by Digital Equipment Corporation. VAX is a high-performance, multiprogramming[8] computer system based on a 32-bit[9] architecture.[10] VAX stands for Virtual Address[11] eXtension.[12]

Alpha AXP is defined as:

> A computer made by Digital Equipment Corporation. Alpha AXP is a RISC-based[13] computer that uses a few simple, fast instructions in order to facilitate faster processing speed.

The Alpha AXP computer was introduced by Digital in November 1992. Although Alpha AXP processors use different sets of instructions than VAX processors, Digital developed a translation of the OpenVMS operating system for the new Alpha AXP computers. For reasons which will become clear later on in this book, this had the effect of transferring the very problem about which this book is written from the VAX computer to the Alpha AXP computer; hence our discussion applies equally to both computer systems.

---

7 *Oxford American Dictionary.*

8 **multiprogramming:** The capability of running two or more programs at the same time without interference.

9 **bit:** See the definition on page 3.

10 **32-bit architecture:** The capability of processing 32 bits of information simultaneously in each cycle of the computer. Like a 32-lane highway, the path on which data flows through the computer carries 32 bits of data at once.

11 **virtual address:** The address of a location in a conceptual memory space that may or may not correspond to a location in the computer's physical memory, but which is translated by the computer in such a way as to make it appear that it does so correspond.

12 This definition of *VAX* is from *The Digital Dictionary*, Second Edition, Digital Press, Bedford, Massachusetts, 1986.

13 **RISC:** *R*educed *I*nstruction *S*et *C*omputer. By using simple sets of instructions, processing speed can be increased considerably.

Since we are going to be talking a lot about disks, let's agree on what a disk is. The maker of both the VAX and Alpha AXP computers, Digital Equipment Corporation, defines *disk* as:

> A thin, round plate with a magnetic surface coating on which data can be stored by magnetic recording.[14]

Disks come in many different sizes and architectures.[15] And, even though we will limit our discussion to fixed (hard, not floppy) disks, there are still a lot of sizes and architectures to consider. Disk architecture is so fundamental to a discussion of fragmentation that an entire chapter (the first) is devoted to it. The chapter consists mostly of definitions of terms, but it contains a lot of pictures and is worth reviewing even if you are already familiar with basic disk concepts.

The purpose of a disk is to store information. This information, or data, is said to be stored in "files."

In computer terminology, any collection of data that is treated as a single unit on a storage medium (such as a disk) is referred to as a "file." Not unlike a manila folder designed to hold sheets of paper in concept, computer files are stored on a disk, with the disk acting as a filing cabinet.

A file can be accessed (found and retrieved), modified (changed in some way) and again stored on the disk. In this way, thousands upon thousands of pieces of information can be stored on a physically small disk, much more than can be stored in a regular filing cabinet.

Now we come to the *real* question: What exactly *is* fragmentation anyway?

The word *fragmentation* means "the state of being fragmented." The word *fragment* means "a detached, isolated or incomplete part." It is derived from the Latin *fragmentum,* which in turn is derived from *frangere,* meaning "break." So *fragmentation* means that something is broken into parts that are detached, isolated or incomplete.

There are two types of fragmentation with which we are immediately concerned: file fragmentation and free space fragmentation. *File fragmentation* concerns computer disk files that are not whole but rather are broken into scattered parts, while *free space fragmentation* means that the empty space on a disk is broken into scattered parts rather than being collected all in one big empty space. File fragmentation causes problems with accessing data stored in computer disk files, while free space fragmentation causes problems creating new data files or extending (adding to) old ones.

---

[14] *The Digital Dictionary*, Second Edition, Digital Press, Bedford, Massachusetts, 1986.
[15] **architecture:** Design, character or style.

In Figure 1, a file consisting of ten records is shown with all ten records contiguous (immediately adjacent to each other) and again with the records scattered around in three different groups. The first arrangement is not fragmented. The second arrangement is fragmented.

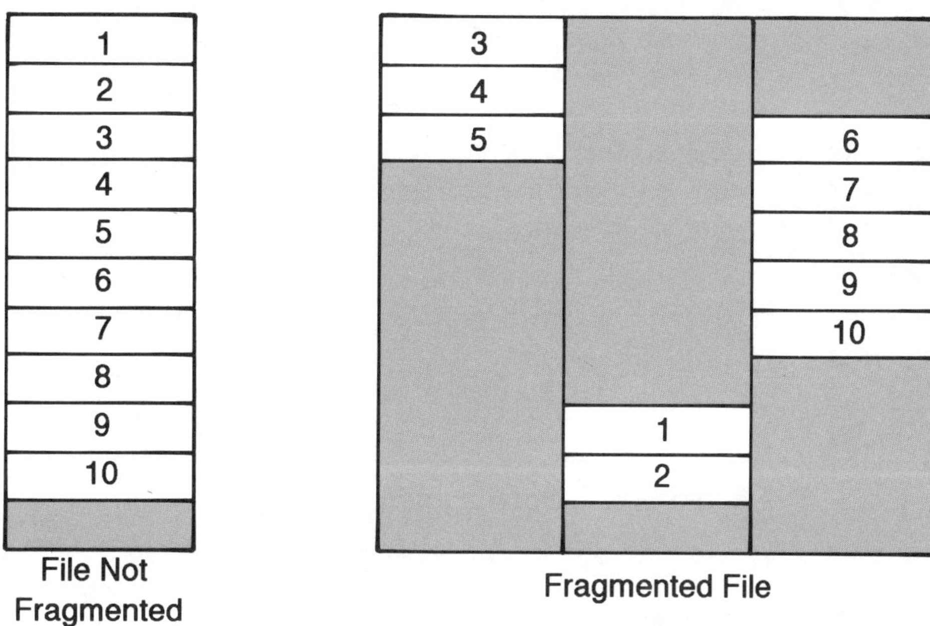

Figure 1 File Fragmentation

In Figure 2, three files are arranged contiguously and again with the files scattered around in three different places. In the first arrangement, the free space is not fragmented; it is consolidated into one large area. In the second arrangement, the free space is fragmented.

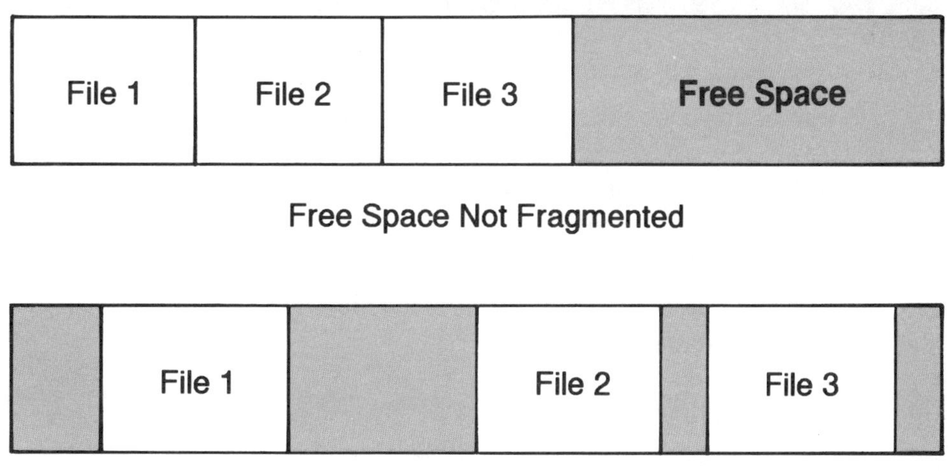

Figure 2 Free Space Fragmentation

Taken together, we refer to the two types of fragmentation as *disk fragmentation*. It is important to note that, when talking about fragmentation, we are talking about the file as a container for data and not about the contents (data) of the file itself. People sometimes use the word *fragmentation* to describe the condition of a file which has its records (contents) scattered about within the file, separated by numerous small gaps. This type of fragmentation may be a problem with the application which maintains the file; it is not inherent in the operating system or disk file structure.[16]

In Figure 3, three records are arranged first contiguously and then again with the records separated by empty record space. In the first arrangement, the record space is not fragmented; it is consolidated into one large area. In the second arrangement, the record space is fragmented.

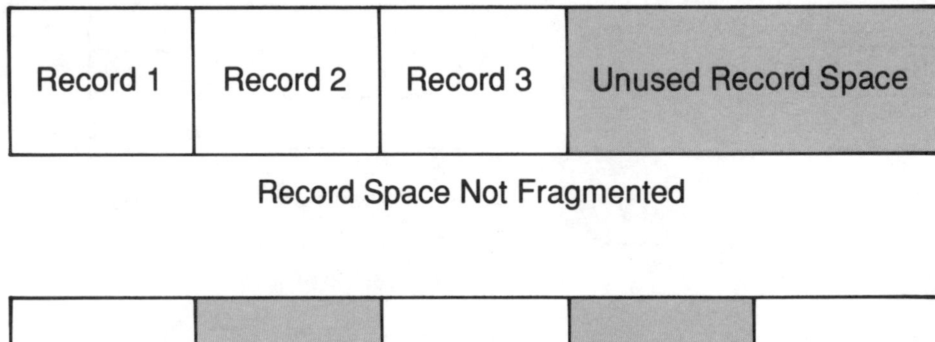

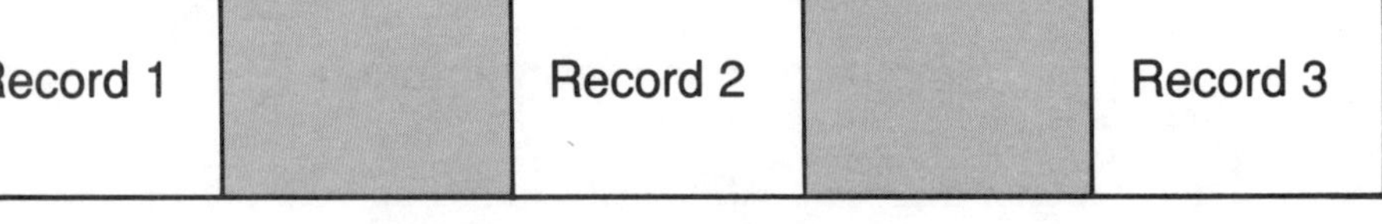

Figure 3 Record Space Fragmentation

Since record space fragmentation is the concern of applications and not of the operating system or file system, this book does not address the subject any further.

The various solutions to fragmentation are collectively referred to as *defragmentation,* meaning something that gets rid of the fragmentation problem.

This book will tell you all about fragmentation and defragmentation, and do it in a way that is clear and understandable.

The material will be presented with care taken to define technical terms. Lots of diagrams and pictures will be used and the material will be presented on a gradient, bit by bit from the simplest material to the more complex, so you do not have to be an expert in later areas to understand earlier areas. For your part, take care to look up the definitions of any words you do not understand or are uncertain of, even non-technical words. If you are unfamiliar with the physical objects discussed, arrange to look at or touch them. For

[16] **file structure:** The standard format used for arranging files on a disk.

intangibles, of which there are many in this subject, try drawing pictures of them to develop a more solid concept.

Finally, if you are having trouble in an area, go back to where you were last doing well, and check to see if there were any words you did not fully understand. If so, look up the definition in a good (not complicated) dictionary. If you do this thoroughly, you will find the material much easier to read. (This works for any subject.)[17]

The Approach

Here is the approach that will be used to present the story of fragmentation:

After explaining how a disk works, and taking a quick look at the OpenVMS file system, fragmentation will be explained in detail. Then you will learn how to tell whether your system suffers from fragmentation, and if so, how badly. We will then look at the effects of fragmentation on the VAX or Alpha AXP system – what's wrong with fragmentation? After that, we'll see what you can do about it, and how you can get your computer to take care of fragmentation by itself. This will include a view to the future, anticipating the extinction of fragmentation for OpenVMS computer systems. The final chapter is devoted to the ultimate solution to the fragmentation problem. Along the way, we will view how this problem came about, why it wasn't detected and prevented early on, Digital's viewpoint, some of the controversy over defragmentation, and some of my personal opinions on the whole subject.

Appendices are included with fill-in-the-blanks solutions for organizational problems that get in the way of solving the fragmentation problem: how to determine the cost of fragmentation, how to justify the cost of a solution and how to get your company to agree to spend the money you need to handle it.

The single most important thing to keep in mind is that *a computer is used to get work done,* so fragmentation is not a problem unless it interferes with doing useful work. Similarly, any solution must be one which allows us to get more useful work done with our computer system.

Actually, fragmentation *does* interfere with our use of the computer to do work. It slows things down – little by little, more and more. If left unhandled for a year or more, it can bring any computer running the OpenVMS operating system close to a complete standstill. I have personally experienced a VAX with a system disk[18] so badly fragmented it took half an hour just to log in to a user account! After defragmenting, it took only a few seconds to log in – good as new.

---

[17] The concept of defining misunderstood words is more fully explained in *The Basic Study Manual,* by L. Ron Hubbard, Chapter Two: The Barriers to Study. Bridge Publications, Los Angeles, 1990.

[18] **system disk:** That disk from which the operating system is loaded into memory when the computer is booted up.

Now let's start at the beginning and unravel the whole story of fragmentation.

CHAPTER 1

HOW A DISK WORKS

You can skip this chapter if you already know all about disks. However, you need to understand disks well to really understand fragmentation. The rest of this book depends heavily upon the terms and concepts presented in this chapter. Rather than skipping this chapter altogether, I recommend that the experienced System Manager skim it or read it quickly, if only to ensure that we agree on all the essential terminology.

There are many different kinds of disks. We can omit some of them from discussion. Read-Only disks, for example, such as CD-ROM,[19] cannot become fragmented after manufacture and, if they are already fragmented when created, there is nothing you can do about it. They are unchangeable. RAM[20] disks and semiconductor disks are really memory,[21] not disks, though they appear as disks to the computer system. While it is theoretically possible for such disks to become fragmented, little additional overhead is caused by their fragmentation, since there are no moving parts to cause delays finding data in "distant" parts of the disk. Floppy disks are usually too small to suffer from fragmentation and they are not ordinarily used for on-line[22] storage. They are typically used once to store a small amount of data and then stored in a box on a shelf somewhere. Such usage does not suffer from the effects of fragmentation.

The disks with which we will concern ourselves are hard (not floppy) disks used for storing frequently-accessed information in a computer. In an OpenVMS system, the disk is an essential, central part of the computer itself. Without a hard disk, there could be no *Virtual Memory System,* which is the VAX operating system itself.

Throughout this book, when the word *disk* is used, the above is the type of disk being referred to.

Now let's take a look at the basic parts of a disk and the terminology that describes them:

---

19 **CD-ROM:** *C*ompact *D*isc *R*ead *O*nly *M*emory. A disk identical in form to audio CDs.

20 **RAM:** *R*andom *A*ccess *M*emory. Storage which can be accessed directly, without having to search through other storage locations.

21 **memory:** A part of the computer in which data can be stored and retrieved rapidly (in about one millionth of a second).

22 **on-line:** Directly connected to the computer system and available for use. The opposite, **off-line**, means that the object referred to is either not directly connected to the computer system or is otherwise inaccessible.

The Physical Parts Of A Disk

A disk looks like this, conceptually:

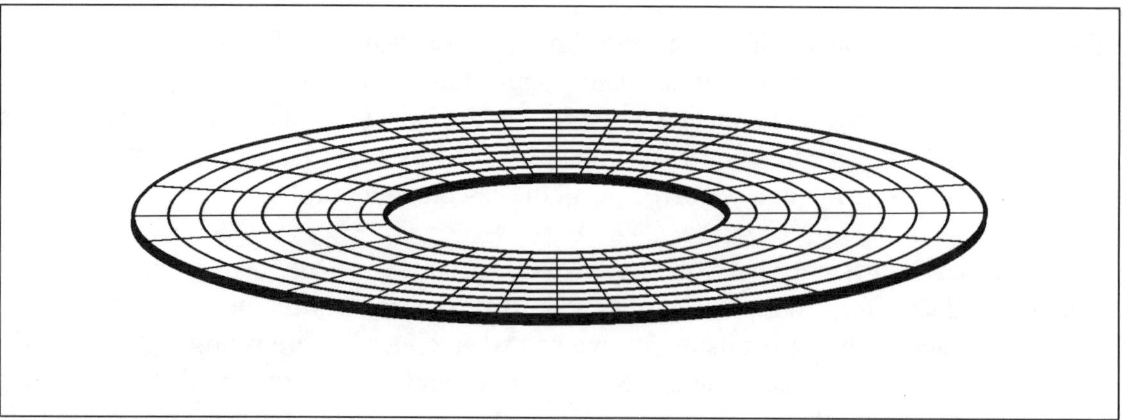

Figure 1-1 A Disk

Magnetic Surface

Any disk has, as a critical part, a *surface* on which to record data. That surface is usually *magnetic,* meaning that it is capable of storing a small amount of magnetism. Perhaps the most remarkable aspect of disk technology is the number of distinct amounts of magnetism that can be stored on a single surface of a disk. At the time of this writing, commercially available disks selling for a few hundred dollars are capable of storing hundreds of millions of separate, distinguishable bits of information on each square inch of surface. These numbers have been multiplying so fast for so long that I dare not even speculate on the future of disk storage capacities.

The surface of a disk is shaped like a platter, similar to a phonograph record.

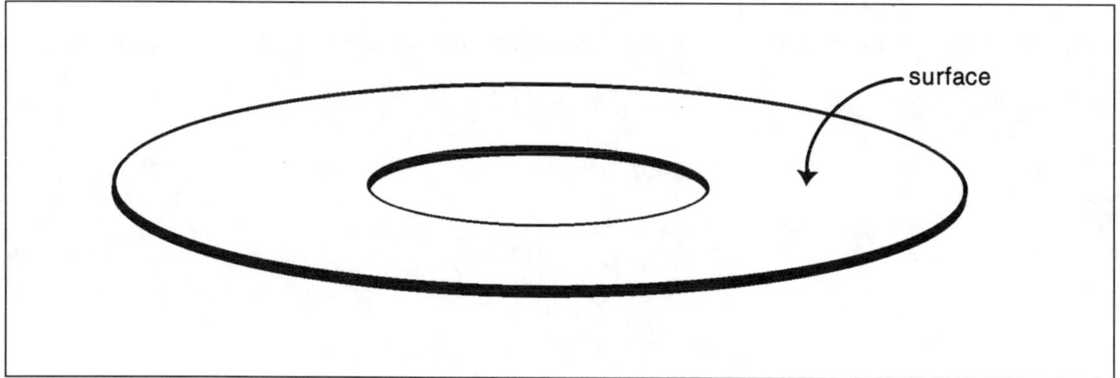

Figure 1-2 Disk Surface

Bits

Each single magnetic entity is used by the computer as a binary symbol. *Binary* means "having two and only two possible states" such as *on* or *off, true* or *false,* and so on. Each such entity is called a *bit,* which is short for *bi*nary digi*t.* Binary digits are represented in written communication as zeros and ones. The use of numbers to represent bits, however, is only a convenience and does not mean that bits have anything to do with mathematics. They do not. Bits are in the realm of logic, which is a matter of reasoning and not arithmetic calculation.

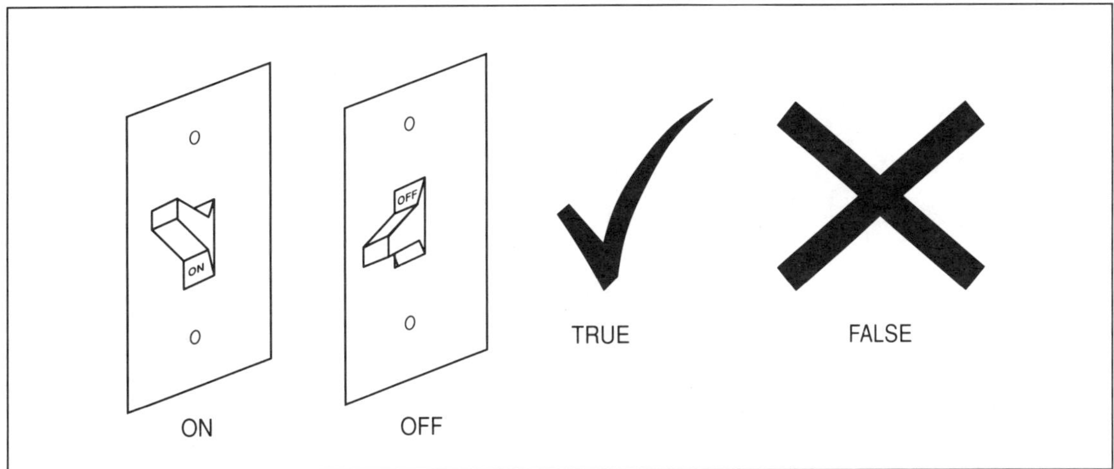

Figure 1-3 Bit

Byte

When eight bits are considered together, they are referred to as a *byte.* A single eight-bit byte is the amount of computer storage typically used to store a single letter of the alphabet or other symbol of human communication. The word *animal* could thus be stored in six bytes of computer storage.

The byte is so common to computers that disks are referred to in terms of how many millions of bytes can be stored on them. Disks that can hold hundreds or even thousands of millions of bytes are commonplace today.

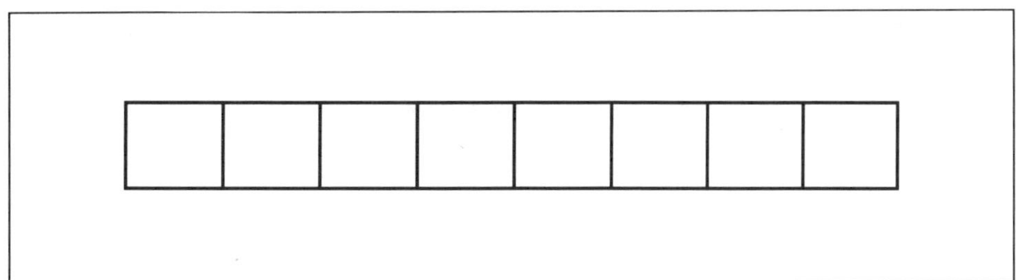

Figure 1-4 Byte

Block, Sector

The surface of a disk is divided into sections. This sectioning is not a physical marking on the surface, but rather it is just an idea that the disk is so divided. These sections are called *sectors* or *blocks*. The term *sector* is more common to personal computers and VAX or Alpha AXP hardware, while *block* is common OpenVMS terminology. In OpenVMS, a block is a collection of 512 bytes. OpenVMS disks are formatted[23] into blocks of 512 bytes each. With a disk so formatted, it is common to talk about *blocks* of disk capacity. A 456 megabyte[24] disk, for example, could also be said to have a capacity of about 890,000 blocks (890,000 x 512 = about 456 MB).

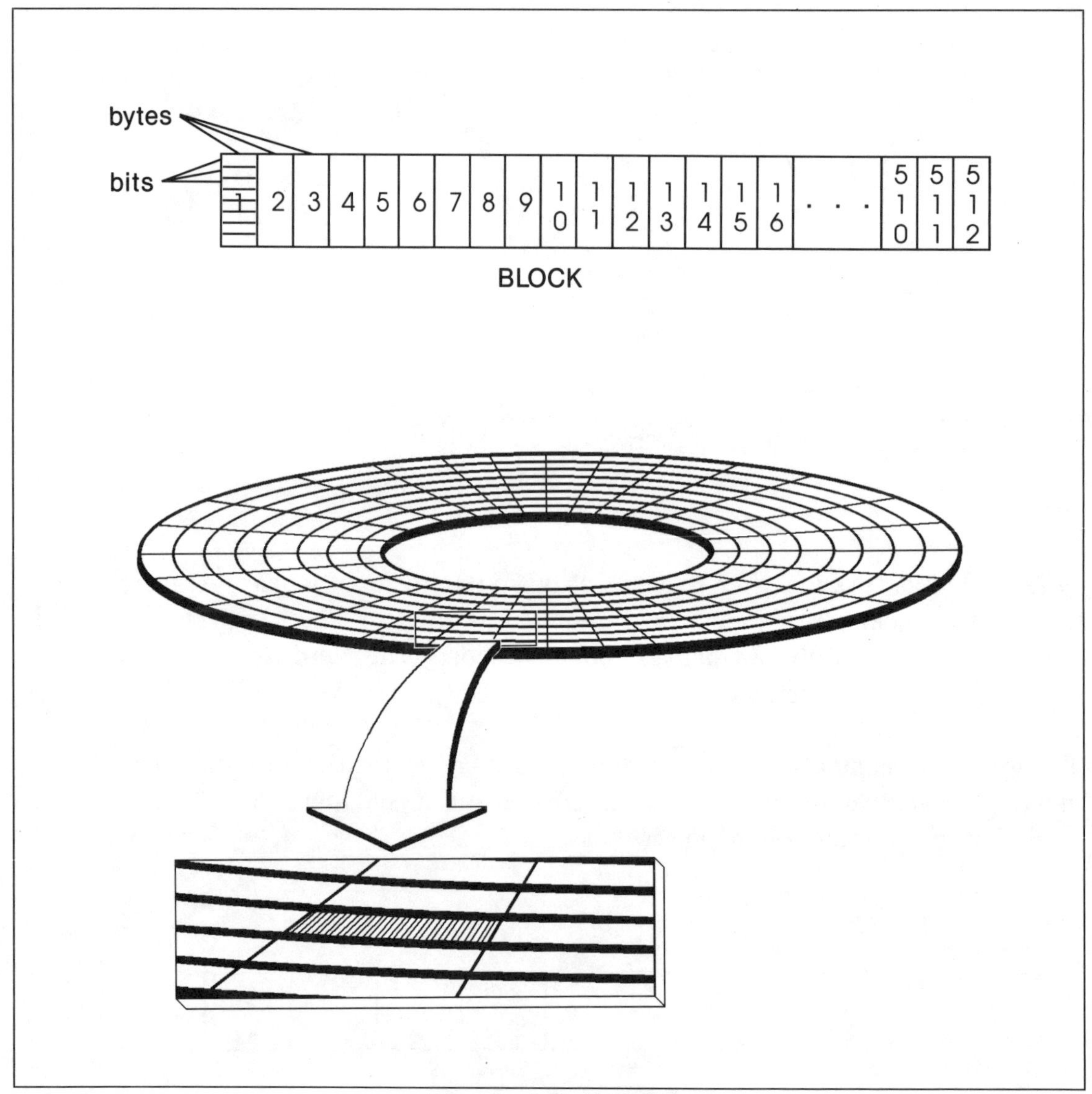

Figure 1-5 Block

[23] The term **formatted** is used to mean that the disk has certain marks that trigger reading and writing of data in particular spots, allowing storage and retrieval of data in groups of a particular size; in this case, 512-byte blocks.
[24] **megabyte, or MB:** 1,048,576 bytes, or approximately one million bytes.

Cluster

With larger disk capacities, it is inefficient for the computer system to deal with millions of individual blocks one at a time. The operating system's map of the disk's blocks is too big to be useful unless single bits in the map can represent more than one disk block. Accordingly, disk blocks are grouped into *clusters,* which are groups of blocks read and written as a unit. In other words, a *cluster* is the minimum allocation[25] quantity for a disk. The cluster size, in terms of number of blocks per cluster, can be varied by reinitializing the disk.

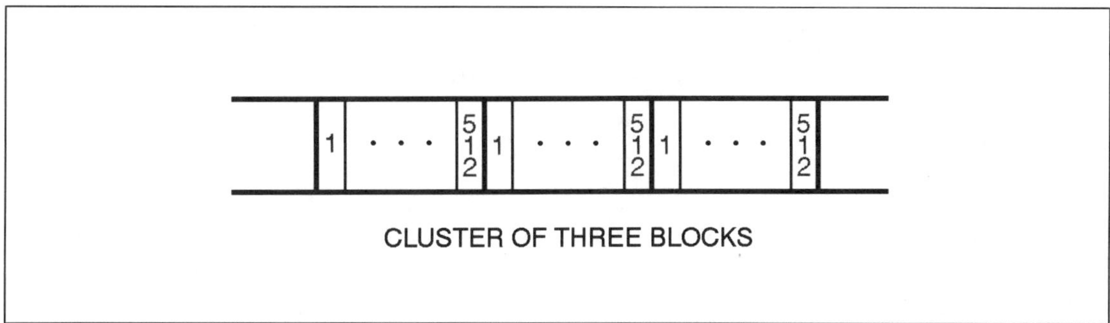

Figure 1-6 Cluster

Tracks

The blocks and clusters of storage space are arranged in groups referred to as *tracks.* A single track is one strip of disk space beginning at one point on the surface and continuing around in a circle ending at the same point. The tracks are concentric rings, not a spiral like the grooves on a phonograph record. Each surface has many tracks.

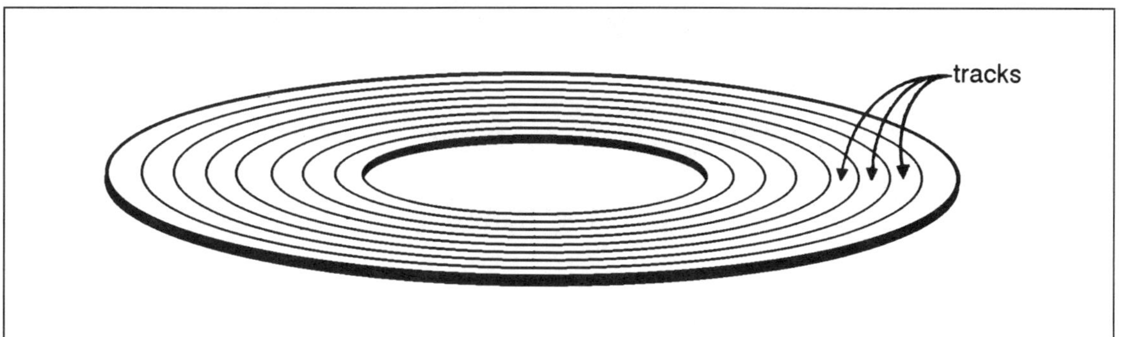

Figure 1-7 Tracks

Platters

A disk may consist of one or more platters, each of which may be recorded on both sides. The platter spins like a phonograph record on a turntable.

---

[25] Before data can be stored on the disk, space for the data must be **allocated** from whatever remains available. One cluster is the minimum number of blocks that can be allocated.

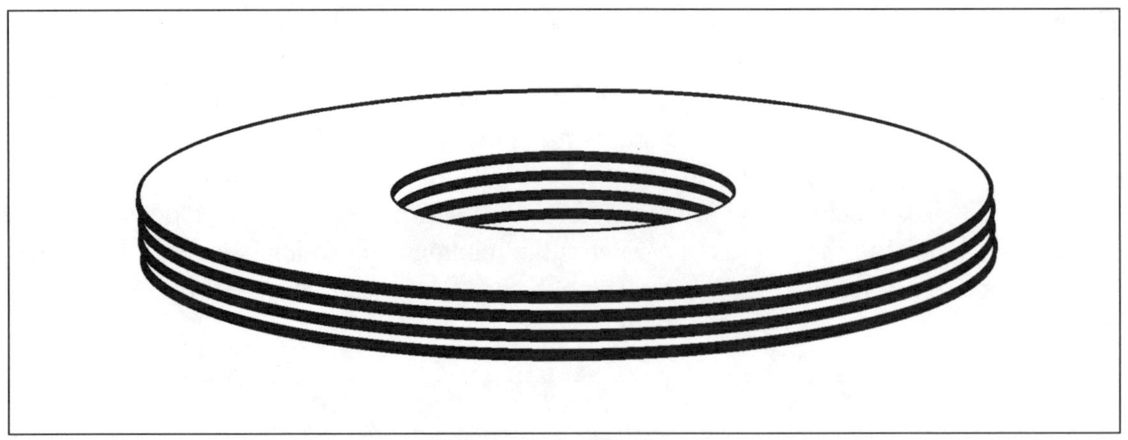

Figure 1-8 Platters

Cylinder

The tracks at the same radius on each platter, taken together, are referred to as a *cylinder*. If you visualized these tracks without any other part of the disk, they would form the shape of a hollow cylinder.

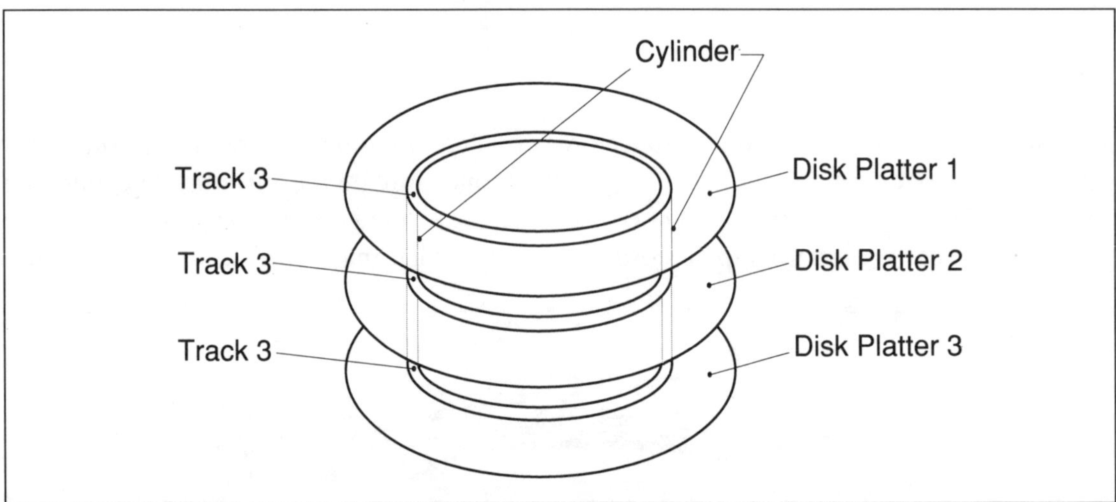

Figure 1-9 Cylinder

Head

To detect magnetic information on the recording surface, the disk has one or more *heads*. A head is a tiny magnetic device capable of reading or writing magnetic bits on the disk surface. The platter spins near the head(s), so that a single track of recorded information is continuously passing under the head, available for reading or writing. The head never touches the surface. Rather, it floats on a cushion of air so thin that a human hair or even a particle of cigarette smoke cannot pass between the head and the surface. As foreign particles that small would cause the disk to fail, such disks are sealed in air-tight containers.

While some disks have had one head hovering over each track, it is far more common to have movable heads capable of moving from track to track as needed. The movement of a head from one track to another is called a *seek*. This term will be important when we are talking about disk speeds. The time it takes for a head to seek is one of the most critical factors in determining the speed of a disk.

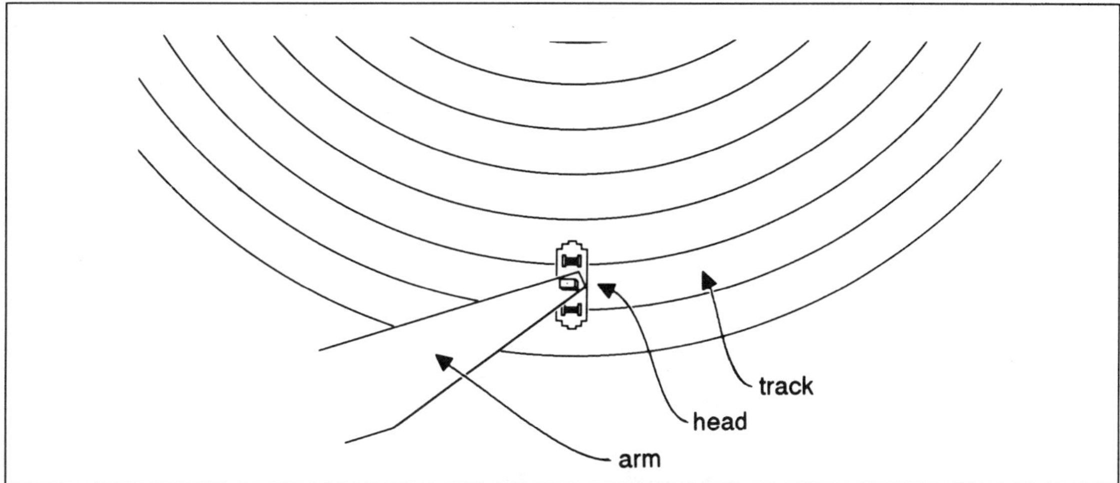

Figure 1-10 Head

Arms

Disk heads are mounted on *arms* that hold the heads close to the platter surface at precisely the right point to read or write data. There may be one arm for each head, but on multiple-platter disks a single arm may support two heads – one for the platter above the arm and one for the platter below. Some disks mount *all* the heads on a group of arms that move in unison. Imagine your spread fingers moving between the fanned pages of a book and you will get the idea of multiple disk arms moving together in and out of disk platters.

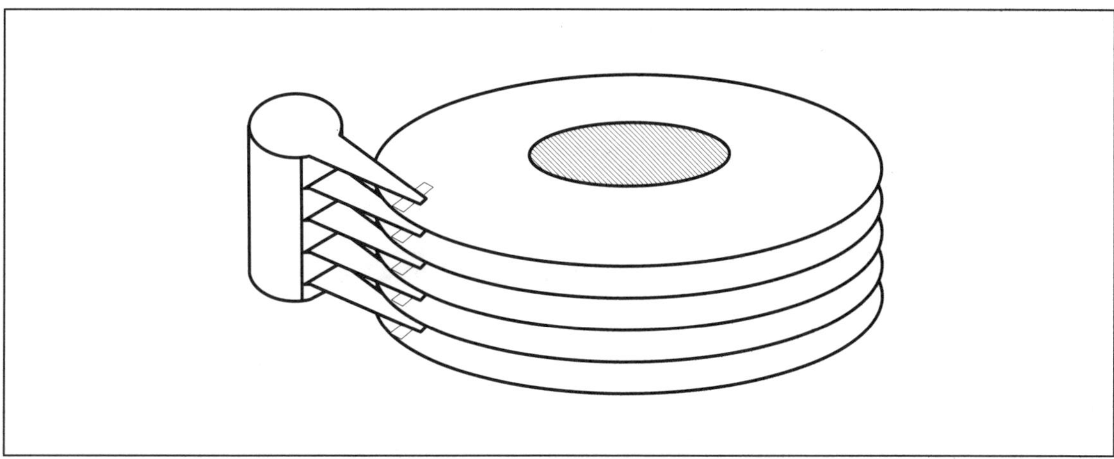

Figure 1-11 Arms

Spindle

A disk platter is attached to a *spindle* around which it rotates like a wheel on the axle of a car. The spindle is at the exact center of the platter. The arm moves the head from the outer edge of the platter toward the spindle at the center and back out again. Though most disks have only one spindle, some complex disks are made up of two or more single-spindle disks treated as one large disk. These are called multi-spindle disks. However, no platter ever has more than one spindle.

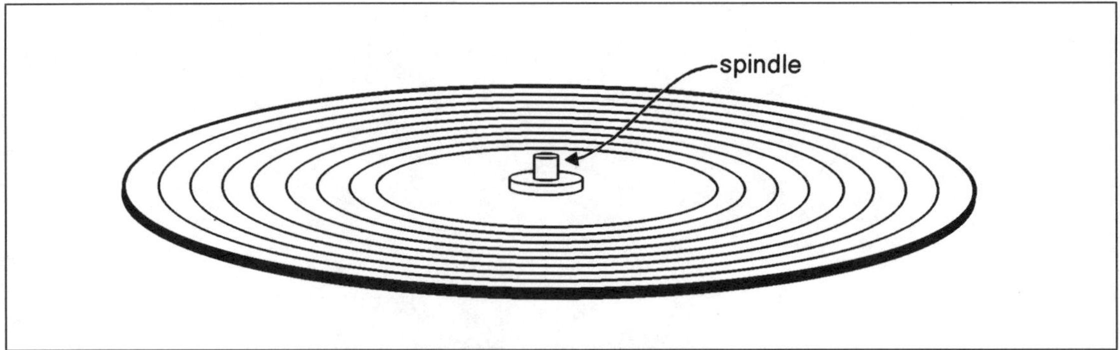

Figure 1-12 Spindle

Electronics

Electronic circuitry is required to sense and record the magnetism on the surface of the platters and to move the heads. This circuitry is commonly referred to as the *electronics* of the disk. The electronics communicate data between the physical disk and the computer.

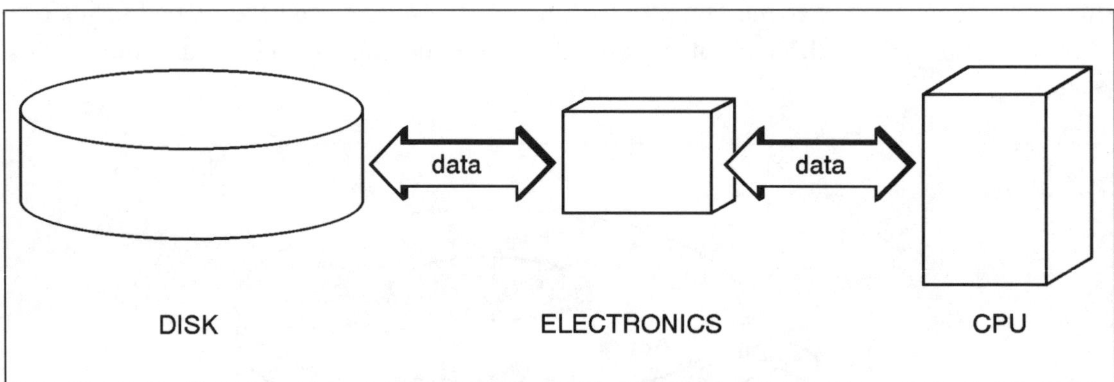

Figure 1-13 Electronics

Drive

The combination of one or more spindles, arms, heads, platters and electronics into a single physical device for storing and retrieving data is known as a disk *drive*. In this book, the term *drive* will be used often to refer to the disk drive. Viewed outside its cabinet, a disk drive is a sealed metal object that looks something like this:

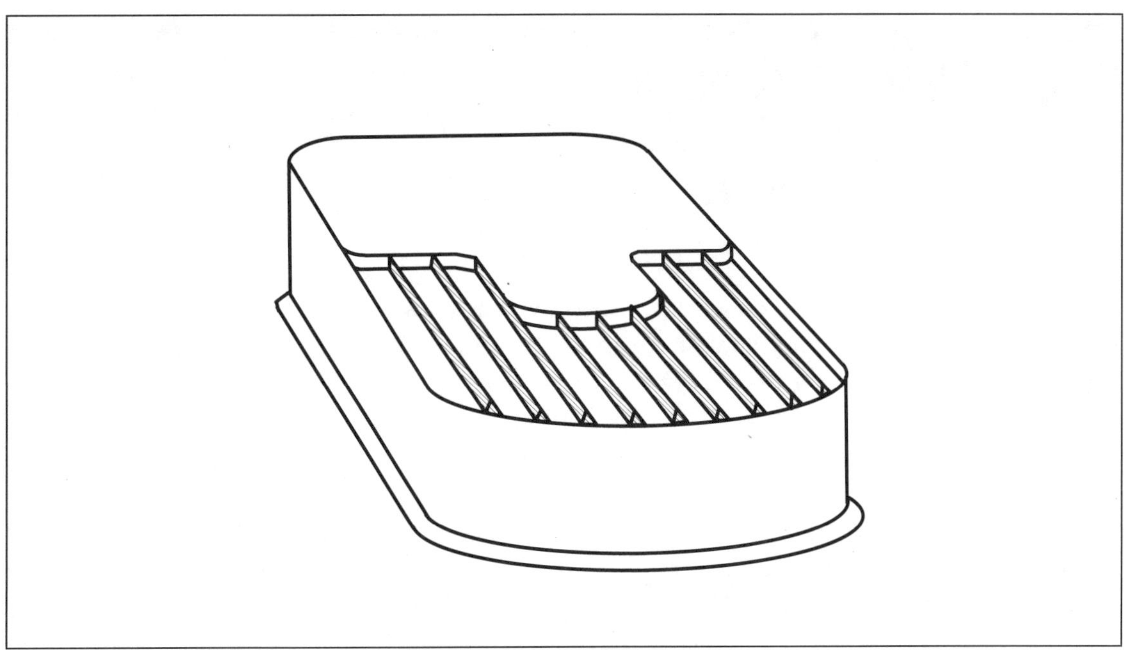

Figure 1-14 Disk Drive

Cable

The electronics in the disk drive are connected to circuitry in the computer by means of *cables,* which are no more than wires with a certain type of connector on each end. Often, the individual wires are color-coded for clarity.

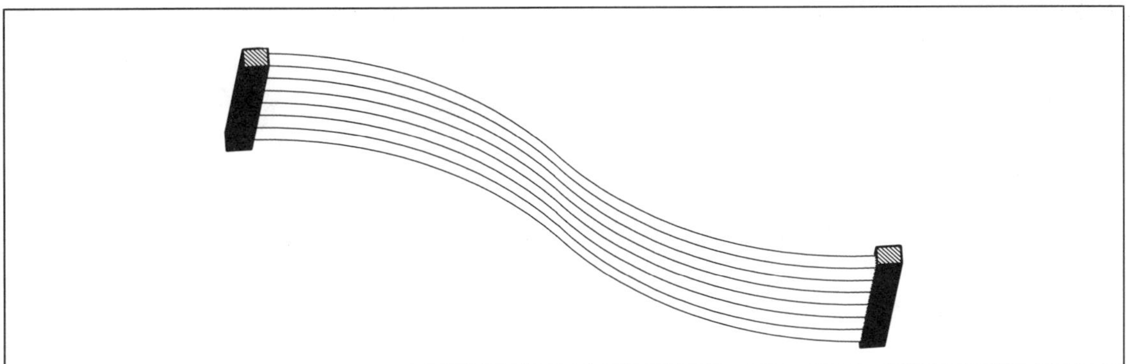

Figure 1-15 Cable

Controller

While the cables attach directly to the electronics of the disk drive on one end, they do not really attach directly to the computer on the other end. On the computer end, the cables attach to a *controller,* which is sometimes referred to as an *interface.* The controller, which is attached to the computer, decodes instructions from the computer and issues instructions to the disk drive to do what the computer has instructed. The controller also receives data and status information from the disk drive, which it passes on to the computer in a form the computer can understand. A single controller may service more than one disk drive.

Intelligent Disk Controller Functions

Disk controllers range in complexity from a very simple controller that merely relays instructions and data, to an intelligent controller that uses its information about the status of the disk to help the computer process data faster. Two examples of intelligent disk controller functions are *seek ordering* and *data caching*.

Seek Ordering

By keeping track of the exact position of the heads at all times, the controller can determine which one of multiple requests from the computer can be serviced in the shortest time. Then, instead of servicing the computer's requests in the order received, the controller can service first the requests for data nearest the heads and then the requests for data farther away. This is called *seek ordering,* which simply means putting the seeks in a better order.

For an over-simplified example, let's say the head is hovering over track 7. The computer is waiting for data from track 2 and from track 5. To go from track 7 to track 2 to service the first request and then back to track 5 for the second would require more time than it would to just stop off at track 5 on the way to track 2. So, the intelligent controller reorders the two requests and services the track 5 request first, then the track 2 request. The result is faster access to disk data *on average*.

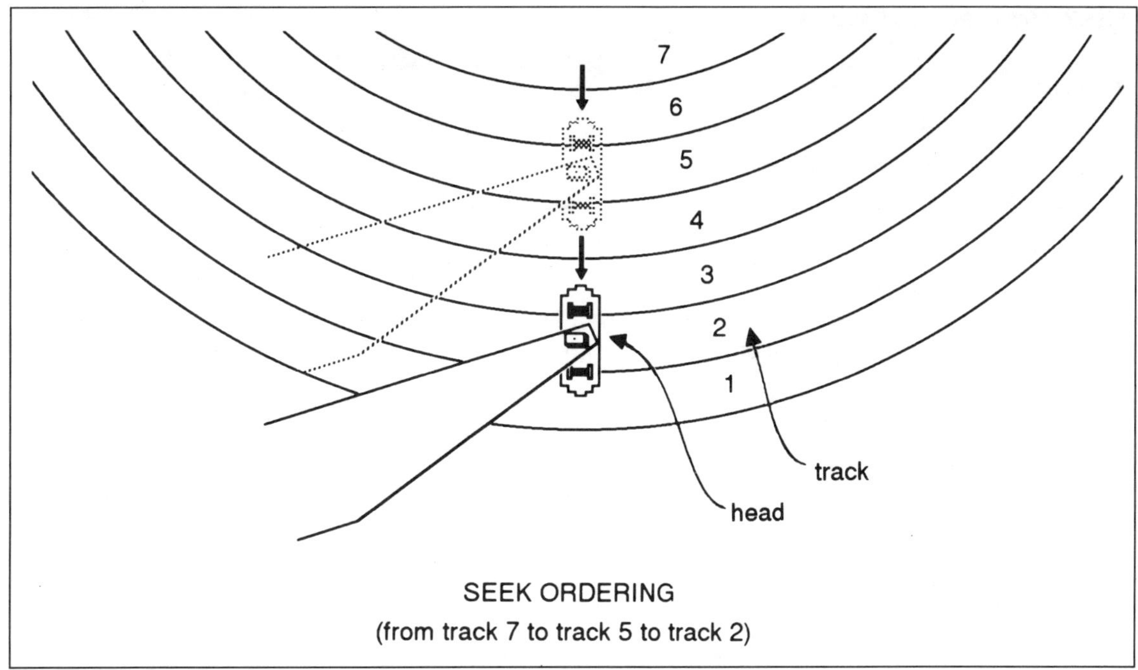

Figure 1-16 Seek Ordering

Data Caching

Dramatic performance improvements can be gained by placing a significant amount of memory inside the disk controller. This local memory is called a *cache*[26] and is used to store data recently retrieved from the disk by the computer. Then, if the computer should happen to request exactly the same data again, the controller can service the request from the local cache *at memory speed* (microseconds[27]) instead of at disk speed (milliseconds[28]). Of course, these dramatic gains are only available when the same disk block is retrieved more than once and when that block has been saved by the controller in its local cache. The amount of performance gain from such a system is wildly variable, being largely application-dependent.

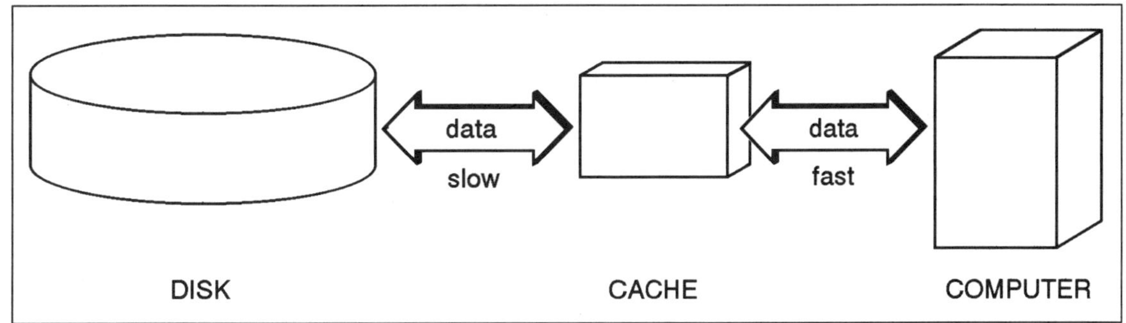

Figure 1-17 Data Caching

---

[26] **cache:** A very fast memory that can be used in combination with slower, large capacity memories.
[27] **microsecond:** One one-millionth of a second.
[28] **millisecond:** One one-thousandth of a second.

Disk-Related Software

Driver

Just as there are many different types of disks, there are also many different types of disk controllers. Different computer instructions are needed to deal with each different type of controller. The set of instructions used to manipulate a controller is a software component known as a *driver*. The driver resides at the lowest levels of a computer's operating system, where it can interact directly with the hardware. The driver translates the instruction codes of the disk controller into standardized instructions recognizable and usable by the more generalized parts of the computer system, and vice versa. Conversely, the driver enables an application program to issue a generic "get data" instruction, for example, to the disk without having to concern itself with the peculiarities of that particular disk (the number of tracks, platters, and so on). A single disk driver may service more than one disk controller.

users
applications software
system services (software)
drivers
hardware

Example 1-1 Drivers in the OpenVMS Hierarchy

Input/Output (I/O) Request Queue

A driver has associated with it a queue[29] for holding input/output (I/O)[30] requests. This queue is merely a data structure[31] enabling the computer to store an I/O request while it carries on with its work without having to wait for the I/O processing to complete. Entries can be added to the queue or deleted from it and, under certain conditions, the entries in the queue can be rearranged.

QIO

The OpenVMS operating system contains a mechanism for queuing (inserting) an I/O request to the queue of a driver. This mechanism is called the *$QIO system service*. The dollar sign indicates that this abbreviation is Digital's. *QIO* stands for "Queue Input Output," where *queue* is used as a verb. An application program or a higher level of the operating system uses the $QIO system service to cause I/O to occur.

---

[29] **queue:** A sequence of items waiting for service, like people in line at the checkout counter in a store.
[30] **I/O:** Refers to the transfer of data between the CPU and a peripheral device, such as a disk device.
[31] **data structure:** A design for the way data is laid out in a program.

Application

An *application* is a computer program which controls the computer system to perform some useful work for the user.

Disk File Structures

OpenVMS deals with disk blocks from two different points of view.

Physical Block

The actual arrangement of information on the surface of a disk platter is referred to as a *physical block.* The *Physical Block Number* (PBN) is an address used for identifying a particular block on the surface of the disk.

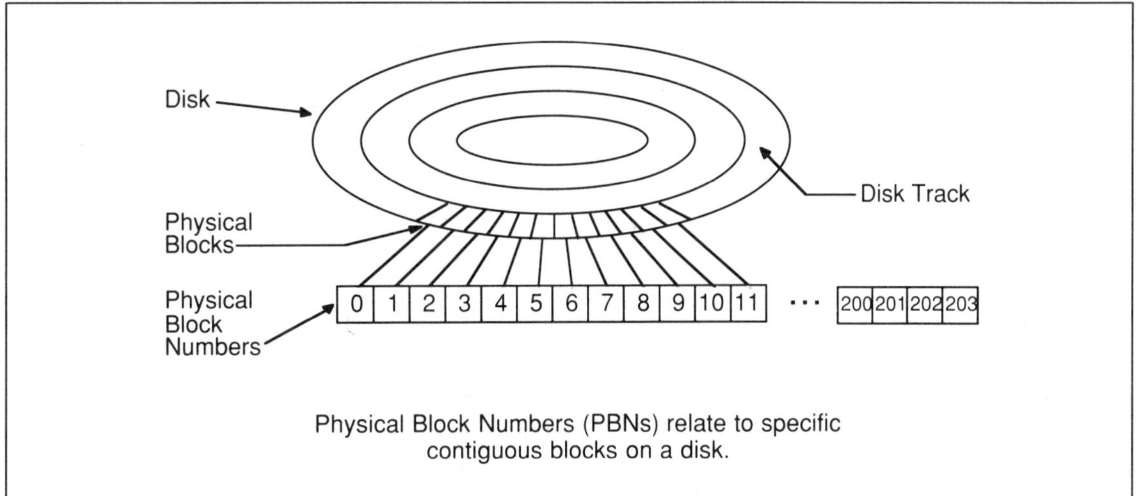

Physical Block Numbers (PBNs) relate to specific contiguous blocks on a disk.

Figure 1-18 Physical Block Numbers

Logical Block

When the blocks on a disk are considered from a programming point of view, they are viewed as *logical blocks.* The address of a logical block on a disk is its *Logical Block Number (LBN).* LBN 0 (zero) is the first LBN on a disk. Logical blocks correspond one-for-one to physical blocks, but the logical block *number* might not correspond directly to the same physical block numbers.

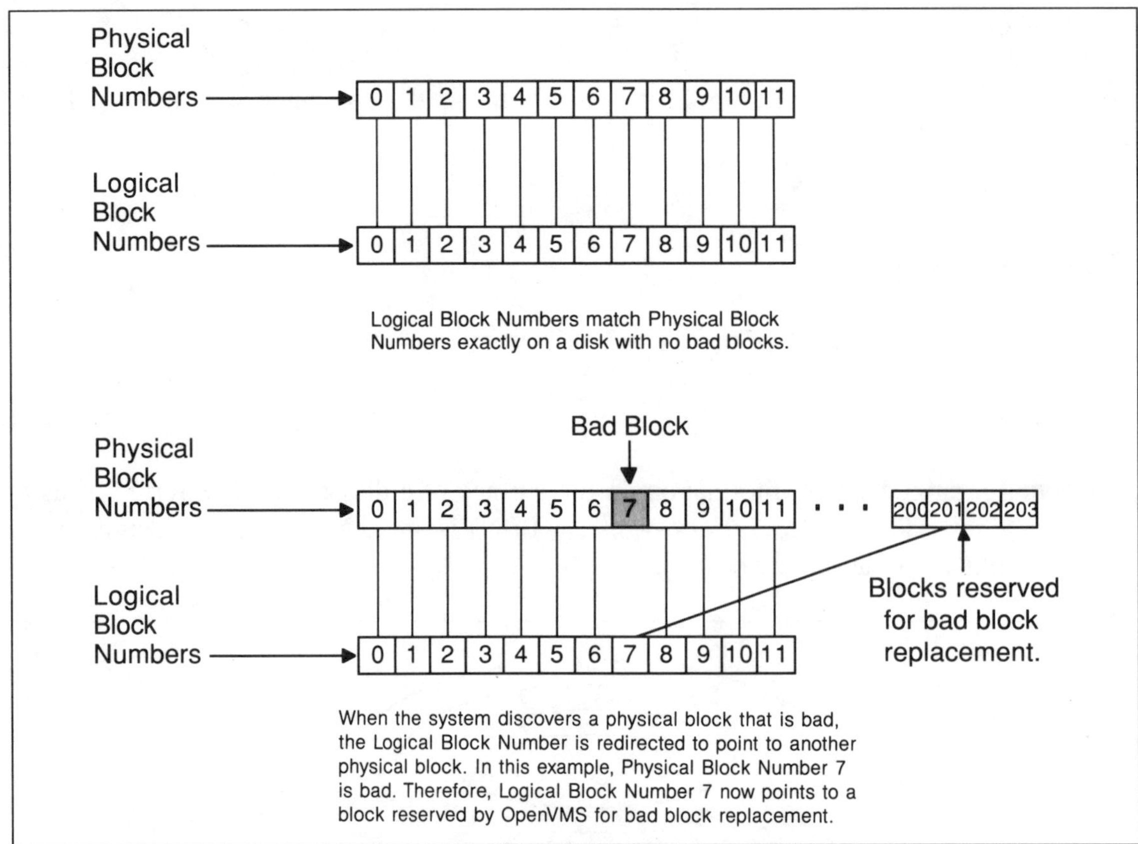

Figure 1-19 Logical Block Numbers

OpenVMS drivers, controllers and some disk electronics are capable of detecting a physical block that is unreliable for storage of data and replacing it with a spare block from the same disk. When this occurs, the logical block number does not change, even though the physical block number is now different. In this book, when discussing blocks or block numbers, we will be referring to *logical blocks* unless otherwise specified.

Volume

In OpenVMS, the word *volume* refers to a structured (formatted) disk. When considering a disk as a logical (conceptual) unit of storage, rather than a physical unit of storage, it is referred to as a *volume.* OpenVMS has the capability of treating one or more physical disk drives as one disk. This capability is implemented by the use of software and does not involve any additional electronics or cabling. When two or more disks are so combined, the combination is referred to as a *volume set,* which is described more fully later.

Storage Bitmap

For each disk, OpenVMS maintains a map indicating which clusters of logical blocks are in use and which are free. Each cluster consists of one or more logical blocks. Each bit in the map represents one cluster. Therefore, a cluster is the minimum amount of disk space that can be allocated to anything. The map is called the *Storage Bitmap*. When OpenVMS allocates space on the disk for a file, it can scan the storage bitmap to find available clusters.[32]

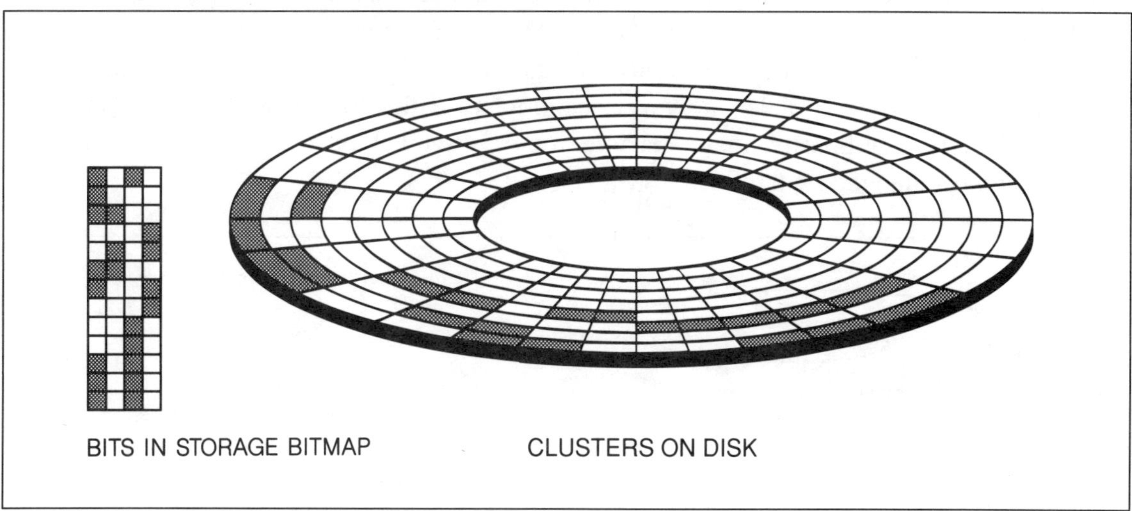

Figure 1-20 Storage Bitmap Relationship To Clusters

Extents

When OpenVMS allocates space on a disk for a file, it is not always possible to allocate all the needed space contiguously on the disk. Sometimes it is necessary to allocate part of a file in one place and the remainder in another. Files have been known to be allocated in dozens and even hundreds of pieces scattered around the disk. Each piece of a file so allocated is called an *extent*. The concept of an extent is inherent in a study of file fragmentation, as the allocation of multiple extents for a single file *is* file fragmentation. A contiguous file has only one extent.

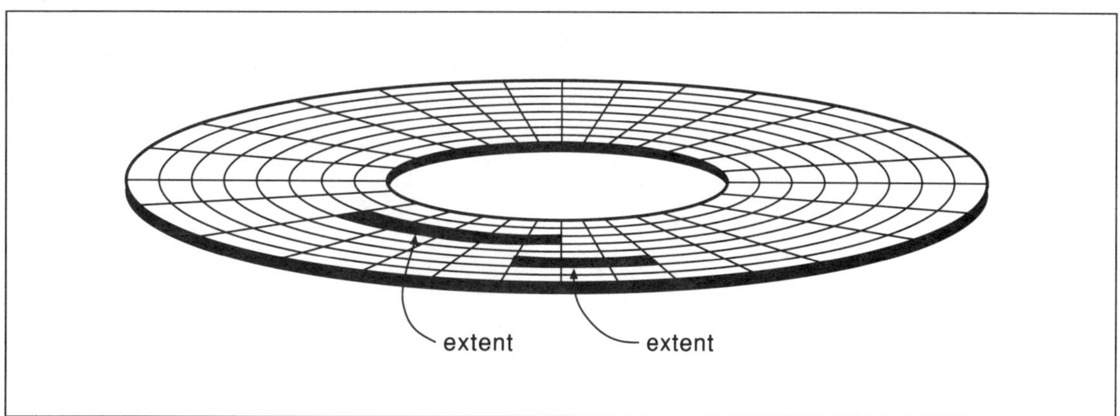

Figure 1-21 Extents

[32] **Note:** OpenVMS also uses the extent cache to allocate storage. The extent cache is defined on page 16.

Extent Cache

The *extent cache* is a portion of the system's memory that is set aside solely for the use of the OpenVMS file allocation mechanism. The extent cache stores the addresses of deallocated clusters, making it fast for OpenVMS to find free disk space by reusing these same clusters. This saves the overhead of scanning the Storage Bitmap of a disk to find free space. The extent cache, however, cannot store the logical block numbers of all deleted clusters. Ordinarily, there is room for only 64 LBNs to be stored, though this number can be changed by the System Manager.

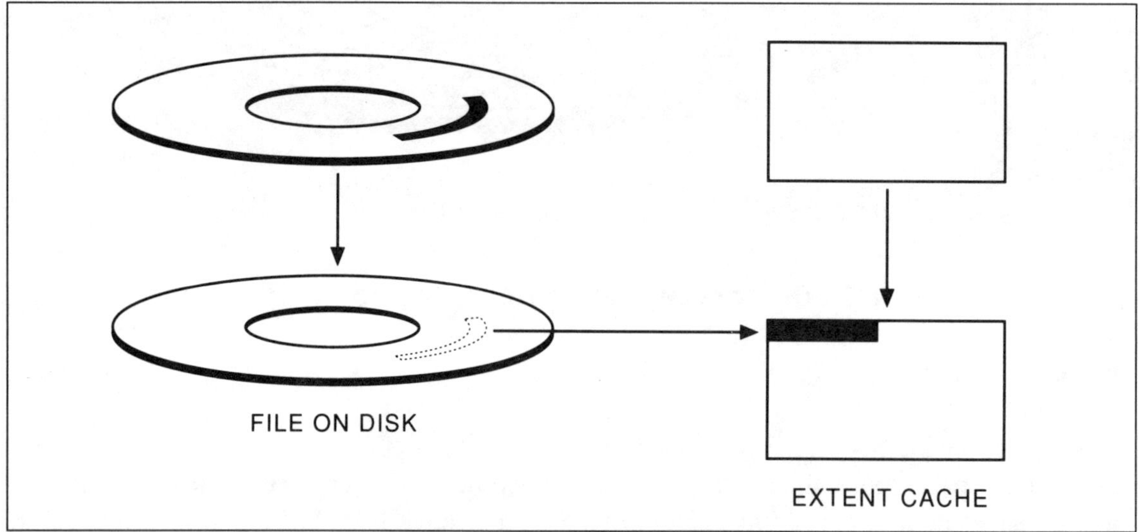

Figure 1-22 Extent Cache

File

Information stored on a disk is ordinarily stored in a *file*. In fact, for any OpenVMS disk using the ODS-2[33] structure, no information can be retrieved from a disk unless it is contained in a file. A *file* is "a collection of related records treated as a unit and usually referenced by a . . . name."[34] While a record is a unit of *data* within a file, an extent (see above) is a unit of the file as a *container* for data.

---

[33] **ODS-2:** *On-Disk Structure Level 2.* The name of the file structure used on most OpenVMS disks.
[34] *The Digital Dictionary.*

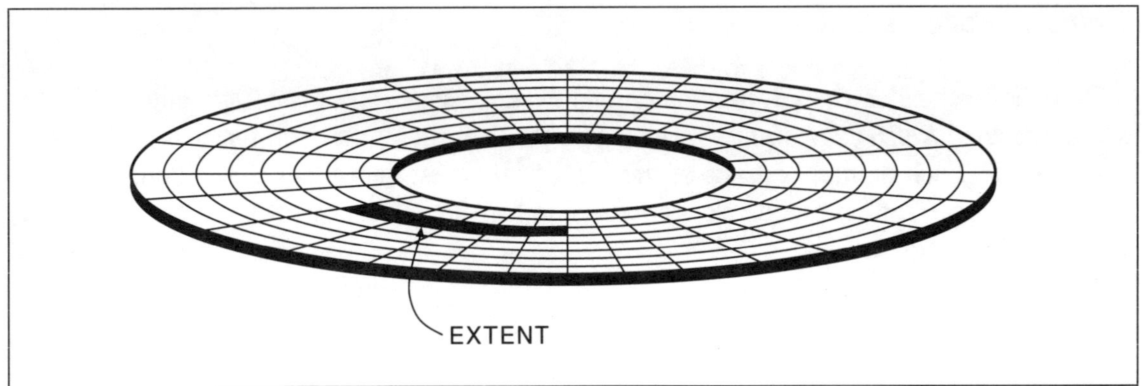

Figure 1-23 File With One Extent

Index File

The Digital Dictionary defines *index file* as "The file on a . . . volume that contains the access information for all files on the volume and enables the operating system to identify and access the volume." The index file is a catalog of all the files on a particular disk. In fact, the header (identifying information) of a file resides within the index file. All the information needed to access a file is contained here.

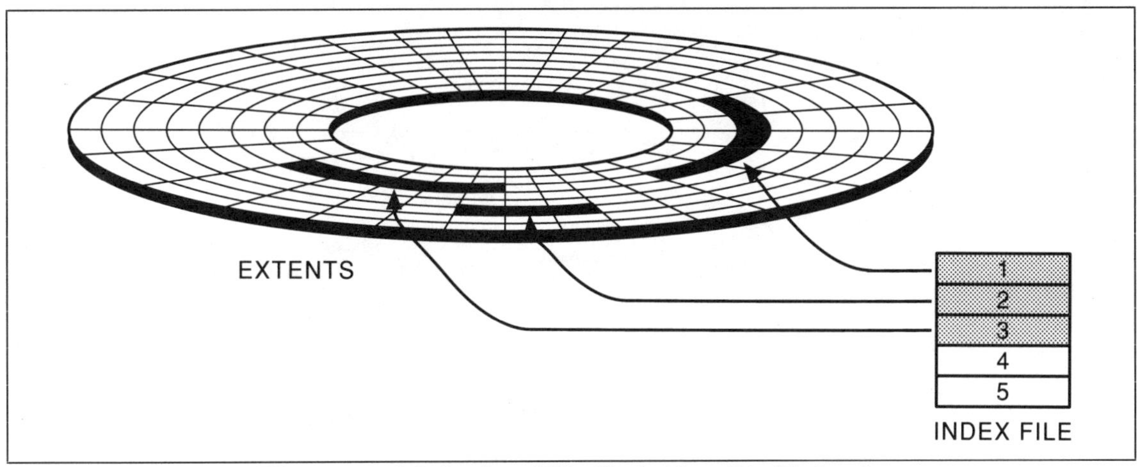

Figure 1-24 Index File Pointing To Extents

File Header

"A block in the index file that describes a file on a . . . disk. Every file residing on the disk has at least one header, which provides the location of the file's extents."[35] While the header actually contains much more information than this, this is all we need to know about it for the purposes of this book.

35 *The Digital Dictionary.*

Retrieval Pointers

Within the file header, the information critical to our discussion of file fragmentation is the section headed *Retrieval Pointers*. These pointers indicate where the file's data is located on the disk. Each pointer consists of the LBN of the first data block and a count of how many successive contiguous blocks contain data for that file. For example, this file has a single retrieval pointer:

```
Map area
   Retrieval pointers
       Count:          12          LBN:       27990
```

Example 1-2 File With One Retrieval Pointer

The first data block of this file is at Logical Block Number 27990. The entire file is contained in that block plus the 11 blocks following it in LBN sequence. This 12-block file is contiguous (not fragmented). It has only one extent.

In the following example, the file is broken into four fragments. The first consists of 6 blocks starting at LBN 5; the second is 3 blocks at LBN 297; the third, 3 blocks at LBN 200460; and the fourth, 4104 blocks at LBN 200760. This file is fragmented. It has four extents.

```
Map area
   Retrieval pointers
       Count:           6          LBN:           5
       Count:           3          LBN:         297
       Count:           3          LBN:      200460
       Count:        4104          LBN:      200760
```

Example 1-3 File With Four Retrieval Pointers

Directory

A *directory* is "a file that briefly catalogs a set of files stored on a disk. . ."[36] From the user's point of view, a directory is a catalog of the names of files that are grouped in a particular way.

---

36 *The Digital Dictionary.*

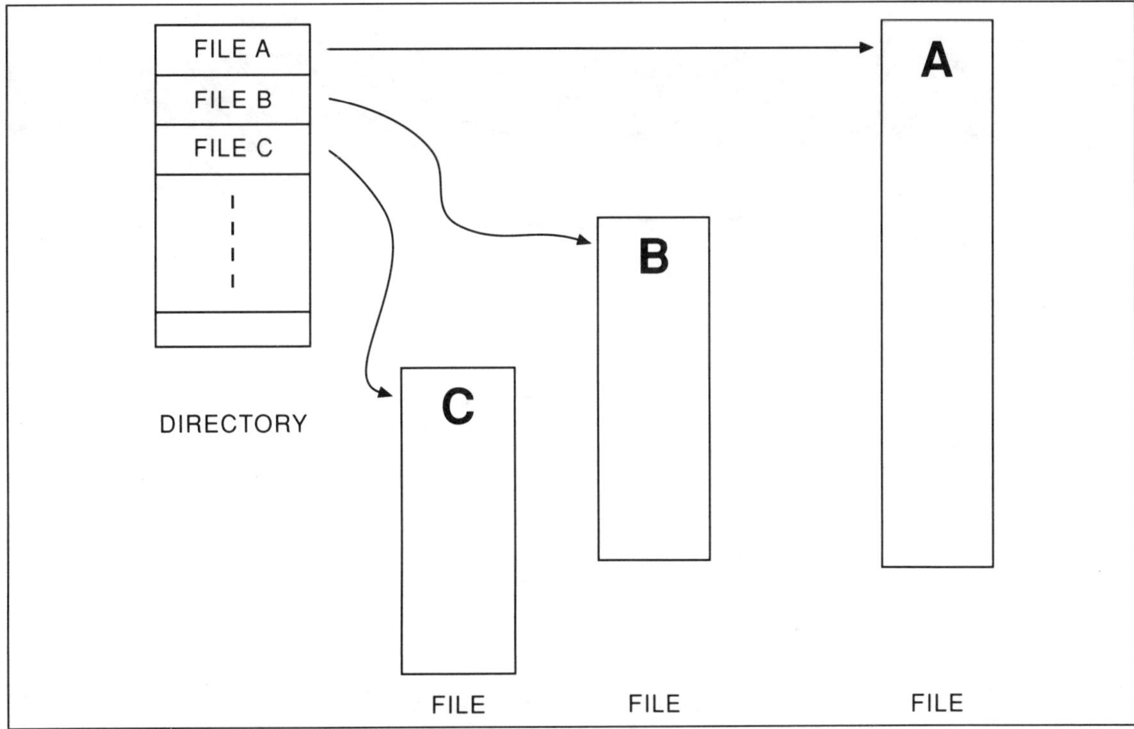

Figure 1-25 Directory

Disk Performance Terminology

Seek Time

As mentioned earlier, the movement of a disk head from one track to another is called a *seek.* The time it takes for a head to seek is the most critical factor in determining the speed of a disk. This is known as the disk's *seek time.* It consists of three parts: the time to start the head in motion and get it up to speed, the time to move the head from one track to another, and the time it takes to stop the head. Additional overhead is required to identify the correct track and, if necessary, reposition the head.

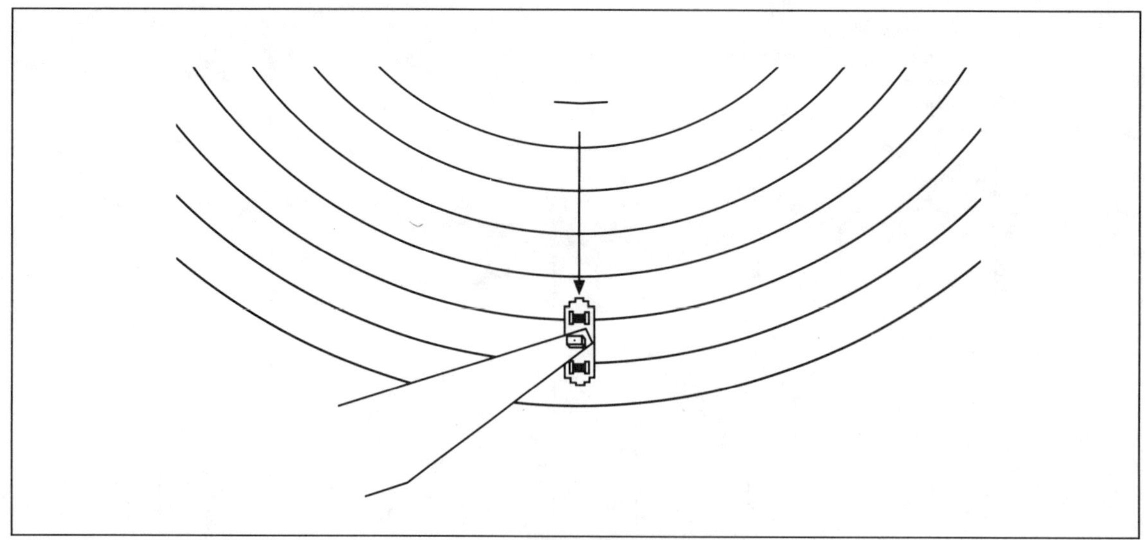

Figure 1-26 Seek Time

Rotational Latency

As a disk platter spins around the spindle, the blocks in a single track of recorded data are brought near a disk head. The head can only read or write a block when that block is immediately under the head.[37] Accordingly, the time to access a block of data on the disk varies. It is much quicker to access a block that is currently or about to be under the head than it is to access a block that has recently passed under the head and is moving away. The block that has just passed under the head has to wait nearly a full rotation of the disk for another access opportunity. This delay is known as *rotational latency.*

A common disk rotational speed is 3600 RPM,[38] meaning that the disk spins completely around 3600 times each minute. At this speed, each revolution of the disk takes 16.67 milliseconds. Naturally, rotational latency on this disk varies from zero to 16.67 milliseconds, and the average rotational latency is half the maximum, or 8.33 milliseconds.

---

[37] The phrase "under the head" is figurative. Sometimes the head is underneath the platter, so the data would have to be "over the head." Nevertheless, the phrase "under the head" is used to describe both conditions.

[38] **RPM**: *R*evolutions *P*er *M*inute

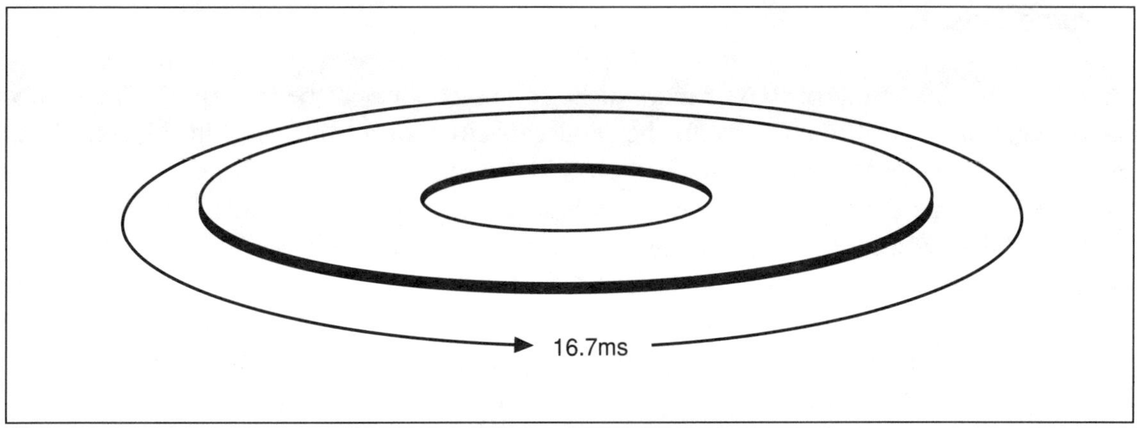

Figure 1-27 Rotational Latency

Average Access Time

To compute the time it takes to access any block on a disk, it is necessary to combine the seek time and the rotational latency. Clearly, if the head is over the proper track and the desired block is immediately under the head, the access time is approximately zero. If the head is over the proper track, the access time is the same as the rotational latency. If the head has to move from one track to another, however, you must *add* the rotational latency to the seek time to compute the *average access time.*[39] The average access time for modern-day disks falls roughly in the range of 8 to 25 milliseconds.

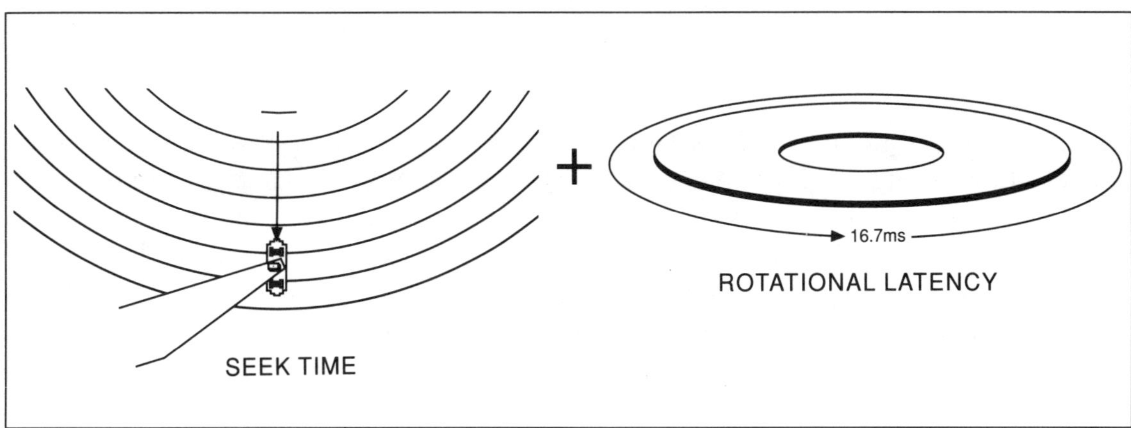

Figure 1-28 Seek Time + Rotational Latency

Disk Sets

Several methods of combining disks into sets are in current use. One reason for combining disks into sets is to improve performance by reducing the average access time when figured for the set as a whole.

---

[39] The average access time is not exactly equal to half the sum of the rotational latency plus the seek time, as the rotation and the seek occur at the same time. The average access time, therefore, is somewhat less than the total.

Volume Sets

A *volume set* is a group of two or more disks combined so as to be treated by OpenVMS as a single disk equal in capacity to the total capacities of all the disks in the set. In a volume set, a file can span two or more disks in the set. The primary benefit of a volume set over separate disks is *size* – the volume set can accommodate a file larger than any individual disk in the set. The volume set also reduces average access time by spreading the disk accesses over two (or more) disks instead of one. Theoretically, half the disk accesses will occur on one disk in a two-volume set, while the other half occur on the other disk. If the theory were borne out in practice, this would allow twice as many disk operations in the same time, but actual results are not greatly improved.

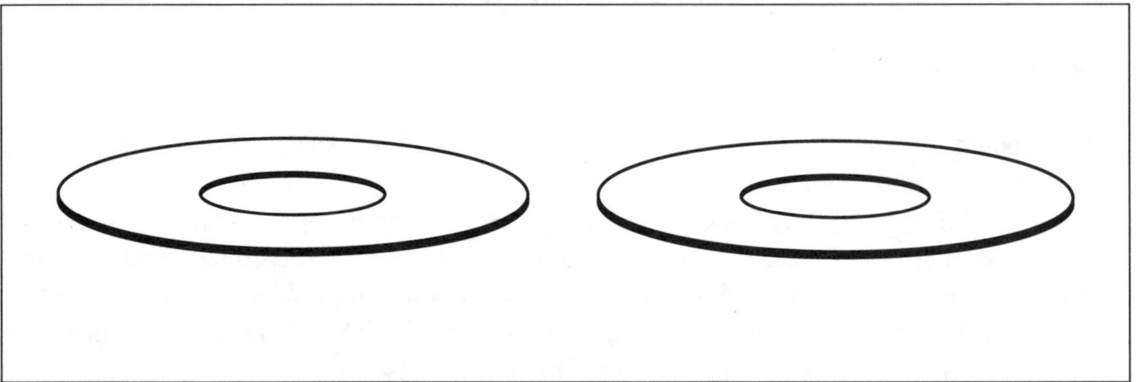

Figure 1-29 Volume Set

Shadow Sets

A *shadow set* is a group of two (or more) identical disks combined so as to be treated by OpenVMS as a single disk equal in capacity to only one of the disks in the group. Each time data is written to the shadow set, the same data is written to all the disks in the set. That way, the data can be retrieved even if all but one of the disks fails. The primary benefit of a shadow set over separate disks is safety. The likelihood of losing the data on two or more disks at the same time is much more remote than that of losing the data on just one disk.

A shadow set also alters performance by increasing the time needed to write data (as it has to be written to all disks in the set) and by reducing the time it takes to read data. The two or more disks in the set are unlikely to have exactly the same block under their heads at exactly the same time, so OpenVMS will direct the read to the one which can retrieve the data faster, either because the data is closer to its head or because there is less work outstanding for that drive to do. Therefore, on average, the read time for the set is faster than that for either disk.

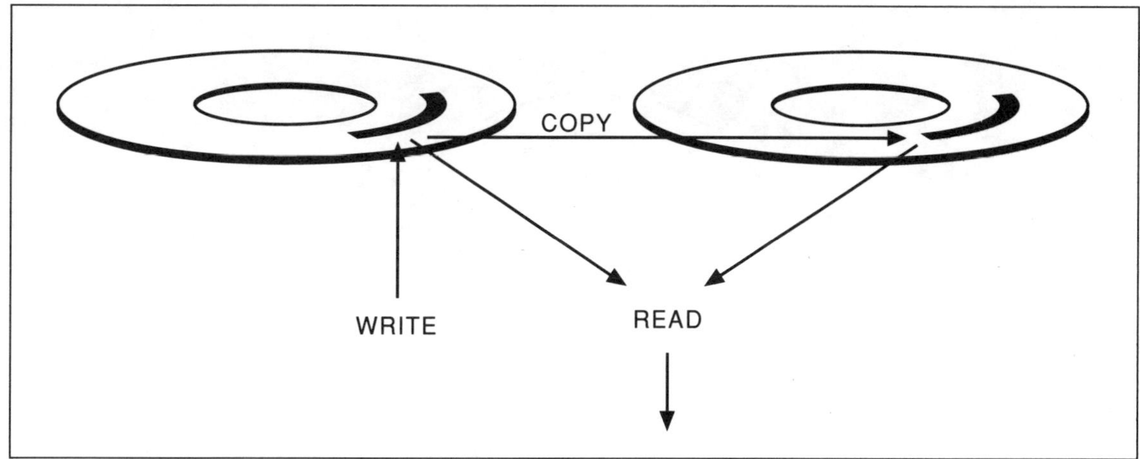

Figure 1-30 Shadow Set

Stripesets

Two or more disks can also be combined into a *stripeset.* A stripeset is similar to a volume set in that the full capacity of all the disks in the set is available for data storage, and the whole set is treated by OpenVMS as a single large disk. Also, the *virtual* disk (the disk which is treated by OpenVMS as a single large disk) is divided into "chunks"[40] rather than clusters.

The main difference is that, while each file extent must reside entirely on a single disk in a volume set, in a stripeset file extents are deliberately spread across multiple disks. One chunk (which could contain one or more extents) resides on one disk, the next chunk in sequence resides on the next disk, the next chunk on the next disk, and so on, starting over at the first disk when the last disk in the set is reached.

The primary benefit of a stripeset is application performance. Data read from a single file will come from several disks simultaneously, greatly reducing the application wait time. For example, if each disk has a 24 millisecond (ms) access time, the average time to collect a chunk from two disks simultaneously is the same – 24 ms. But that is 24 ms for *two* chunks instead of one.

---

[40] **Chunk:** Due to the way OpenVMS disks are structured, disks in a stripeset are divided into "chunks" rather than clusters, chunks consisting (usually) of more blocks than clusters.

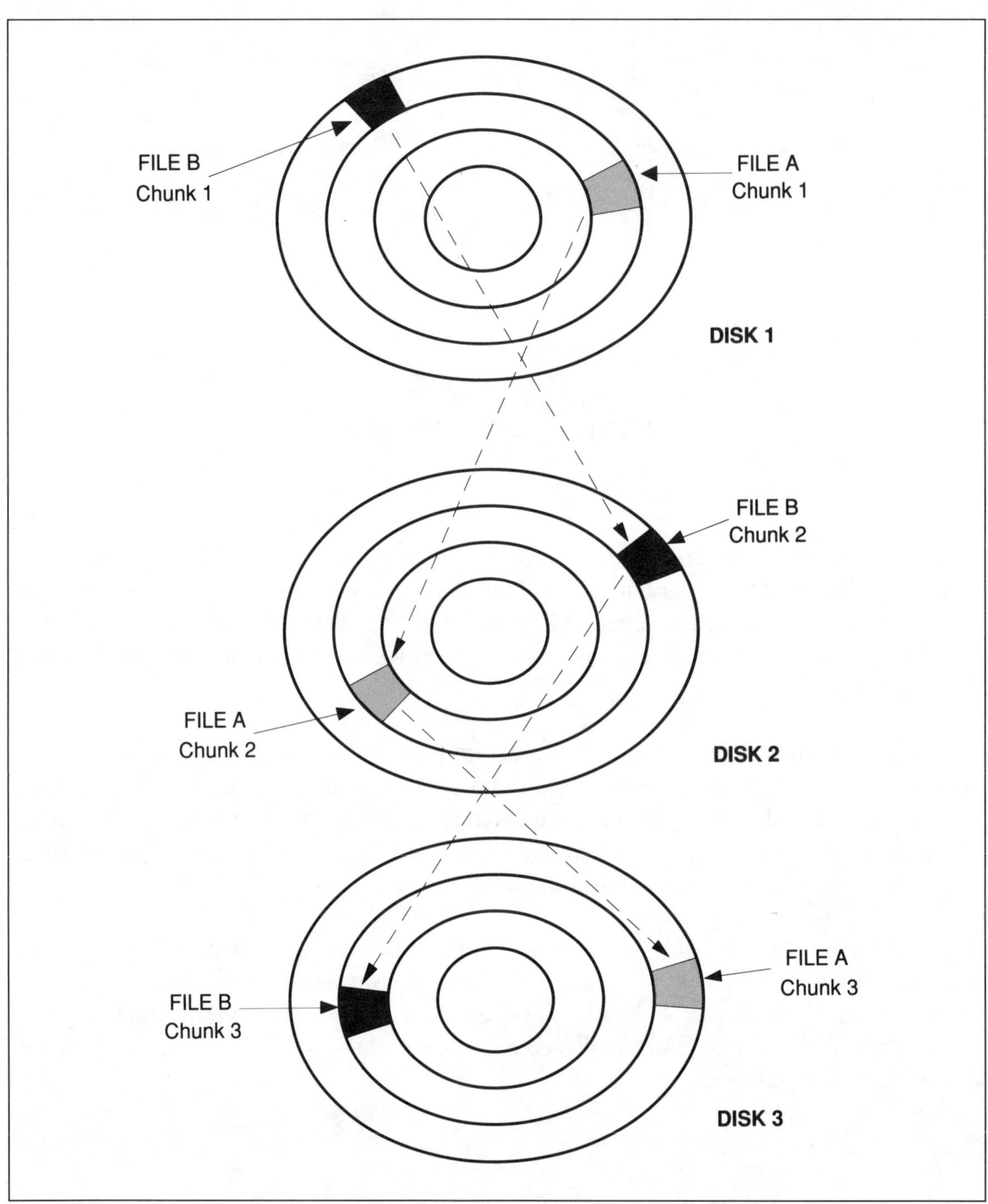

Figure 1-31 Stripeset

Disk Architecture Evolution

Perhaps the most interesting question that comes up with respect to fragmentation is, "Why is the OpenVMS operating system designed so badly as to suffer from fragmentation?"

The answer to this question is that age-old saw, "It's a feature, not a bug!"

It's true. Originally, the VAX/VMS operating system, as it was called then, was deliberately designed to allow fragmentation and to deal with it efficiently. This design was actually the solution to an older and more serious problem.

The Original Problem

You see, when computers first appeared on the scene, they had no disks at all. Obviously, disk fragmentation was not a problem. No one had even had the idea yet, so the operating systems of that age had no mechanism to deal with fragmentation at all. *If* the computer even *had* an operating system.

This ancient era extended into the late 1960's, before the VAX and before even the PDP-11,[41] on which the VAX was based. In the Digital world, these were the days of the PDP-8.[42]

Then, disks happened. The first disks were small – unbelievably small by today's standards. They were measured in thousands of bytes rather than millions, never mind the billion-byte disks now available. Nevertheless, this was a fabulous advance in the days when memory sold for a dollar a *byte*. (At this writing, memory sells for $40 a megabyte retail – 25,000 times less!)

Later, the early PDP-11 operating system, called RT-11 (*Real Time-11),* was capable of storing data on disks in files, and the files were organized in a formal file structure. This file structure, however, *required* that all files be contiguous. That is, no file could be split into two or more pieces. It was not a question of performance; the system simply had no capability to create or access a file split into pieces. A file had a single location on a disk and that was that.

This requirement for contiguous files meant that a newly-created file had to fit within a single gap on the disk or not at all. It was not possible to allocate a part of the file to one gap and the rest to another, as can be done with today's OpenVMS. This was true even when there were no individual gaps large enough to accommodate the file, in spite of the fact that the total free space on the disk far exceeded the size of the new file. There had to be a large enough *contiguous* free space, period.

---

[41] **PDP-11:** *P*rogrammable *D*ata *P*rocessor-*11.* A 16-bit computer on which the VAX (originally, the VAX-11/780) was based. The PDP-11 introduced virtual memory to the Digital world, although early versions of the PDP-11 lacked this capability.

[42] **PDP-8:** *P*rogrammable *D*ata *P*rocessor-*8.* A 12-bit computer preceding the PDP-11. The PDP-8 is widely regarded as the first minicomputer which, at that time, was simply defined as a computer which cost less than $100,000. Considering inflation, the cost of such a computer would be closer to $1 million today.

Naturally, this problem (of not enough contiguous free space to create a file) occurred every time a disk filled up, and small disks fill up *very* fast. With frequent file deletions, it was not unusual to have a disk reach the point where no more files could be created even though the disk was little over half full.

The *SQUEEZE* Solution

The solution to this problem was the *SQUEEZE* command. *SQUEEZE* compacted the disk, rearranging the files so they were all together near the beginning (LBN 0) of the disk, leaving all the free space in one large, contiguous area at the end. After a *SQUEEZE,* any file could be created, provided it would fit in the total free space remaining.

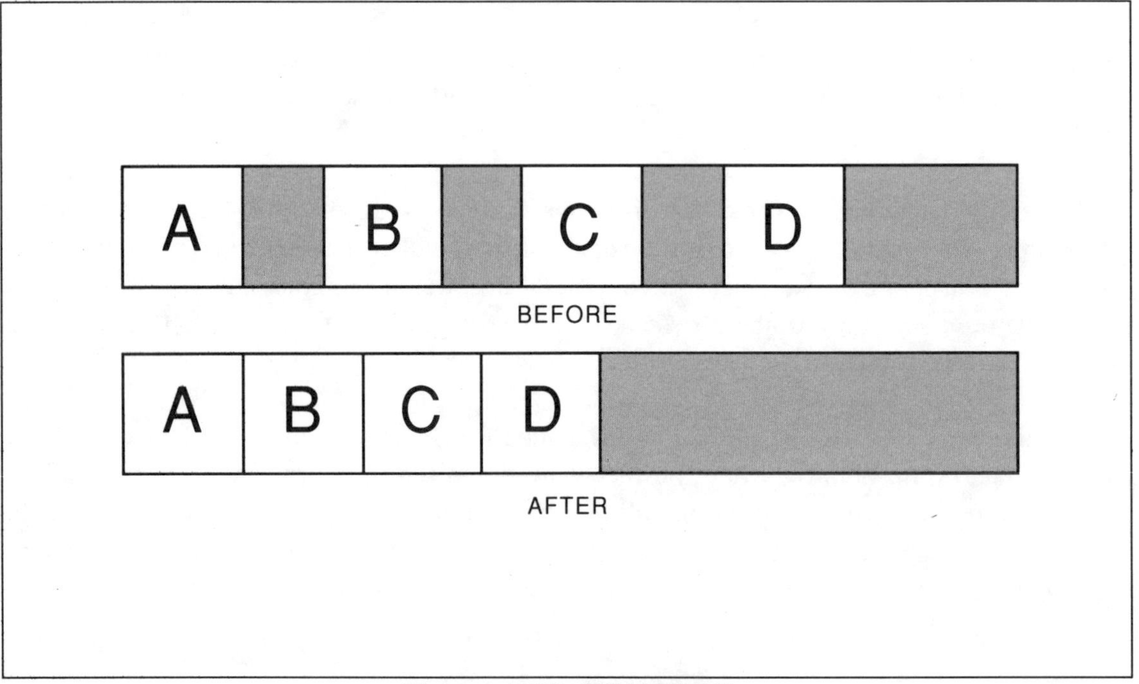

Figure 1-32 SQUEEZE

Nothing else could be done on that disk while the *SQUEEZE* was in progress, but this was not a big drawback, as RT-11 was a single-user system anyway. The only person inconvenienced was the one who wanted that new file created, so the benefit always outweighed the inconvenience.

The Fragmentation Solution

Then a wondrous new operating system came along, one that allowed multiple simultaneous users of the same PDP-11 computer – RSX-11.[43] Now the inconvenience of a *SQUEEZE* would certainly outweigh the benefit, as *all* the users would have to stop working, not just the one who wanted to create the new file. Clearly, *SQUEEZE* was no longer a viable solution.

The designers of RSX-11 cleverly created a file structure that included the revolutionary capability to locate parts of a file in different places on the disk. Each file had a header that gave the location and size of each piece of the file, so the file could be in pieces scattered around the disk. Now a file could be created anytime there was sufficient free space *anywhere* on the disk; the space did not have to be contiguous.

Nor was there any drawback to this mechanism whatsoever. It really was "a feature, not a bug." Performance losses due to fragmentation, even when taken to extremes, caused very little difficulty for anyone. You must realize that at this time, in the early 1970's, disks were very small. Let's take a look at a real example:

The RK05 disk, which was in common use at the time, held 2½ megabytes (5,000 blocks). Suppose the disk was totally and utterly fragmented, that is, no two consecutive data blocks were contiguous. Every single disk access likely required moving the head and waiting for rotational latency. Even so, the whole disk could be read in 250 seconds (50 ms times 5,000 blocks). That's a little over four minutes – worst case. The same action on today's 700MB disk, even with a 16 ms access time, takes over *6 hours*. During the same period of time, disk capacities have increased to over 500 times that of the RK05, and CPU speeds have increased to over 400 times that of the original PDP-11. Even though disk speeds have increased by a factor of three, they have not kept pace with the rest of computer technology. This makes the speed of the disk a major bottleneck in the computer system. This point is critical to an understanding of the fragmentation problem.

Clearly, today's larger disks brought with them more than higher capacities and speeds. They brought a susceptibility to a new kind of computer disease – fragmentation.

---

43 **RSX-11:** Real-time *R*esource *S*haring e*X*ecutive for the PDP-11 computer.

Here is a table showing the time required to access every block on a disk:

		AVERAGE ACCESS TIME IN MILLISECONDS							
		70.00	50.00	40.00	33.00	25.00	16.00	10.00	8.00
	0.032	4.48	3.20	2.56	2.11	1.60	1.02	0.64	0.51
S	0.5	70.00	50.00	40.00	33.00	25.00	16.00	10.00	8.00
I	1	2.33	100.00	80.00	66.00	50.00	32.00	20.00	16.00
Z	2	4.67	3.33	2.67	2.20	100.00	64.00	40.00	32.00
E	5	11.67	8.33	6.67	5.50	4.17	2.67	100.00	80.00
	10	23.33	16.67	13.33	11.00	8.33	5.33	3.33	2.67
I	20	46.67	33.33	26.67	22.00	16.67	10.67	6.67	5.33
N	40	93.33	66.67	53.33	44.00	33.33	21.33	13.33	10.67
	100	3.89	2.78	2.22	110.00	83.33	53.33	33.33	26.67
M	206	8.01	5.72	4.58	3.78	2.86	109.87	68.67	54.93
B	456	17.73	12.67	10.13	8.36	6.33	4.05	2.53	2.03
	700	27.22	19.44	15.56	12.83	9.72	6.22	3.89	3.11
	1200	46.67	33.33	26.67	22.00	16.67	10.67	6.67	5.33

Legend: seconds | minutes | hours

Table 1-1 Time Required To Access Every Block On A Disk

So the ability to deal with fragmented files, which was carried over from the RSX-11 operating system to the OpenVMS operating system, was a solution to an earlier problem that failed to anticipate the enormous capacities to which disks would grow. There is no end to this growth in sight. Deliberate fragmentation is no longer only a feature; it is now a problem, too.

Summary

In this chapter, the inner workings of a disk have been explained, with care taken to define the terms needed to truly understand fragmentation. To be sure, there is a lot more to know about disks, but our concern here is not to learn disk design, construction or maintenance. Our purpose is to understand enough about disks so that fragmentation and its cure make sense. To this end, the first chapter has also devoted time to the basic concepts of files and file structure. With these concepts and terms well understood, we are ready to tackle the real problem – the fragmentation disease.

CHAPTER 2

WHAT IS FRAGMENTATION?

File Fragmentation and Free Space Fragmentation

Fragmentation means two things:

1) a condition in which individual files on a disk are not contiguous but are broken up in pieces scattered around the disk; and

2) a condition in which the free space on a disk consists of little bits of free space here and there rather than only one or a few free spaces.

Condition 1 is referred to as *file fragmentation,* while Condition 2 is referred to as *disk fragmentation* or, more precisely, *free space fragmentation.* File fragmentation causes performance problems when *reading* files, while free space fragmentation causes performance problems when *creating* and *extending* files.

Neither condition has anything to do with the *contents* of a file. We are concerned only with the files as *containers* for data and with the arrangement of these containers on the disk.

Internal Fragmentation

The term *fragmentation* is sometimes applied to the contents of a file. This type of fragmentation will be explained here only to differentiate it from our real subjects, file and free space fragmentation.

Files consist of records. Each record is a collection of fields[44] considered as a unit. There are three basic kinds of files, each affected by file content fragmentation differently:

Sequential: In a sequential file, every record except the first falls immediately after the preceding record. There are no gaps. An illustration of a sequential file is a music cassette. You cannot get to any selection without searching through the tape. Accordingly, sequential files are not subject to internal fragmentation. The situation simply cannot exist.

Random: In a random access or direct access file, every record is the same size. Because of this, records can be deleted and replaced with new ones easily. An illustration of a

[44] **field:** An area reserved for data.

direct access file is a bookshelf full of books which are all the same size. You can go directly to any book desired and withdraw it from the shelf. You can also replace it anywhere there is a space on the shelf. Fragmentation of the contents of such a file causes virtually no performance problems, as the file is designed to be accessed in random order and any new record is guaranteed to fit precisely within any free space in the file.

Indexed: Indexed files, however, do suffer from internal fragmentation. An illustration of an indexed file is a floor of offices in a building. The directory in the lobby tells you what floor the office is on, but you still have to search the floor to find the right office. Such files have an index that contains pointers to organized data records elsewhere in the file. In such a file, variable length data records are stored in *buckets*[45] of a certain number of blocks each. If a record will not fit in a bucket (because the bucket is already full of other records), the bucket is split into two buckets to accommodate all the records. An indexed file with numerous split buckets is said to be *fragmented.* This type of fragmentation affects performance of only those applications accessing the affected file (unless such activity is so intense that it degrades the performance of the entire system). It is cured by reorganizing the data records within the file, usually by creating a better-organized copy of the file to supersede the fragmented one. This reorganization can be done safely only when access to the file has been suspended.

This *internal* file fragmentation is not the type of fragmentation with which this book is concerned.

Pagefile Fragmentation

Another type of fragmentation which occurs on OpenVMS systems but is beyond the scope of this book is *pagefile fragmentation.*

As information is added to the pagefile and deleted from it, the space in the pagefile can become fragmented, leaving no single space large enough to hold more information. This type of fragmentation causes severe performance degradation and can even cause the system to become unusable. It is cured by rebooting the system, and is prevented by increasing the size of the pagefile or adding secondary pagefile(s) to the system.

---

[45] **Bucket:** A storage structure of 1 to 32 disk blocks that is used to store and transfer data in files. Unlike a block, a bucket can contain only entire records.

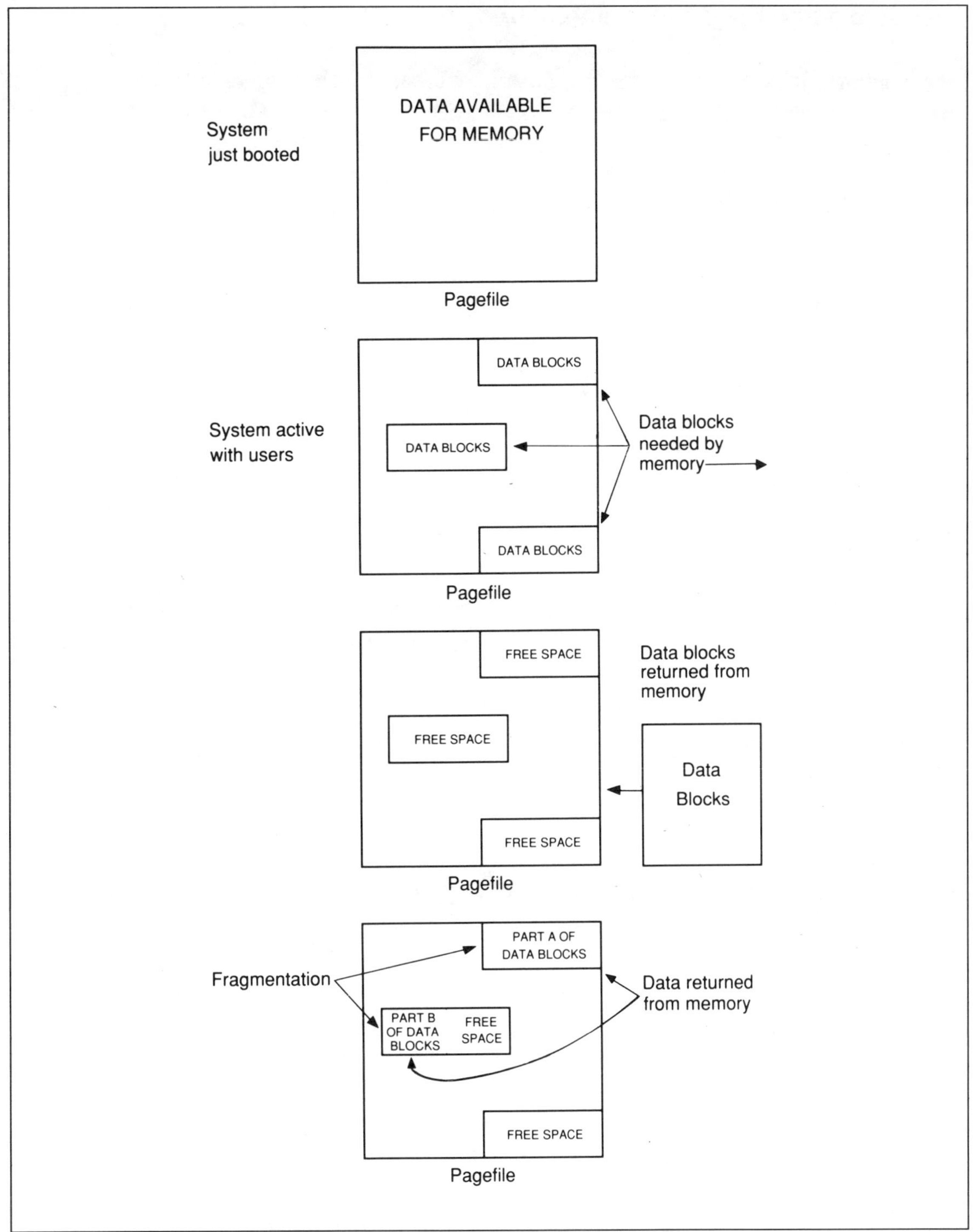

Figure 2-1 Pagefile Fragmentation

Note: The type of defragmentation described in this book does nothing to remedy pagefile fragmentation.

Deliberate and Needful Fragmentation

It sometimes happens that a file is deliberately created in a fragmented state. The best example of this is a standard OpenVMS file, needed for every OpenVMS disk volume, called INDEXF.SYS.[46] This file contains the headers for all the files on that volume.[47] It also contains certain information critical to the system's ability to access data on that disk volume, like the location of the INDEXF.SYS file itself. This information is so important, it is separated into four pieces and stored in four different places on the disk, minimizing the risk of losing all four pieces at once and maximizing the ability to recover data from a damaged disk. As these four copies are part of the INDEXF.SYS file, the file must be fragmented at all times, but only to the degree described here. The part of the file containing file headers can be made contiguous and kept so.

Why Fragmentation Occurs

The OpenVMS File Allocation Strategy

When OpenVMS allocates disk space for a file, it looks in the storage bitmap to find what clusters are available. In so looking, it always begins its scan of the storage bitmap from the beginning (LBN 0) when the disk has been recently mounted.[48] Thus, there is a tendency on the part of OpenVMS to group files near the logical beginning of a disk, leaving the higher LBNs free. This tendency is modified (for better or for worse) by the *Extent Cache* (see page 34 for a more complete explanation), but it is worth understanding clearly to grasp one of the primary causes of file and free space fragmentation on an OpenVMS disk.

Starting with a completely empty disk, allocating space by choosing the first available clusters in the storage bitmap is a reasonable approach. At least it is until some files are deleted. Until file deletions begin, you would see the storage bitmap bits changing steadily from "free" to "allocated," from beginning to end, like mercury in a thermometer rising from the bulb to the boiling point. The state of the disk is clear: every cluster before a certain point is allocated to one file or another, while every cluster after that same point is free, waiting to be allocated to a new file. Additionally, every file is contiguous – the ideal state for maximum disk I/O performance under most circumstances.

---

[46] **INDEXF.SYS:** The name of the file that contains the information necessary for OpenVMS to identify and access the disk and the files contained on it. **INDEXF** stands for *index file.* The file type **.SYS** indicates that this is a system file, reserved for use by the OpenVMS operating system.

[47] In a volume set, there is an INDEXF.SYS file on each disk in the set.

[48] **Mounted:** The term *mounted* is used to describe a volume that has been introduced to the system and made available for use.

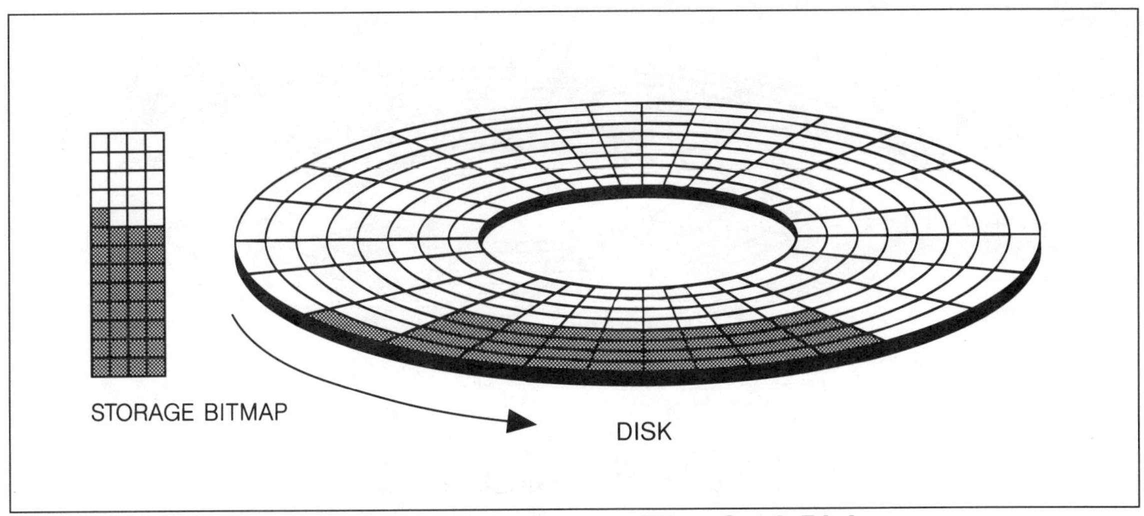

Figure 2-2 Contiguous Files On A Disk

Once even a single file is deleted, however, the OpenVMS scan-from-the-beginning allocation strategy begins to trip over itself. When the file is deleted, naturally, its clusters are marked "free" in the storage bitmap. Our elegant thermometer is now broken, having a gap in the mercury somewhere between the bulb and the mercury's highest point.

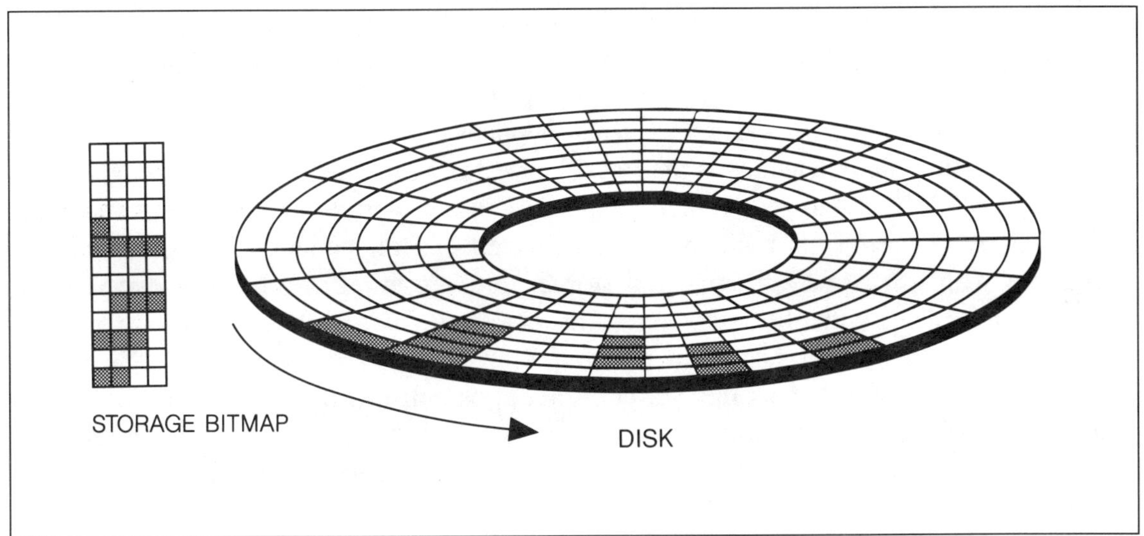

Figure 2-3 Fragmented Files On A Disk

The scan-from-the-beginning allocation strategy is going to find that gap on the next allocation scan and allocate the space to the new file. This is fine, presenting no performance problem or fragmentation susceptibility, *provided the new file fits entirely within the gap vacated by the deleted file.*

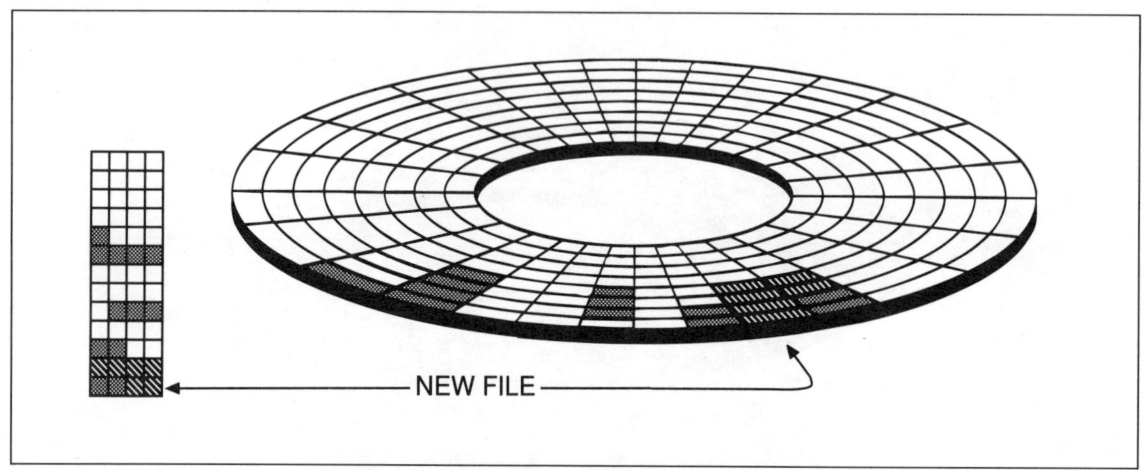

Figure 2-4 New File Allocation

But what if it doesn't fit? What if the new file is larger than the one deleted? OpenVMS will allocate the entire gap (or what is left of it if part has been used already) to the new file and then continue its scan of the storage bitmap to find more space to allocate. With only a single gap in the storage bitmap, this continued scan will take us all the way to the end of the allocated portion of the storage bitmap and there we will find the space to allocate for the remainder of the file. Not so bad. The file has only two extents (fragments). And OpenVMS, as we have seen, was specifically designed to deal with files broken into multiple fragments. This two-fragment file is not a serious problem for OpenVMS, causing only a slight degradation of performance. But what happens when more than a few files are deleted? What happens when dozens, hundreds or even thousands of files are deleted, as is the typical case for an interactive time-sharing system like OpenVMS? What happens is that the mercury in our thermometer becomes shattered into a zillion[49] pieces, with a zillion gaps into which file fragments can be allocated. In fact, even with a maximally fragmented storage bitmap, in which precisely every other cluster is allocated, with the intervening clusters free, OpenVMS continues to merrily allocate disk space on a first-come-first-served, scan-from-the-beginning basis. Space for a 100 block file allocated under these circumstances on a disk with a one-block cluster size would be allocated in 100 separate pieces, giving you a file requiring 100 separate disk I/O operations to service, where a single I/O operation would serve for the same file existing in only one piece.

Why? Well, scanning the storage bitmap takes precious time. Ending the scan at the first available cluster makes for shorter scans and saves time. At least it saves *scanning* time. But what about the 100 times greater overhead required to access fragmented files?

The Extent Cache

As we have seen in Chapter 1, a decade ago there were good reasons for this now seemingly awful blunder. Before inspecting its true impact, however, we have to take into consideration the *extent cache*. The extent cache is a portion of the system's memory that

[49] **Zillion:** A technical term meaning "a lot."

is set aside for the use of the OpenVMS file allocation mechanism. The extent cache stores the LBNs of released clusters, making it easy for OpenVMS to reuse these same clusters without the overhead of a storage bitmap scan.

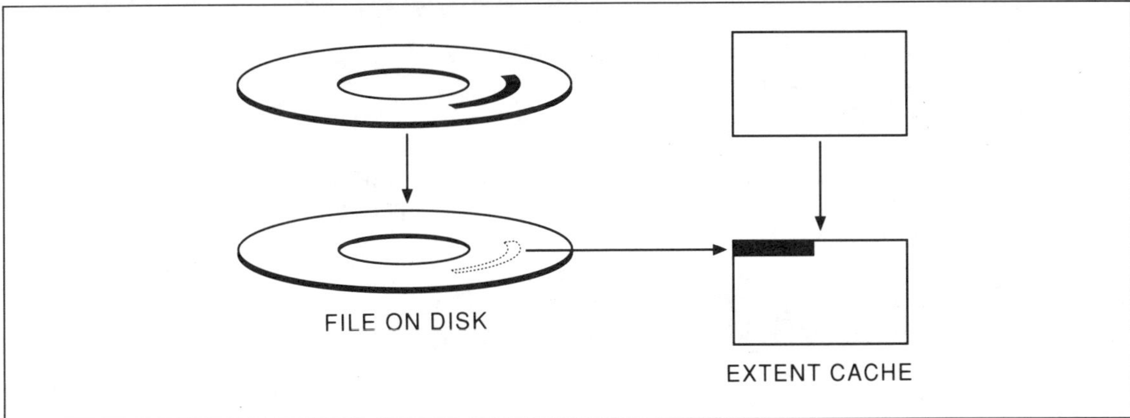

Figure 2-5 Extent Cache

Some argue that the extent cache completely overcomes the drawbacks of the scan-from-the-beginning allocation strategy, claiming that the majority of deleted files (the ones whose clusters will be loaded into the extent cache) tend to reside in the higher LBNs of a disk. While this may be true in a contrived laboratory environment, it is not the case in a typical production environment. In a production environment, with lots of users running programs that create and delete files willy-nilly, the deleted files tend to occur randomly over the entire range of LBNs on a disk.

Seeing It With Your Own Eyes

The above description of the OpenVMS file allocation strategy may seem beyond belief or exaggerated. If you lean towards skepticism, here is a way to demonstrate the matter for yourself.

You need a disk that can be initialized.[50] Of course, this means all files on the disk will be lost, so don't go initializing a disk containing data you need. Use a floppy disk, if you have one on your system, or use a spare disk. If you have neither, use a data disk only after you have backed it up carefully.

You will need two test files: one very small (1 to 4 blocks) called TEST_SMALL.DAT and one somewhat larger (about 100 blocks) called TEST_BIG.DAT. It does not matter what is in these files. Pick any two files you have on hand that are about the right size and copy them, or create a new file using the DCL CREATE command, a text editor or some other procedure of your choice.

[50] **initialize:** The process by which the computer prepares a . . . disk for handling user information. This process erases any information that was on the disk. *(Digital Dictionary)*

Then create the following command procedure, using your own disk device designation[51] in place of **DUA1:**

```
$! Demonstrate Fragmentation Occurring
$
$  initialize /index=end DUA1: DEMO
$  mount DUA1: DEMO
$  count = 0
$LOOP:
$  copy /contiguous TEST_SMALL.DAT DUA1:[000000]TEST_SMALL.TMP
$  copy /contiguous TEST_SMALL.DAT DUA1:[000000]
$  count = count + 1
$  if count .LT. 10 then goto LOOP
$  delete /nolog DUA1:[000000]TEST_SMALL.TMP;*
$  copy /log TEST_BIG.DAT DUA1:[000000]
$  dismount DUA1:
$  mount DUA1: DEMO
$  dump /header /blocks=END:0 DUA1:[000000]TEST_BIG.DAT
$  exit
```

This command procedure initializes the scratch disk so it consists entirely of one big contiguous free space, less the necessary system files. It then creates ten pairs of small files and deletes every other one, leaving ten small files separated by ten small gaps. Next, it copies one large file onto the disk. This large file is invariably broken up by OpenVMS into ten small pieces (occupying the ten small gaps) and one large piece (the remainder). In other words, the file is created by OpenVMS in a badly fragmented condition even though there is plenty of free space further along on the disk in which the file could have been created contiguously.

In the display resulting from the DUMP /HEADER command at the end of the command procedure, file fragments are represented by the Retrieval Pointers. If there is more than one pointer, the file is fragmented. In this example, you should see eleven retrieval pointers. In the dump, the counts and number of map area words are not important for our purposes; it is the number of pointers that you should pay attention to. As you can see from the dump of the header, the file TEST_BIG.DAT is split into many fragments even though far more than 100 free blocks remain on the disk in a single contiguous free space.

When you consider the long-term effects of this allocation strategy on a disk in continuous use, you can see readily that fragmentation can become extreme.

---

[51] **Disk device designation:** In OpenVMS, a disk is referred to by a unique code consisting of letters and numbers that indicate exactly which disk is meant. In the example, "D" means it is a disk device, "U" indicates the type of disk, "A" indicates that it is the first controller for disks of that type on this computer (the second would be "B", the third "C" and so on), and "1" indicates that it is the second disk drive associated with that controller (the first would be "0").

Multi-Header Files

Fragmentation at its worst comes in the form of the multi-header file. As its name implies, this is a file with more than one header or, to be more precise, with a header containing so many retrieval pointers they won't fit into a single one-block header. OpenVMS, therefore, allocates a second (or third or fourth!) block in the INDEXF.SYS file to accommodate storage of the extra retrieval pointers. Just for the record, the first block of a file header will hold all the information there is to know about a file, plus approximately 70 retrieval pointers. A full header block, therefore, can accommodate a file fragmented into as many as 70 pieces. This is pretty miserable, as fragmentation goes, but it can get worse – much worse.

A second header block can be allocated to hold approximately another 102 retrieval pointers. This gets us up to the positively gross level of 172 fragments in a single file. Not wanting to underestimate the depths to which disk management can fall, the VMS developers provided for even more additional header blocks – each one holding another 102 pointers or so. I don't want to take this line of discussion any further, though. Fragmentation to the tune of *hundreds* of fragments per file borders on outright sabotage.

The Magnitude Of The Fragmentation Problem Today

How widespread is the fragmentation disease? *Pandemic* is the word doctors use to describe a disease when virtually everyone has it. Fragmentation is unquestionably pandemic. It occurs on every computer running the OpenVMS system, except:

- a diskless system
- a system with pre-formatted, Read-Only disks (like a CD-ROM server)
- a system that is turned off (expensive doorstop)

If you have a computer system that you don't use very often, its fragmentation problem will be slight. But if you don't use it, who cares?

That leaves us with all the other systems – the vast majority by far. These systems are typically running 24 hours a day, used interactively by the users from somewhere around 8:00 AM to the vicinity of 5:00 PM, with peaks of usage around 10:00 AM and 2:30 PM, and a real dead spot at lunch time. Such systems typically have sporadic usage in the evening, then slam to 100% utilization at midnight when a barrage of batch jobs kick off and run for several hours; usage then tapers off to nearly nothing until the users arrive again in the morning.

Such a system typically has several disk drives dedicated to user applications. These disks get a lot of use, with hundreds of files being created and deleted every day. Naturally, more are created than are deleted, so the disk tends to fill up every few months and stay that way (nearly full) until the System Manager forces users to delete excess files.

Under these circumstances, a disk will fragment badly. You can expect to see a 10% to 20% increase in fragmentation each week. That is, if you had 10,000 files, all contiguous at the beginning of the week, by the same time the next week, you could expect those same 10,000 files to consist of 11,000 pieces or more. A week later, there would be over 12,000 pieces, then 13,000 and so on. After a month, the fragmentation level would exceed 40% with over 14,000 pieces. In three months, the level multiplies to over 240%, with over 34,000 pieces. After a year, the problem would theoretically reach astronomical proportions, with those same 10,000 files fragmented into some 1.4 million pieces. But it doesn't really, as there aren't enough disk blocks to hold that many pieces (on this "typical" disk) and the performance degradation is so bad that users aren't able to use the system enough to keep up the fragmentation rate.

It is true however, that a poorly managed disk, with no handling done for fragmentation will, over time, degrade so badly that it becomes for all practical purposes unusable simply because each file is in so many pieces that the time to access all the files a user needs is just not worth the effort.

CHAPTER 3

HOW CAN YOU TELL IF YOU'VE GOT IT?

Like someone first hearing about a terrible new disease, you may find yourself wondering, "Do *I* have fragmentation? How do I know if I've got it?"

Some System Managers just know they've got it, while others wait for outraged users to complain (tar, feathers and shotguns loaded with peppercorn and rock salt) of rotten performance and use *that* as a measure of fragmentation. Professional System Managers actually look into their VAX or Alpha AXP computer systems.

It is not difficult to find out whether you have fragmentation or not, though it is easier if you have the right tools.

Fragmentation Analysis Tools

The DUMP Utility

The simplest and most direct method for determining whether a file is fragmented is the *DUMP* command, used as follows:

```
$ DUMP /HEADER /BLOCKS=END:0 filespec
```

This command allows you to examine the header of a specific file for multiple retrieval pointers. Each pointer represents one fragment (extent) in the file. So, if there is only one pointer, the file is contiguous (not fragmented at all). If there are two pointers, the file is fragmented into two pieces. Three pointers means three fragments, and so on.

The drawbacks of the *DUMP* command are that it can only be used on one file at a time, requiring an unacceptable amount of time to examine all the files on a disk, and it gives you a lot of irrelevant information, with the map pointers appearing at the end of all the information displayed.

The MONITOR Utility

To determine whether fragmented files are causing your computer to do excessive disk I/O, you can use Digital's *MONITOR* utility, which comes free with OpenVMS. Type this command:

```
$ MONITOR IO
```

You should see a screen that looks something like this:

	CUR	AVE	MIN	MAX
OpenVMS Monitor Utility **I/O SYSTEM STATISTICS** on node CURLY 6-SEP-1993 11:26:20				
Direct I/O Rate	9.50	6.42	0.00	11.58
Buffered I/O Rate	0.66	0.89	0.00	9.27
Mailbox Write Rate	0.71	0.12	0.00	0.96
Split Transfer Rate	1.00	0.81	0.00	6.33
Log Name Translation Rate	0.00	0.22	0.00	0.99
File Open Rate	0.20	0.27	0.00	0.40
Page Fault Rate	3.42	3.08	0.95	20.86
Page Read Rate	3.01	2.21	0.00	6.29
Page Read I/O Rate	1.46	1.03	0.00	3.99
Page Write Rate	0.41	0.87	0.00	0.89
Page Write I/O Rate	0.19	0.63	0.00	0.50
Inswap Rate	0.00	0.00	0.00	0.00
Free List Size	48048.00	48042.65	48042.00	48049.00
Modified List Size	252.00	247.31	246.00	252.00

Example 3-1 MONITOR IO Display

In example 3-1, the word "CUR" indicates the *current* rate of I/O transfers per second. "AVE" means *average*, "MIN" means *minimum* and "MAX" means *maximum.*

The fourth line in the table is the *Split Transfer Rate*. This line tells you how many times the computer is having to do two or more I/O transfers when one would serve. A split transfer is the result of fragmentation. *If there are any split transfers at all, you are suffering performance losses due to fragmentation.*

Now enter this command:

```
$ MONITOR FCP
```

(*FCP* stands for *File Control Primitive*)

You should see a screen that looks something like this:

```
                     OpenVMS Monitor Utility
                   FILE PRIMITIVE STATISTICS
                         on node MOE
                    6-SEP-1993 13:28:53

                                 CUR        AVE        MIN        MAX

FCP Call Rate                    0.66       0.62       0.00       9.63
Allocation Rate                  0.00       0.03       0.00       1.32
Create Rate                      0.00       0.03       0.00       1.98

Disk Read Rate                   0.00       0.61       0.00      17.94
Disk Write Rate                  0.33       0.26       0.00       3.98
Volume Lock Wait Rate            0.00       0.01       0.00       0.66

CPU Tick Rate                    0.33       1.00       0.00      21.85
File Sys Page Fault Rate         0.00       0.03       0.00       0.66
Window Turn Rate                 3.65       0.37       0.00       3.98

File Lookup Rate                 0.33       0.31       0.00       8.97
File Open Rate                   0.33       0.24       0.00       6.31
Erase Rate                       0.00       0.00       0.00       0.00
```

Example 3-2 MONITOR FCP Display

The critical entry in this table is *Window Turn Rate,* which tells you how many times OpenVMS had to load new retrieval pointers from a file's header to gain access to the desired portion of a file. The term *window,* as it is used here, means the set of retrieval pointers the system keeps in memory to access the file. If the file is contiguous, only one pointer is needed to access the file, so a window turn would never occur. A window typically holds seven pointers,[52] so a file can be fragmented in up to seven pieces and still can be accessed without causing a window turn. When there are eight or more pieces, however, one or more pointers have to be flushed and new pointers loaded into the window in memory to get at the later parts of the file. If a file is fragmented into many pieces, windows turns can become a major performance bottleneck.[53]

Split transfers and window turns are not the only consequences of fragmentation, but they are the only ones you can detect with the OpenVMS *MONITOR* utility. If you do not have the *Disk Analysis Utility, Software Performance Monitor* or *VAX Performance Advisor, MONITOR* will have to do.

---

52 While seven is the default number of pointers, a file can be opened using "cathedral" windows that can accommodate a great many more pointers.

53 The severity of the performance bottleneck due to window turns is largely dependent upon the type of file being accessed. It is most severe for indexed files, minor for sequential files and rare for direct (random) access files.

Digital's Performance Utilities

Digital Equipment Corporation offers two system utilities that include some fragmentation analysis capability: the *Software Performance Monitor (SPM)* and *VAX Performance Advisor (VPA)*.[54] Both will tell you a little about fragmentation on your disk, but neither will tell you a lot, as they were designed primarily for other things. And they are a bit pricey, especially when compared to Executive Software's *Disk Analysis Utility*.

Software Performance Monitor (SPM)

Digital's *Software Performance Monitor,* or *SPM* for short, produces two reports that can be used to detect performance problems due to fragmentation. One reports system performance problems in terms of Window Turns and Split I/Os and the other reports information about fragmentation of files and free space on a disk. Unfortunately, the Window Turns and Split I/Os information is only reported on a system-wide basis, so the performance problem cannot be traced to a particular disk. Without knowing which disk is the cause of the problem, there is nothing you can do about it except "fix everything" or use other tools to narrow the search.

We'll look first at the report on Window Turns and Split I/Os. Before you can generate the report, you have to collect data for a while. The DCL command to invoke SPM is "PERFORMANCE" and the parameters for this DCL command are the commands acted upon by SPM.

First, collect the necessary data:

```
$ PERFORMANCE COLLECT=TUNE /CLASS=ALL /OUTPUT=filename
```

In this command, *filename* is the name you want given to the output file. When you have finished collecting your sample of performance data, use this command to stop SPM:

```
$ PERFORMANCE COLLECT=TUNE /STOP
```

Then, generate the report using the same file name as above with this command:

```
$ PERFORMANCE REPORT=LOG_FILE filename
```

This produces an eleven-page report. Only the second page is of interest here, and even that one contains far more data than we need. The report is 132 columns wide, so it is difficult to view on a screen or reproduce on the page of a book. Nevertheless, here is a sample of page 2 of the SPM *SYSTEM* report:

---

[54] Digital has released a product, *DECps,* which replaces SPM and VPA, incorporating the functionality of both products.

```
Report Date: 11-NOV-1991 09:34                         NODE1                                   VAX SPM V3.3-03      Page    2

************************                                FINAL Statistics                                   ***********************
************************     Data Analyzed: from    1-NOV-1991 00:00:00.00  to   8-NOV-1991 15:30:00.00    ***********************

+--- AVE Process-Memory Counts ---+------- Memory Utilization -------+- AVE Mem/CPU -+------------- Swapper Counts --------------+
!                                 !                                  !    Queues     !                                          !
!  Proc   Balset   Free    Modify !  Total   Paged   User    Modify  !               !                    Header  Header  Swaper  !
!  Count  Count    Pages    Pages ! MEMutl  MEMutl  MEMutl  MEMutl   ! Mem      CPU  !  InSWP    Outswp   InSWP   Outswp  CPU %   !
! ------  ------  -------  ------ ! ------  ------  ------  ------   ! -----  ----- ! ------   ------   ------  ------  ------   !
!     42      40   201327    5371 !  23.2%   15.1%   15.3%    2.3%   !     0      0 !      0        0        0       0    0.3%   !
+---------------------------------+----------------------------------+---------------+------------------------------------------+

+------------------------- CPU Statistics -------------------------+-----------------+
!  CPU   Total   Busy   Inter                                      !                 !
!  ID     Idle   Wait   Stack   Kernel   Exec   Super    User  Compat !  System   Task  !
!  ---   ------  ------ ------  ------  ------  ------  ------ ------ !  ------  ------  !
!   1    66.1%   0.2%    4.0%    6.6%    1.9%    4.7%   16.4%   0.0% !   12.8%   21.1% !
!   2    56.3%   0.3%    0.4%   10.5%    3.3%    7.0%   22.2%   0.0% !   14.5%   29.2% !
+------------------------------------------------------------------+-----------------+

+-------- Lost CPU --------+----------- CPU and I/O Overlap ----------+
!                   Page   !                                          !
!  Page    Swap   or Swp   !  CPU+IO   CPU     I/O    Multi   CPU+IO  !
!  Wait    Wait    Wait    !   Idle    Only    Only    I/O     Busy   !
!  ------  ------  ------  !  ------  ------  ------  ------  ------   !
!   2.9%    0.0%    3.0%   !    6.7%   10.7%   54.5%   30.1%   28.1%   !
+--------------------------+------------------------------------------+

+------------------------------------- Paging Rates (per second) ------------------------------------+    +----------------+
!                                                                                                    !    !                !
!  Page   System   Pages   Read    Pages   Write   Free   Modify   Bad    Dzero   Gvalid  Trans  WritIN !    !  Hard    Soft  !
! Faults  Faults   Read    I/Os   Writen   I/Os    List    List    List  Faults  Faults  Faults  Prog  !    ! Faults  Faults !
! ------  ------  ------  ------  ------  ------  ------  ------  ------ ------  ------  ------ ------ !    ! ------  ------ !
!  44.1     0.0    18.7     1.5     0.9     0.1     7.1     8.3     0.0   17.1     9.9     0.1    0.0 !    !  3.3%   96.7%  !
+----------------------------------------------------------------------------------------------------+    +----------------+

+---------- I/O Rates (per second) --------+             +------ File I/O Rates (per second) -----+           +----------+
!                                          !             !                                         !           !   AVE    !
!  Direct  Buffrd  Lognam  Mailbx  Mailbx  !             ! Window  Window   Split   Erase   File   !           !   Open   !
!   I/Os    I/Os   Trans    Reads  Writes  !             !  Hits    Turns    I/Os    I/Os   Opens  !           !   Files  !
!  ------  ------  ------  ------  ------  !             ! ------  ------  ------  ------  ------  !           !  ------  !
!   28.6    32.7    20.3     6.2     6.2   !             !  25.5     0.4     0.2     0.0     3.7   !           !    383   !
+------------------------------------------+             +-----------------------------------------+           +----------+

+---------- File Cache Attempt Rate (per second) ----------+     +---------------- File cache Effectivness ----------------+
!                                                          !     !                                                        !
!   Dir     Dir             File    File             Bit   !     !   Dir     Dir             File    File             Bit  !
!   FCB     Data   Quota    Id      Hdr    Extent    Map   !     !   FCB     Data   Quota    Id      Hdr    Extent    Map  !
!  ------  ------  ------  ------  ------  ------  ------  !     !  ------  ------  ------  ------  ------  ------  ------ !
!    2.1     3.6     0.0     0.2     9.0     0.7     .0.1  !     !  97.8%   92.7%   99.9%   99.0%   66.1%   91.3%   60.7%  !
+----------------------------------------------------------+     +--------------------------------------------------------+
```

Example 3-3 SPM *SYSTEM* Report

If you look closely at this report, in the fifth row of boxes, the middle box is headed *File I/O Rates (per second).* This box contains the two numbers that interest us most: *Window Turns* and *Split I/Os.* Use these numbers to determine the impact of fragmentation on the performance of your VAX. *Any Window Turns or Split I/Os at all* means fragmentation is probably slowing down your VAX or Alpha AXP.

Next we'll look at the report on disk files and space. This time you do not have to collect data before you can generate the report. The command to generate the report is:

$ PERFORMANCE REPORT=DISK_SPACE *diskname*

This produces a report of three pages. There is a lot of useful information in this report, but the key information is *Mean no. extents/file* on Page 2 and the listing of *Files with extension headers* on Page 3. Here is a sample of the SPM DISK_SPACE report:

```
11-NOV-1993 09:43:32.27                         VAX SPM V3.3-03     Page   1

****  Detailed volume analysis for     _HSCOOO$DUA5: *****

Items preceded by 'I','M' or 'S' are controlled by Initialize,
Mount  or Sysgen.

(I  ) Volume name  is 'USERDISK1    '.
(I  ) Serial number is           0.
(I  ) Creation date was  4-NOV-1987 15:22:23.77.
(I  ) Volume owner is 'CAMPBELL      '.
(IM ) Owner uic is [SYSTEM].
(I  ) Format type  is 'DECFILE11B  '.
(IM ) Volume protection is [RWED,RWED,RWED,RWED].
(IMS) Default data checking is NOREAD-CHECK, NOWRITE-CHECK.
(I  ) Structure level is   2, version   1.
(I  ) Allocation cluster size is     3 blocks.
(I  ) Index file bitmap is located at LBN     445614.
(IM ) Default file extension is     5 blocks.
(IM ) Default window size is  10 retrieval pointers.
(I  ) Maximum number of files allowed is     111384.
(IMS) Default number of cached directories is    3.

      Volume size is      891072 blocks with
                              51 blocks/track,
                              14 tracks/cylinder,
                            1248 cylinders/volume.
```

***** Summary of FREE STORAGE for _HSC000$DUA5: *****

Free Storage		Extent Sizes	No. Extents	Cum % Space
>= 3,	<	6	17	0.1
>= 6,	<	9	8	0.1
>= 9,	<	15	6	0.2
>= 15,	<	30	3	0.3
>= 30,	<	60	10	1.1
>= 60,	<	90	2	1.2
>= 90,	<	150	4	2.0
>= 150,	<	300	8	4.1
>= 300,	<	600	2	5.2
>= 600,	<	900	7	12.7
>= 900,	<	1500	14	39.4
>= 1500,	<	3000	18	89.6
>= 3000,	<	6000	2	100.0
>= 6000,	<	9000	0	100.0
>= 9000.	<	15000	0	100.0
>= 15000.	<	30000	0	100.0
>= 30000,	<	60000	0	100.0
>= 60000,	<	90000	0	100.0
>= 90000,	<	150000	0	100.0
>= 150000			0	100.0

Total free blocks = 68736.
No. of extents = 101.
Mean blocks/extent = 681.
Smallest extent = 3.
Largest extent = 3957.

11-NOV-1993 09:43:32.27 VAX SPM V3.3-03 Page 2

**** Summary of ALLOCATED SPACE for _HSC000$DUA5: *****

Space Allocated per Header			No. Headers	Cum % Headers
>= 3,	<	6	5603	41.1
>= 6,	<	9	1905	55.0
>= 9,	<	15	1883	68.8
>= 15,	<	30	1753	81.7
>= 30,	<	60	883	88.2
>= 60,	<	90	544	92.2
>= 90,	<	150	447	95.4
>= 150,	<	300	322	97.8
>= 300,	<	600	84	98.4
>= 600,	<	900	126	99.3
>= 900,	<	1500	34	99.6
>= 1500,	<	3000	27	99.9
>= 3000,	<	6000	9	99.8

```
 >=      6000,  <      9000             6          99.9
 >=      9000,  <     15000            10         100.0
 >=     15000,  <     30000             3         100.0
 >=     30000,  <     60000             2         100.0
 >=     60000,  <     90000             0         100.0
 >=     90000,  <    150000             0         100.0
 >=    150000                           0         100.0

Minimum allocated extent =         3.
Maximum allocated extent =     47262.
Total allocated blocks   =    820965 ( 92.1% of volume).
Total used blocks        =    801995 ( 97.7% of allocated).
No. extents allocated    =     13682.
Mean alloc blocks/extent =        60.
Total no. of files       =     13688.
Mean alloc blocks/file   =        60.
Mean no. extents/file    =         1.
No. extension headers    =         4.
No. multi-volume files   =         0.
No. directories          =       468.

11-NOV-1993 09:43:32.27                           VAX SPM V3.3-03     Page   3

****  Files with extension headers for _HSC000$DUA5: *****

 File name                                                        Ext. headers
 -----------------------------------------------------------      ------------

 [CRANDALL.PJT]M4WC_26SEP.DAT;1                                              1

 [FAIR.CMS.EOF.33]EXEC.LIS;1                                                 3
```

Example 3-4 SPM Disk Space Report

VAX Performance Advisor (VPA)

Before you can produce any report, graph or analysis from VPA, data must be collected from the system over a period of time. You can tell VPA to start collecting the data immediately:

```
VPA> ADVISE /COLLECT /START
```

or you can have it start collecting the data at a later specified time:

```
VPA> ADVISE /COLLECT /BEGINNING="dd-mmm-yyyy hh:mm:ss.cc"
```

Then you have to tell VPA when to stop collecting data. Again, you can tell it to stop immediately:

```
VPA> ADVISE /COLLECT /STOP
```

or at a later specified time:

```
VPA> ADVISE /COLLECT /ENDING="dd-mmm-yyyy hh:mm:ss.cc"
```

Note: You can generate VPA reports while the data capture is running. You do not have to stop VPA to request graphs, reports or an analysis.

Window turns can be reported as a graph. To display a graph of window turns, type the following:

```
VPA> ADVICE /GRAPH=GRAPH /TYPE=CUSTOM=SYSTEM=(WINDOW)
```

Here is a sample of the VPA output showing the Window Turn Rate:

```
                               VPA CUSTOM GRAPH
                                  Node: BOOT
                          Date: 16-SEP-1993 00:00-10:09

                                                LEGEND:
                                                1 =  WINDOW_TURN
                                                (Metric Values are  Stacked)
Y-Units: Window Turn Rate

0.300 !
0.285 !
0.270 !           1
0.255 !           1
0.240 !           1
0.225 !           1
0.210 !           1
0.195 !          11
0.180 !          11
0.165 !          11
0.150 !          11    1
0.135 !          11    1
0.120 !          11    1
0.105 !          11    1
0.090 !          111   1
0.075 !          111   1                                    1
0.060 !          111   1                                    1
0.045 !          111 1 1                                    1
0.030 !  1      1 1111 1 1                                  1             1
0.015 !11111111111111111 111111 11111 111111 11111 111111 11111 111111 11111 111
      +--------------------------------------------------------------------------
       0       1       2       3       4       5       6       7       8       9      10

VPA Command:  ADVISE/GRAPH/NODE=BOOT/TYPE=CUSTOM=SYSTEM=(WINDOW)
```

Example 3-5 VPA Output Showing Window Turns

Example 3-5 shows the Window Turn Rate over a period of ten hours (midnight to 10:09 AM) running generally at about 0.015 window turns per second. Around 2:00 AM, however, there is a burst of activity, with the Window Turn Rate peaking at 0.270 window turns per second.

What does this mean in terms meaningful to fragmentation analysis? *Any window turns at all* indicate a fragmentation problem severe enough to degrade the performance of your system. The more window turns you have, the worse the performance degradation is. The only acceptable number here is zero.

Another useful report you can get from VPA is one showing Split I/Os. To produce this report, enter the following command:

```
VPA> ADVISE /REPORT=PERFORMANCE_EVALUATION=(NOALL_STATISTICS,-
VPA>_ DISK_STATISTICS) /NODE=BOOT
```

On the next page is a sample of such a report:

```
Reporting on Node1
VPA V2.0 Performance                   CLUSTER                          PAGE 1
         Evaluation        Monday 16 SEP  00:00 to 10:16


    +-----------------------------------------------------------------------+
    | The following table gives the summary of all disk activity as seen    |
    | by the indicated node.  An "*" for service node indicates that more   |
    | than one was detected.                                                |
    +-----------------------------------------------------------------------+


Disk     Avg I/O  Avg    Avg     IOsz  Source Service  %     % IO  % IO        # of
Volume   per Sec Queue Kb/sec  in pgs   Node    Node   Busy  Read  Split Type Samples
------   ------- ----- ------  ------ ------ ------ ------ ---- ----- ---- -------
BOOTDISK       (BOOT$DUA0)
            0.21  0.01   0.6     5.6   NODE1 NODE1   0.75   86     0  RD54     309
WORK1       (WORK1$DKA0)
            0.00  0.00   0.0     0.0   NODE1 NODE2   0.00    0     0  UNK      309

CORPDISK       (BOOT$DUC0)
            2.49  0.12   6.7     5.3         NODE1          84     0  RA81
            0.04  0.12   0.1     5.3   NODE1         8.91   84     0           309

DATASHADOW     (USER1$DKB200)
            0.00  0.00   0.0     0.0   NODE1 NODE4   0.00    0     0  UNK      309
WORK2       (WORK2$DUB0)
            0.00  0.00   0.0     0.0   NODE1 NODE3   0.00    0     0  RD54     309
FINDISK        (USER1$DKB400)
            0.00  0.00   0.0     0.0   NODE1 NODE5   0.00    0     0  RD54     309
USERDISK2       (USER2$DKB0)
            0.29  0.03   1.3     8.6   NODE1 NODE4   1.07   88     5  UNK      309

Totals      3.20  0.16   8.66    5.41                       82     0


User Command: ADVISE/REPORT=PERFORMANCE_EVALUATION=(NOALL,DISK_STAT)/NODE=BOOT
```

Example 3-6 VPA Report Showing Split I/Os

The important information in this report, for purposes of fragmentation analysis, is the third column from the right, headed *% IO Split*. This indicates the percentage of I/O requests that resulted in Split I/Os. In this example, you can see that only one disk, USERDISK2, is suffering from Split I/Os and that 5% of the I/O requests to that disk result in Split I/Os. Therefore, you would conclude from this report that about 5% of the USERDISK2 I/O load is resources wasted due to fragmentation.

Disk Analysis Utility

The best tool, in my opinion, is the *Disk Analysis Utility* from Executive Software. This is a program I designed and wrote originally in 1986 with my associate Rick Cadruvi. He has since reworked it and enhanced it to the point where it probably qualifies as a total rewrite now, but it remains the only tool designed specifically and solely to determine the extent of fragmentation on an OpenVMS disk.[55]

The *Disk Analysis Utility* can provide anything from a quick summary to a very detailed analysis. It can be run at any time on any Digital-supported disk and it is not necessary to allocate the disk, dismount it, or stop users from accessing it.

The *Disk Analysis Utility* is invoked with the command:

```
$ DAU disk_name /qualifiers
```

where *disk_name* is the device name of the disk to be analyzed. If *disk_name* is omitted, the *Disk Analysis Utility* will prompt for the disk name. The optional */qualifiers* represents *Disk Analysis Utility* qualifiers, which you can find described in its manual.

Sample Disk Analysis Utility Output

The example on the following pages was produced using the command:

```
$ DAU BOOT$DUA0: /FULL
```

```
                               Disk Analysis Utility
DISK_ANALYSIS V6.0
Copyright (c) 1993 Executive Software International, All Rights Reserved.
_BOOT$DUA0    :                            1-AUG-1993 12:16:39.58
Number of Usable Blocks:   311100       Cluster Size             :        3

<<<<<<<<<<<<<<<<<<<<<<<<<<<<  Free Space Summary  >>>>>>>>>>>>>>>>>>>>>>>>>>>>

Total Free Space Size  :     78260       Smallest Free Space     :      676
Number of Free Spaces  :        16       Largest  Free Space     :     9366
#Spaces =  82% of Total:        10       Mean Size of Free Space:      4891

<<<<<<<<<<<<<<<<<<<<<<<<<<  16 Largest Free Spaces  >>>>>>>>>>>>>>>>>>>>>>>>>>

Start LBN   Size     Start LBN   Size     Start LBN   Size     Start LBN   Size
--------- --------- --------- --------- --------- --------- --------- ---------
   204828      9366    196610      6760     68198      4852     73886      3166
    98304      8232    190860      5748     78336      4126     57390      1516
   118748      7576     51854      5524     36978      3982    165152      1036
   139196      6774     59472      5302     90274      3624     47986       676
```

---

[55] For a free copy of the *Disk Analysis Utility,* write to Executive Software at 701 North Brand Boulevard, 6th Floor, P.O Box 29077, Glendale, California 91209-9077 USA or call 1-800-829-4357.

```
<<<<<<<<<<<<<<<<<<<<<<<<< Free Spaces Distribution >>>>>>>>>>>>>>>>>>>>>>>>>

     Size Range          # Spaces          Size Range          # Spaces
--------------------   ---------   --------------------   ---------
       1 to       2   -        0        511 to     1022   -        1
       3 to       6   -        0       1023 to     2046   -        2
       7 to      14   -        0       2047 to     4094   -        3
      15 to      30   -        0       4095 to     8190   -        8
      31 to      62   -        0       8191 to    16382   -        2
      63 to     126   -        0      16383 to    32766   -        0
     127 to     254   -        0      32767 to    65534   -        0
     255 to     510   -        0      65535 to   311198   -        0

<<<<<<<<<<<<<<<<<<<<<<<<<<<< Free Space Detail >>>>>>>>>>>>>>>>>>>>>>>>>>>>

Start LBN   Size    Start LBN   Size    Start LBN   Size    Start LBN   Size
--------- --------- --------- --------- --------- --------- --------- ---------
    36978      3982     59472      5302     90274      3624    165152      1036
    47986       676     68198      4852     98304      8232    190860      5748
    51854      5524     73886      3166    118748      7576    196610      6760
    57390      1516     78336      4126    139196      6774    204828      9366

<<<<<<<<<<<<<<<<<<<<<<<<<<<< Special Case Files >>>>>>>>>>>>>>>>>>>>>>>>>>>>

Reserved File     : (1,1,0)  [000000]INDEXF.SYS;1
Reserved File     : (2,2,0)  [000000]BITMAP.SYS;1
Zero Length File  : (3,3,0)  [000000]BADBLK.SYS;1
Reserved File     : (3,3,0)  [000000]BADBLK.SYS;1
Reserved File     : (4,4,0)  [000000]000000.DIR;1
Zero Length File  : (5,5,0)  [000000]CORIMG.SYS;1
Reserved File     : (5,5,0)  [000000]CORIMG.SYS;1
Zero Length File  : (6,6,0)  [000000]VOLSET.SYS;1
Reserved File     : (6,6,0)  [000000]VOLSET.SYS;1
Zero Length File  : (7,7,0)  [000000]CONTIN.SYS;1
Reserved File     : (7,7,0)  [000000]CONTIN.SYS;1
Zero Length File  : (8,8,0)  [000000]BACKUP.SYS;1
Reserved File     : (8,8,0)  [000000]BACKUP.SYS;1
Zero Length File  : (9,9,0)  [000000]BADLOG.SYS;1
Reserved File     : (9,9,0)  [000000]BADLOG.SYS;1
Zero Length File  : (36,31,0)  [SYS6.SYSMGR]ACCOUNTNG.DAT;1
Zero Length File  : (581,15,0)  [SYS6.SYSMGR]VMSIMAGES.DAT;14
Placed File       : (1132,20,0)  [SYSE.V4COMMON.SYSEXE]JBCSYSQUE.DAT;3
Zero Length File  : (1478,1,0)  [SYSE.V4COMMON.SYSEXE]NOTICE.TXT;2

<<<<<<<<<<<<<<<<<<<<<<<<<< Most Fragmented Files >>>>>>>>>>>>>>>>>>>>>>>>>>>

      77: (866,2,0)  [SYSE.V4COMMON.SYSLIB]BASIC$STARLET.TLB;1
      73: (86,24,0)  [SYS1.SYSERR]ERRLOG.SYS;1
      34: (116,7,0)  [SYS3.SYSERR]ERRLOG.SYS;1
      19: (26,73,0)  [SYS0.SYSERR]ERRLOG.SYS;1
      10: (81,68,0)  [SYS2.SYSERR]ERRLOG.SYS;1
       9: (1132,20,0)  [SYSE.V4COMMON.SYSEXE]JBCSYSQUE.DAT;3
       7: (1,1,0)  [000000]INDEXF.SYS;1
       6: (24,1,0)  [SYS0.SYSEXE]PAGEFILE.SYS;1
```

```
        4: (34,6,0) [SYS2.SYSEXE]PAGEFILE.SYS;1
        4: (1051,3,0) [SYS3.SYSEXE]PAGEFILE.SYS;1
        3: (1009,8,0) [SYS0.EASYLINK]INMAIL.LOG;1
        3: (1206,24,0) [SYS6.SYSEXE]PAGEFILE.SYS;1
        3: (1225,20,0) [SYS3.SYSMGR]OPERATOR.LOG;70
        2: (230,2,0) [SYS5.SYSEXE]PAGEFILE.SYS;1
        2: (316,11,0) [SYS0.EASYLINK]EMC.LOG;72
        2: (618,8,0) [SYS1.SYSMGR]OPERATOR.LOG;92
        2: (1112,15,0) [SYS2.SYSMGR]OPERATOR.LOG;68

<<<<<<<<<<<<<<<<<<<<<<<<<<<<<  File Information  >>>>>>>>>>>>>>>>>>>>>>>>>>>>>>

Maximum Number of Files:    51866       # Reserved      Files   :        9
Total Number of Files  :     1545       # Placed        Files   :        1
Total Size of all Files:   230607       # Multi-Header Files    :        2
Smallest File Size     :        1       # Multi-Volume Files    :        0
Largest  File Size     :    50000       # Directory     Files   :      125
Mean  Size of all Files:      150       # Zero Length Files     :        9
# Extent Headers       :        1       # Files with Frags >= 2:        17
Total File Fragments   :     1763       Lost Blks/Extent Cache :      2333
Mean Fragments per File:     1.10       Total Split I/Os        :     1291

<<<<<<<<<<<<<<<<<<<<<<<<<<<<  File Sizes Summary  >>>>>>>>>>>>>>>>>>>>>>>>>>>>

     Size Range            # Files            Size Range            # Files
--------------------     ---------      --------------------     ---------
       1 to       2   -       335          511 to    1022   -         11
       3 to       6   -       288         1023 to    2046   -          8
       7 to      14   -       179         2047 to    4094   -          4
      15 to      30   -       267         4095 to    8190   -          1
      31 to      62   -       187         8191 to   16382   -          4
      63 to     126   -       134        16383 to   32766   -          2
     127 to     254   -        81        32767 to   65534   -          1
     255 to     510   -        34        65535 to  311198   -          0

<<<<<<<<<<<<<<<<<<<<<<<<<<<  File Fragments Summary  >>>>>>>>>>>>>>>>>>>>>>>>>>

  Fragments     # Files      Fragments     # Files      Fragments     # Files
 -----------   ---------    -----------   ---------    -----------   ---------
      0     -          9        6      -          1       12     -          0
      1     -       1518        7      -          1       13     -          0
      2     -          5        8      -          0       14     -          0
      3     -          3        9      -          1       15     -          0
      4     -          2       10      -          1       16     -          0
      5     -          0       11      -          0       17+    -          4
```

Example 3-7 DAU Output

How to Read the Disk Analysis Display

The heading includes the title, the version of the program used, a copyright notice, the physical device name of the disk analyzed and a date/time stamp indicating when the report was generated. The physical device name of the disk is provided to ensure there is no mistake about which disk is being analyzed, because the utility accepts logical as well as physical disk names as input.

Number of Usable Blocks is the total number of usable blocks on the disk, whether allocated or free.

Cluster Size is the minimum allocation quantity for that disk. It is the number of blocks represented by each bit in the storage bitmap. The cluster size is set by the System Manager at the time the disk is initialized.

The *Free Space Summary* section gives information about free space on the disk so you can determine the degree of free space fragmentation.

Total Free Space Size is the number of disk blocks that are unoccupied, including the number of blocks in the extent cache for this disk on the local node.[56]

Number of Free Spaces is the total number of free spaces (of any size) on the disk.

#Spaces = nn% of Total indicates how many free spaces combined represent 80% or more of the free space on the disk. In the example, ten free spaces constitute 82% of the free space on the disk.

Smallest Free Space is the size in blocks of the smallest free space on the disk.

Largest Free Space is the size in blocks of the largest free space on the disk.

Mean Size of Free Space is the average size of a free space, calculated by dividing the total free space size in blocks by the number of free spaces.

The table headed *16 Largest Free Spaces* shows the location and size in blocks of the 16 largest contiguous free spaces on the disk. Space held in system caches is considered only if the user has the privileges required to access such information.

The table headed *Free Spaces Distribution* shows the number of free spaces on the disk categorized by size in blocks. In the example, there is one free space from 511 to 1022 blocks in size, two more in the range 1023 to 2046, three in the range 2047 to 4094, eight in the range 4095 to 8190 and two between 8191 and 16382.

The table headed *Free Space Detail* shows the size and location of unallocated free spaces on the disk, in order from LBN 0 to the end of the disk. Again, space held in system caches is considered only if the user has the privileges required to access such information.

---

56 If the user does not have system privileges, the *Total Free Space Size* can be misleading because it omits free space in the extent cache in other nodes of a cluster.

The table headed *Special Case Files* shows files that may be of special interest to the System Manager. The list includes files reserved for use by the file system, directory files, zero length files, multi-header files, placed files and any multi-volume files if the disk is part of a volume set. The files are listed both by File ID and by name.

The table headed *Most Fragmented Files* shows the files that have the most fragments, in order from most fragmented to least. Only files that have two or more fragments are listed, but the size of the list (64 files by default) can be limited by the use of the /MOST_FRAGMENTED_FILES=*n* qualifier. The number of fragments in each file is shown as well. Multi-header files appear several times, as these are listed once for each header.

The *File Information* table is a collection of statistical information about the files and fragments on the disk.

Maximum Number of Files is the total number of files that can be created on the disk.

Total Number of Files is the total number of files (headers) currently on the disk, including zero-length files.

Total Size of all Files is the number of disk blocks that are occupied. Blocks allocated to a file but not yet written are included in the total as well.

Smallest File Size is the size in blocks of the smallest file on the disk.

Largest File Size is the size in blocks of the largest file on the disk.

Mean Size of all Files is the average size of all files, calculated by dividing the total size of all files by the total number of files, excluding zero-length files.

 # Extent Headers is the number of extra (extension) file headers. This does not include the primary header required for each file.

Total File Fragments is the total number of pieces of files on the disk. Note that it is possible for this number to differ from, and even be less than, the *Total Number of Files* figure, because zero-length files are included in the *Total Number of Files,* but such files consist of zero fragments.

Mean Fragments per File shows how many fragments there are in the typical file on the disk (total number of fragments divided by total number of non-zero-length files). This is an index of how fragmented the files on the disk are. If the mean fragments per file is 1.00, the files are all contiguous. If the figure is 1.10, then 10% of the files, on average, are in two pieces. 1.20 means 20%, 1.30 means 30%, etc. A figure of 2.00 means the files average two fragments each. 1.00 is the best figure attainable, indicating that all files or nearly all files are contiguous.

Reserved Files is the number of files reserved for use only by the file system.

Placed Files indicates how many files on the disk are fixed at their current location using OpenVMS placement control.

Multi-Header Files indicates the total number of headers associated with files that have more than one header.

Multi-Volume Files indicates how many files on the disk span two or more disks in a volume set.

Directory Files indicates how many directory files there are on the disk.

Zero Length Files indicates how many files have no blocks allocated to them.

Files with Frags >= 2 indicates how many files have two or more fragments, meaning these files are fragmented (not contiguous).

Lost Blks/Extent Cache is the result of the following calculation:

Number of Usable Blocks – (Total Free Space Size + Total Size of all Files)

In other words, this value is derived from two arithmetic operations. The number of blocks known to be free is added to the number of blocks known to be in use. This sum is subtracted from the size of the disk to arrive at Lost Blks/Extent Cache. Therefore, this value represents all the blocks that are not accounted for. They are not in use and they are not available for use. Their status is unknown. On an active disk, this is not alarming. These blocks may be any combination of:

- blocks marked allocated that are not yet actually part of a file (due to space being allocated in anticipation of writing data);

- blocks held in another node's extent cache for this disk; or

- blocks that were added to this node's extent cache while the *Disk Analysis Utility* was running.

Total Split I/Os indicates how many I/O operations since system boot time have been split into two or more I/O operations to retrieve data split across two or more fragments of a file. This is the most meaningful indicator of the actual cost of fragmentation on your system. It is important to note, however, that this value is the total split I/Os for the entire system, not just for one disk. Therefore, defragmenting only one disk on a multi-disk system may only cause this value to decrease slightly. It may be necessary to defragment all the disks on the system to see this value reduced to zero (following the next reboot).

The table headed *File Sizes Summary* shows the number of files on the disk categorized by size in blocks. In the example, there are 335 1 to 2 block files, 288 files from 3 to 6 blocks in size, and so on.

The table headed *File Fragments Summary* shows the number of files on the disk categorized by number of fragments. In the example, there are 9 zero-length files, 1518 files with one fragment each (contiguous), 5 files with two fragments each, and so on.

Note: The figures provided by the *Disk Analysis Utility* constitute a rolling snapshot of the state of the disk, so the figures can appear inconsistent at times.

Customized Analysis

Another, more direct approach, is this: Run some tests on your system to get some idea of how good or bad its performance is. If you don't have tools to do this, you can make some up. Time the system response. How long is it from the time a user hits the RETURN key after a command until the first characters are displayed on the screen in response to that command? How many users can log in before the system starts to bog down? How long does a major batch job take to complete? These are tests you can run on your own system that tell you how well *your* system is performing under *your* conditions at *your site*. Be sure to run these tests when the system is in use by everyday users. Otherwise, you get a distorted picture that reflects a laboratory environment instead of your real environment.

Then, once you have run these tests and documented the results, backup your disks. You probably do this once a week or so anyway, so it doesn't cost you any extra work if you time your testing to occur shortly before the backup.

Then, initialize each disk and restore the complete disk from backup. (Be very, very sure you have a valid, usable backup before initializing the disk because, once you do, the data on that disk is *gone*. The /VERIFY qualifier on the BACKUP command is useful for this purpose.) When you initialize the disk, be sure to use sensible values for such qualifiers as /CLUSTER_SIZE=*n*, /DIRECTORIES=*n* and /HEADERS=*n*. Low values for these will cause your INDEXF.SYS file to be excessively fragmented and may contribute to fragmentation in other ways. (See Chapter 5 for recommendations on minimizing fragmentation by proper initialization of disks.)

After initializing each disk, restore the data from backup, making sure you use the /NOINITIALIZE qualifier on the BACKUP command to prevent BACKUP from overriding your initialization parameters. This results in disks that are, for the moment at least, free of fragmentation.

Now run your tests again, under conditions as similar to the first test as possible. Compare the results and see just how much fragmentation was costing your own site in terms of performance.

CHAPTER 4

WHAT'S WRONG WITH FRAGMENTATION?

When you find out you have fragmentation, your next concern might be, "How bad is it?" If the *Disk Analysis Utility* reveals a Mean Fragments Per File (fragmentation rating) of 1.2 (badly fragmented) or more, you may be in trouble. You had better do something about that *fast,* before the system stops altogether.

If you think I am exaggerating, consider this: One site, with a combination system/user disk with 4.9 fragments per file required nearly half an hour for each user to log on. This dropped to a few seconds once the main disk was defragmented. Another system, with an incredible 18.7 fragments per file, was literally unusable until defragmented.

A fragmentation rating of 1.2 means there are 20% more pieces of files on the disk than there are files, indicating perhaps 20% extra computer work needed. It should be pointed out that these numbers are merely *indicators.* If only a few files are badly fragmented while the rest are contiguous, and those few fragmented files are never accessed, the fragmentation may have no performance impact at all. On the other hand, if your applications are accessing the fragmented files heavily, the performance impact could be much greater than 20%. You have to look further to be sure. For example, if there were 1,000 files and only one of those files is ever used, but that one is fragmented into 200 pieces (20% of the total fragments on the disk), you have a serious problem, much worse than the 20% figure would indicate. In other words, it is not the fact that a file is fragmented that causes performance problems, it is the computer's attempts to access the file that degrade performance.

To explain this properly, it is first necessary to examine how files are accessed and what is going on inside the computer when files are fragmented.

What's Happening to Your Disks?

Here's a diagram of a disk:

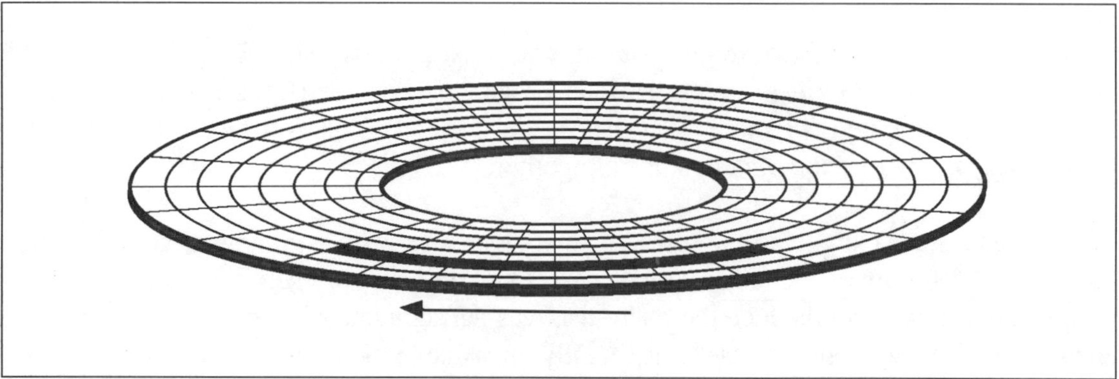

Figure 4-1 Disk

This diagram represents one side of a single platter. The circles represent tracks, though in reality there would be far more tracks on one side of a platter. Within one track is a shaded strip representing a file. Imagine a head on an arm, not much different from the needle on the tone arm of a phonograph, moving from file to file as the platter spins. The contents of the file can be scanned from the disk in one continuous sweep merely by positioning the head over the right track and then detecting the file data as the platter spins the track past the head.

Now here is a diagram of a disk with one file broken into two parts:

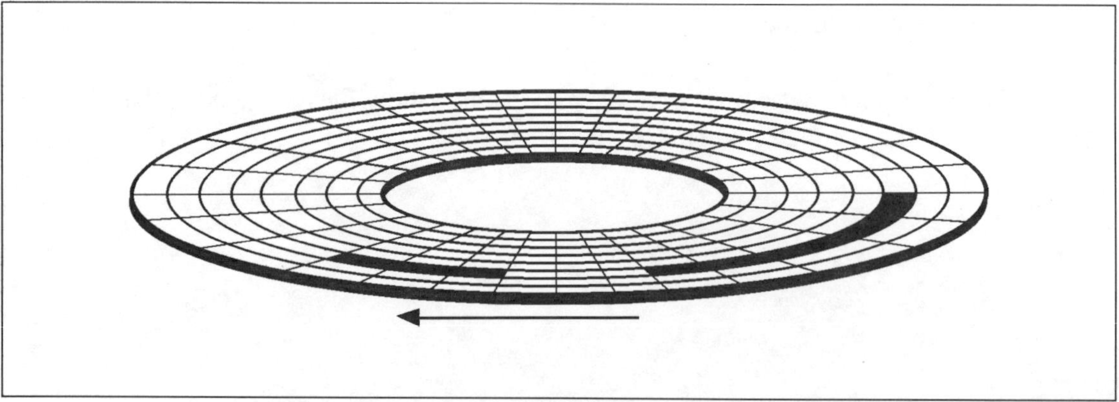

Figure 4-2 Disk With File In Two Parts

In this case, the file is fragmented into two parts on the same track. Thus, to access this file, the head has to move into position as described above, scan the first part of the file, then suspend scanning briefly while waiting for the second part of the file to move under the head. Then the head is reactivated and the remainder of the file is scanned.

As you can see, the time needed to read the fragmented file is longer than the time needed to read the unfragmented (contiguous) file. The exact time needed is the time to rotate the entire file under the head, *plus* the time needed to rotate the gap under the head. A gap such as this might add a few milliseconds to the time needed to access a file. Multiple gaps would, of course, multiply the time added. The gap portion of the rotation is wasted time due solely to the fragmentation disease. Then, on top of that, you have to add all the extra operating system overhead required to process the extra I/Os.

Now let's look at another disk:

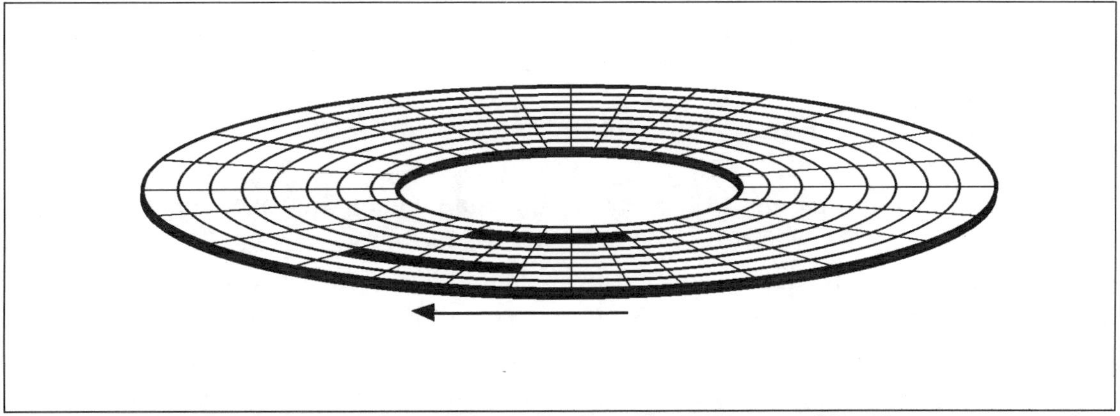

Figure 4-3 Two File Extents On Different Tracks

In this case, the file is again fragmented into two parts. But this time the two parts are on two different tracks. So, in addition to the delay added by the rotation of the disk past the gap, we have to add time for movement of the head from one track to another. This track-to-track motion is usually much more time-consuming than rotational delay, costing tens of milliseconds per movement. Further, this form of fragmentation is much more common than the gap form.

To make matters worse, the relatively long time it takes to move the head from the track containing the first fragment to the track containing the second fragment can cause the head to miss the beginning of the second fragment, necessitating a delay for nearly one complete rotation of the disk, waiting for the second fragment to come around again to be read.

But the really grim news is this: files don't always fragment into just two pieces. You might have three or four, or ten or a hundred fragments in a single file. Imagine the gymnastic maneuvers your disk heads are going through trying to collect up all the pieces of a file fragmented into 100 pieces!

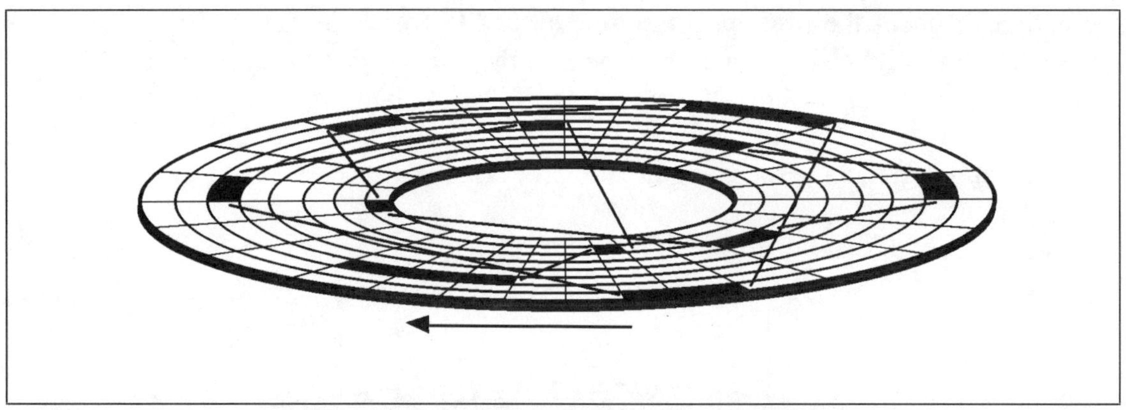

Figure 4-4 File In Many Fragments

When it takes more than one I/O to obtain the data contained in one (fragmented) file, this is known as a *split transfer* or *split I/O*. When a file is fragmented into more than the seven pieces that can be accommodated by a single file window, and the eighth or later fragment is accessed, one or more retrieval pointers are flushed from the window and it is reloaded with seven more retrieval pointers. This is called a *window turn*. When more than 70 pointers are required to map (indicate the location of) a file in its header, a second (or third, or fourth) file header is required. The name for that is a *multi-header file*. Each of these fragmentation symptoms costs overhead, and each one described costs much more than the one before.

For every split transfer, the overhead of a second (or third, or fourth, etc.) disk I/O transfer is added. For every window turn, the overhead of reloading the window, in addition to the I/O required just to access the fragment is added. For every multi-header file accessed, add to each I/O the overhead of reading a second (or third, or fourth, etc.) file header from the INDEXF.SYS file.

On top of all that, extra I/O requests due to split I/Os and window turns are added to the I/O request queue along with ordinary and needful I/O requests. The more I/O requests there are in the I/O request queue, the longer user applications have to wait for I/O to be processed. This means that fragmentation causes everyone on the system to wait longer for I/O, not just the user accessing the fragmented file.

Fragmentation overhead certainly mounts up. Imagine what it is like when there are 300 users on the system, all incurring similar amounts of excess overhead.

What's Happening to Your Computer?

Now let's take a look at what these excess motions and file access delays are doing to the computer.

OpenVMS is a complicated operating system. It is complex because it has a great deal of functionality built into the system, saving you and your programmers the trouble of building that functionality into your application programs. One of those functions is the service of providing an application with file data without the application having to locate every bit and byte of data physically on the disk. OpenVMS will do that for you.

When a file is fragmented, OpenVMS does not trouble your program with the fact, it just rounds up all the data requested and passes it along. This sounds fine, and it is a helpful feature, but there is a cost. OpenVMS, in directing the disk heads to all the right tracks and LBNs within each track, consumes system time to do so. That's system time that would otherwise be available to your applications. Such time, not directly used for running your program, is called *overhead.*

You can see overhead depicted graphically on your system by using the *MONITOR* utility. Type this command:

```
$ MONITOR MODES
```

You should see a display that looks something like this:

```
                          OpenVMS Monitor Utility
          +-----+         TIME IN PROCESSOR MODES
          | CUR |              on node LARRY
          +-----+           10-SEP-1993 13:41:31
                              0         25        50        75        100
                              + - - - - + - - - - + - - - - + - - - - -+
Interrupt Stack            47 |*******************
                              |         |         |         |          |
MP Synchronization            |
                              |         |         |         |          |
Kernel Mode                20 |********
                              |         |         |         |          |
Executive Mode             12 |*****
                              |         |         |         |          |
Supervisor Mode               |
                              |         |         |         |          |
User Mode                  22 |*********
                              |         |         |         |          |
Compatibility Mode            |
                              |         |         |         |          |
Idle Time                     |
                              + - - - - + - - - - + - - - - + - - - - -+
```

Example 4-1 MONITOR MODES Display

The critical line of this display is the *User Mode* line. That's the one that tells you how much of the VAX's computing capacity is being used to run application programs. Everything else is mostly overhead, unless you are running PDP-11 programs in compatibility mode,[57] in which case that would have to be counted as productive (!) time as well.

Idle time, of course, is unused computer time, but that is a type of overhead, isn't it? When you look at this display, you really want to compare the *User Mode* value to the total of the values above it. The modes higher in this table show you how much of your computer's time is being spent doing work on your behalf, other than running the application program itself. In my experience as a System Manager, I have been fairly satisfied to see these values split in a 2-to-1 ratio. That is, I expect to see two-thirds of the system being used directly for running applications in user mode, and one-third being consumed by overhead. If you see more than one-third of the system spent on overhead, as in the example above, you have a performance problem, and fragmentation is a good place to look for the cause.

If there is fragmentation and system overhead is high, as indicated by large values for Interrupt Stack and Kernel Mode, you probably have a situation in which OpenVMS is

[57] **compatibility mode:** Some VAXes have the ability to run PDP-11 programs as if the VAX were a PDP-11 computer running the RSX-11M operating system. When operating in this way, the VAX is said to be in *compatibility mode.*

spending a lot of extra time processing I/O requests because two or three or more actual I/O transfers have to be done to collect up all the pieces of fragmented files. This adds up to a performance problem.

What's Happening to Your Applications?

What's happening to your applications while all this overhead is going on? Simple: Nothing. They wait.

What's Happening to Your Users?

Oh yes, the users. . . .

The users wait, too, but they do not often wait without complaining, as computers do. They get upset, as you may have noticed.

The users wait for their programs to complete, while excess fragments of files are chased up around the disk. They wait for keyboard response while the computer is busy chasing up fragments for other programs that run between the user's keyboard commands. They wait for new files to be created, while the operating system searches for enough free space on the disk and allocates a fragment here, a fragment there, and so on. They wait for batch jobs to complete that used to get done faster on the same computer with the same user load, before fragmentation robbed them of their machine time. They even wait to log in, as the operating system wades through fragmented command procedures and data needed by startup programs. Even backup takes longer – a lot longer – and the users suffer while backup is hogging the machine for more and more of "their" time.

All the users know is this: The system is slow; you're in charge of the system; it's all your fault. And they're right. If you are the System Manager, you are responsible for the computer system and its performance.

If management and finance people are aware of the problem, they view it as paying for 100% of a computer system, but getting something less for their money. The users are not only upset, they're getting less work done and producing less income for the company. That's bad, and it's *your* responsibility.

Something had better be done about it, and quickly.

CHAPTER 5

WHAT CAN YOU DO ABOUT IT?

What can you do about fragmentation? Get rid of it, of course.

How? There are several ways, all of which will be explained here. It's not hopeless. Something can be done about it.

Clear off Disks

First off, you could keep your disks half empty. This discipline, enacted as a matter of policy, would keep enough free space so files would not fragment so badly on creation. It is at the moment of file creation that the fragmentation problem begins. When a disk is nearly full, the free space on the disk tends to fragment badly. This greatly increases the likelihood that a newly created file will be created in many small fragments. When a disk is half empty, the free space tends to occur in larger pools (because there is more of it), increasing the chances that newly created files will be created in a single contiguous piece or, at worst, in only a few larger fragments. So a policy of keeping disks half empty reduces the fragmentation problem by prevention.

Of course, this solution carries the drawback of having to have twice as much disk space as you really need. Nice if you have the budget.

Copy / Contiguous

A second solution is to use the DCL command DUMP /HEADER to examine files that are known to be in heavy use and, when a fragmented file is found, use the DCL command COPY /CONTIGUOUS to defragment the file, purging the old copy once the new one is made. This is a simple and inexpensive solution, but tedious, to say the least. It has the additional drawback of changing the creation and backup dates of each file copied, which means your incremental backups are going to swell with files that have not materially changed. It also changes the File I.D. for the file, which may cause problems for your batch and print queues. Further, you must be very sure not to attempt this at the same time an application is accessing the file. At best, the application could be locked out and may abort processing. At worst, the application could update the *old copy* of the file during your copy-making and the updates would be lost in the purge. Another major drawback of this technique is that it marks the file as having to be contiguous. This causes OpenVMS to recopy the file to another area of the disk whenever the file is extended if there is not enough contiguous free space immediately following the file. Still another major problem is alias file names. OpenVMS allows a file to have two or more different names, called *aliases*. The file must not be open when this method of defragmentation is used, but it is possible, if the file has an alias, that the file could be open under the alias and so this technique could fail.

The exact commands for this technique are:

```
$  DUMP /HEADER /BLOCKS=END:0 filespec
$  OPEN /ERROR=FILE_OPEN INPUT_FILE filespec
$  CLOSE INPUT_FILE
$  COPY /CONTIGUOUS filespec filespec
$  PURGE filespec
$  EXIT
$
$FILE_OPEN:
$  WRITE SYS$OUTPUT "File open, try again later"
$  EXIT
```

Backup and Restore

From the time Digital's users first started complaining about fragmentation, the officially recommended remedy was something called "backup and restore." The "and restore" part of this is the critical part. Omitted from the phrase "backup and restore" is the critical middle step – *initialize.*

"Backup" is easy. You already do that anyway, so it doesn't take any more time or effort than you already expend just to make sure your files are safely backed up. Backing up a disk, however, does absolutely nothing for fragmentation. To cure the fragmentation, it is necessary to then reinitialize the disk after the backup and then restore all the files to the disk.

Initializing the disk, of course, effectively deletes every file from the disk. The data can then be restored from the backup tape (or other media), and the data is restored in a clean unfragmented, contiguous fashion.

There are drawbacks to this solution, too. Not the least of these is the time it takes to restore the information to the disk. This takes just about as long as the backup process itself, which is not exactly quick.

Another drawback is the absolute requirement for a backup that it be precisely accurate in every respect. If the tape is badly flawed or the drive has malfunctioned, your data is lost. You simply cannot get that data back. So you are strongly encouraged to verify your backup tapes before initializing the disk. The verify pass, of course, also takes quite a long time.

Perhaps the most aggravating drawback of backup and restore is that it has to be done after hours. You can't very well erase all the users' files while they are using them, and people get really upset when you take away access to their files during the workday. So you stay late at night or come in on the weekend to handle this chore.

Now, in my experience as a System Manager, my friends weren't working nights and weekends. They used these times for sensible activities like having fun with their families or nights out on the town. And there is nothing like long hours of tedious, boring backup and restore to remind you of that fact. They're out having fun and you're not.

To compound the aggravation, it is nearly impossible to get any other useful work done while doing a backup. If you're using a 9-track tape drive, you have to jump up every ten minutes or so to change the tape. There isn't much useful work you can do that can be interrupted every ten minutes, so you are reduced to an awful lot of busy work or just plain sitting around. And this goes on for *hours*.

I know at least one System Manager who would have been divorced by his wife if he hadn't solved this after-hours backup and restore problem.

To look at this from the dollars and cents viewpoint, if your system doesn't sit idle every night, what does it cost your organization to shut the thing down for a night or two to defragment the disks? It's not cheap. Even a small system costs enough to make you want to avoid downtime like the plague.

For those who don't mind these difficulties or who have no better solution, the commands for doing a backup and restore operation are:

```
$ BACKUP /IMAGE /VERIFY disk-device tape-device
$ INITIALIZE disk-device
$ BACKUP /IMAGE /NOINITIALIZE /VERIFY tape-device /SAVE_SET disk-device
```

Initialization Procedures

As long as you are initializing the disk anyway, there are several things you can do at the same time to make that disk less susceptible to fragmentation and better performing, too.[58] These are explained in detail in the *Prevention* section, later in this chapter.

Disk-to-Disk Copy

An abbreviated form of the *backup and restore* technique that is much faster is the disk-to-disk copy. This technique requires a spare disk drive exactly like the one you want to defragment.

58 After you initialize the disk, however, make very sure you use the /NOINITIALIZE qualifier on the BACKUP command. Otherwise, BACKUP will reinitialize the disk using its default settings.

What you do is make an image backup (a logical copy) of the fragmented disk onto the spare disk drive. The BACKUP utility automatically initializes the new disk unless you initialize it yourself and suppress BACKUP's initialization with its /NOINITIALIZE qualifier. BACKUP then copies the files contiguously to the new disk, leaving all the free space in two large areas. Then you change the disk drive number physically so OpenVMS will know where the data is. Unfortunately, you also have to power down and restart the disk drives for the plug swap to take effect.

This technique is very fast – as fast as you can copy one entire disk onto another. The obvious drawback is the expense: it requires having a spare disk drive. Another drawback is that you still have to backup the data separately, unless you can afford to keep the spare disk drive tied up as a backup to the defragmented disk. Yet another drawback is that, to ensure the data doesn't change in the middle of the copying, you have to block access to both disks, depriving the users of access to their files for the duration of the process.

The commands for this technique are:

```
$ INITIALIZE disk-2 label_name
$ BACKUP /IMAGE /NOINITIALIZE /VERIFY disk-1 disk-2
```

The initialization advice given for the *backup and restore* technique on page 66 applies equally to this method.

Defragmentation Software Products

There are software products available that you can use to defragment disks. These are referred to as *defragmenters.* They come in two forms: off-line defragmenters and on-line defragmenters. We'll examine each separately.

Off-Line Defragmenters

An off-line defragmenter is a computer program used to defragment a disk. It is differentiated from on-line defragmenters in that you have to take a disk out of service (off-line) to use the defragmenter on it.

Why? This type of defragmenter analyzes a disk to determine the state of fragmentation and then maps out a rearrangement of the files on the disk that will reduce or eliminate the fragmentation. After mapping out where the files should go, it rearranges them. This type of defragmentation has to be done off-line to accommodate the drawbacks inherent in such a method:

1. Having a separate analysis pass and then the actual file rearrangement pass presents the biggest problem. If, after calculating the ideal position for each file on the disk, some user application comes along and deletes a file, adds a new file or extends an existing file, the

analysis is instantly obsolete and the planned rearrangement is unlikely to provide ideal results. In fact, rearranging files with an obsolete analysis is downright dangerous. If the defragmenter were to write data into an area it thinks is free but that has become occupied since the analysis, user data could be lost. By taking the disk out of service, so no user application can access any file on the disk, this danger is eliminated.

2. This type of defragmentation is like throwing all the files up in the air and slipping them into the right slots as they come back down. What if something happens while the files are up in the air? I am not talking about adding, changing or deleting a file. I am talking about a disaster. Suppose the system goes down or the disk fails? What happens to the data files that are "up in the air?" Most likely, they are lost.

The remedy for this is a logging facility that keeps track of what files are "up in the air" at any given moment, keeping copies of the files in a scratch space so the file can be reconstructed following a catastrophic interruption. Logging and reconstruction such as this is extremely complicated in a constantly changing environment, so such a defragmenter must be run off-line in an unchanging, laboratory-like environment.

3. Since many sites tend to keep their disks very nearly full, there may not be enough room for the defragmenter to make a copy of a file to be defragmented, particularly a large file. For this reason, the off-line type of defragmenter often uses a scratch area on a second disk for copies of files being defragmented. This may require taking *two* disks out of service – the one being defragmented and the one with the scratch area. It certainly requires that the defragmentation be done off-line to reduce the risk of data loss. Even so, a power failure may leave you with an important file (is there any chance it would be an *unimportant* file?) stranded out in the scratch area, with recovery dependent upon a special procedure you need to run to get the file back. But what if the power failure is in the middle of the night when you're not around? And what if the stranded file is the program image containing the recovery procedure?

Of course, the ultimate drawback for this off-line method of defragmentation is taking the disk out of service. Taking the disk out of service, obviously, means no one can use it. The disk, if not the entire system, is "down" for the duration of the defragmentation activity. The users' data is inaccessible. Like backup and restore, this solution carries a heavy penalty.

Now take a look at this: Let's say it takes two hours to do that defragmentation job (and I have seen reports of off-line defragmentation efforts taking ten times that long). That's two hours of lost computer time. *How much performance increase does your defragmenter have to achieve to make up for two hours of complete downtime?* You're right, it's a lot. It seems to me that the cure is worse than the disease.

Because of these serious drawbacks, because of the outrageous cost of shutting down a computer system for the duration of the defragmentation process and because a much better solution arrived, off-line defragmenters have all but disappeared from the market.

On-Line Defragmenter

An *on-line defragmenter* is one that processes disks while user jobs are active, even while user applications are accessing files on the same disk that is being defragmented. It is not necessary to take the disk off-line or allocate it to the defragmenter process.

An on-line defragmenter eliminates the drawbacks inherent in off-line defragmenters.[59] There is no analysis pass to become obsolete when users add, change or delete files. Rather, each file is analyzed individually as the defragmenter turns its attention to defragmenting that particular file. The files are not "thrown up in the air" and juggled. Instead, each file is copied into a new location and, once safely there, removed from the old location. It doesn't use a scratch area in which files can get lost. The file being defragmented is kept intact in its original position while the new, contiguous copy is created elsewhere on the same disk.

But the real advantage of an on-line defragmenter is that of keeping the disk in service while the defragmenting is done. No more hours of downtime; no more downtime at all. Only with this type of defragmenting can the system performance improve without sacrificing an equal or greater amount of system resources to do so.

How long should a defragmenter take to do its job? Less than the time and resources being lost to fragmentation. If your system loses 20% of its resources to fragmentation, a defragmenter that consumed even 19% would be worthwhile (though not much). Clearly, the fewer resources that are consumed, the more worthwhile that defragmenter would be. The point is that some defragmenters consume 21% or even more of your system's resources. So this cost of defragmentation must be weighed against the cost of performance losses due to fragmentation.

Another major factor to consider is the amount of time and effort spent by you, the System Manager, in managing the defragmenter. The ideal on-line defragmenter would be one of the "set it and forget it" variety. You just install it on your system and it takes care of everything from then on.

---

59 Watch out, however, for supposed "on-line" defragmenters that are really off-line defragmenters modified to run with users active on the system. Such products suffer from the same drawbacks described for off-line defragmenters.

Prevention

There are several major performance problems that should be handled before addressing the quality of defragmentation. These are multi-header files, user files on the system disk, and unnecessary data checking. It is also well worth your while to invest a little system management time in organizing the system so fragmentation occurs less often and is a little slower to creep in. Techniques for doing this are discussed later in this section.

Like the old saying, "An ounce of prevention is worth a pound of cure," a little care taken *before* fragmentation becomes a problem can save a lot of time, effort and headaches cleaning up the mess later.

Clearing unneeded files off the disks is by far the most effective means of preventing fragmentation. The more space you can keep free on the disks, the less likely files are to become fragmented. It should be noted, however, that reducing disk space in use below 50% does not improve things much – not enough to warrant the cost of maintaining so much unutilized disk capacity. On the other hand, even if you cannot keep the disks half empty, keeping them 40% empty, or 30% or even 20% helps a lot. In my own experience, I have observed that VAX disk I/O performance is great when the disk is 50% empty or more. Performance worsens slightly as the disk fills to 80% of capacity. Above 80%, performance really goes to the dogs quite rapidly and, if you are running above 90% full, you have a built-in performance problem of severe proportions.

When I see a disk above 90% full, I lose all interest in fragmentation and get busy clearing off some space on that disk. The performance gains from doing so are clearly noticeable.

It is not as difficult to free up 10% of a disk as you might think. I have personally accomplished this feat numerous times by the simple expedient of issuing a notice to all users (via a NOTICE file in the login procedure). The notice says, "The disks on our computer system are too full. Delete all unnecessary files from the system within 24 hours. If sufficient space is not freed up by then, the System Manager will delete files from the directories of the worst offenders until sufficient space is available. Files not needed now which might be needed later can be stored in archives until they are needed."

This notice *always* gets good results. Sometimes, it brings 20% or more free space with no further action than that. Of course, you have to actually enforce it once in a while, but a check of each user's total file sizes usually reveals a user or two who is abusing the system wholesale, with dozens of versions of old, old files that haven't been touched in months. This is the guy who saves *everything* and consumes as much space as half the other users combined.

To detect this varmint, merely enable disk quotas briefly and run off a report of how many disk blocks each user is consuming. Then you can turn off disk quotas if you don't really need them on. (Disk quotas cost overhead.)

Another source of wasted space is users who have left the organization. Archive their files and delete them from the system.

Time spent in clearing off disks to 20% or more free space will be the best investment you can make in improving disk I/O performance and preventing fragmentation.

Preventive Measures When Initializing a Disk

Disk Cluster Size

Keep in mind that initializing a disk erases everything on that disk. Therefore, it is advisable to use the INITIALIZE command only after first doing the BACKUP/VERIFY step, to ensure that you have a backup of the disk and that its data integrity has been verified.

Make sure you choose the correct cluster size for the intended use of the disk. Disks larger than 50,000 blocks default to a cluster size of three when initialized, but this may not be the best value for your intended use. A cluster size of one incurs the maximum possible overhead in disk I/O, but assures the availability of every last block on the disk. A cluster size of three reduces the size of the storage bitmap on the disk by a factor of three and speeds file allocation, but one or two disk blocks are wasted for every file that is not a multiple of three blocks in size. If your average file size is one, this could be a tremendous waste – two-thirds of the disk!

The next page shows a table displaying the amount of disk space wasted for various cluster sizes when the file sizes vary randomly:

Cluster Size	Avg Blocks Wasted per File	Max Files on 456MB Disk at 80% Full	Blocks Wasted
1	0	712,858	0
2	0.5	356,429	178,214
3	1.0	237,619	237,619
4	1.5	178,214	267,322
5	2.0	142,572	285,143
6	2.5	118,810	297,024
7	3.0	101,837	305,510
8	3.5	89,107	311,875
9	4.0	79,206	316,826
10	4.5	71,286	320,786
11	5.0	64,805	324,026
12	5.5	59,405	326,726
13	6.0	54,835	329,011
14	6.5	50,918	330,970
15	7.0	47,524	332,667
16	7.5	44,554	334,152

Table 5-1 Wasted Space Due To Cluster Size Setting

Check the current cluster size for your disks using this DCL command:

```
$ SHOW DEVICES /FULL
```

When choosing the cluster size, consider first what is most important with respect to that disk: speed of access (large cluster size) or maximum utilization of the available space (small cluster size). Then consider what the average size of a file will be on that disk. If most files will be small and saving space is important, use a small cluster size – perhaps half the size of an average file. If most files will be large and speed is more important than saving space, use a large cluster size – perhaps 16. The maximum is 1/100th the size of the disk. Research shows that the typical disk has an average file size of eight blocks.
The command for setting the cluster size when initializing a disk is:

```
$ INITIALIZE /CLUSTER_SIZE=n diskname label_name
```

Data Checking

When initializing a disk, do not use the /DATA_CHECK qualifier unless you really need the extra level of safety it affords. /DATA_CHECK increases disk I/O by causing read-after-write operation and, optionally, read-after-read to verify data integrity. That is to say, every time an application reads from or writes to the disk, a follow-up read is performed and the data compared for accuracy. *Data checking need not be turned on for this feature to be used.* Critical applications can use it any time, whether it is turned on or not, by specifying data checking in their I/O routines. Having data checking turned on causes this feature to be in effect for *every* I/O to that disk. If this is not what you want, make sure it is turned off. The default is /NODATA_CHECK, so chances are you have not been using this feature anyway.

The command for turning off data checking when initializing a disk is:

```
$ INITIALIZE /NODATA_CHECK diskname label_name
```

Directory File Pre-allocation

The DCL INITIALIZE command allows you to pre-allocate space for directories. Unfortunately, it defaults to only sixteen directories, so most disks require additional directory file space to be allocated. The additional directories are created smack in the middle of production processing, disrupting application I/O and scattering the newly-created directory files all around the disk. When you initialize a disk, estimate how many directories will be created on it, and specify a slightly larger number with the INITIALIZE /DIRECTORIES=*n* qualifier.

The command for preallocating directory space when initializing a disk is:

```
$ INITIALIZE /DIRECTORIES=n diskname label_name
```

File Header Pre-allocation

The DCL INITIALIZE command allows you to pre-allocate space for file headers in INDEXF.SYS. Unfortunately, like INITIALIZE /DIRECTORIES, it defaults to only sixteen files, so most disks require additional space to be allocated to INDEXF.SYS after the disk has been initialized. The extra space allocated is often not contiguous to INDEXF.SYS, so this all-important file becomes fragmented right from the start. When you initialize a disk, it is very important for consolidation of free space on your disk that you estimate how many files will be created on it and specify a slightly larger number with the INITIALIZE /HEADERS=*n* qualifier.

The command for preallocating space for file headers when initializing a disk is:

```
$ INITIALIZE /HEADERS=n diskname label_name
```

Index File Location

When initializing a disk, the disk's index file can be forced to the beginning of the disk (toward LBN 0), the middle of the disk, the end of the disk, or to any specific block desired. I recommend that the index file be placed at the end of the disk using the INITIALIZE /INDEX=END qualifier. This frees up the maximum amount of space near the beginning of the disk, where OpenVMS will be allocating new files. Having few or no files near the beginning of the disk guarantees the fastest possible file creation times and increases the likelihood that new files will be contiguous when created.

The command for locating the index file when initializing a disk is:

```
$ INITIALIZE /INDEX=END diskname label_name
```

Preventive Measures After a Disk Has Been Initialized

Even if you cannot reinitialize your disks to obtain better performance, you can modify volume characteristics to improve the situation somewhat. The following commands can be used after a volume has been initialized and should be considered for use on all your disks.

Turn Off Data Checking

Use the DCL command SHOW DEVICES /FULL to find out whether a disk has data checking enabled for read, write or both. If it does, you will see in the SHOW DEVICES display heading the words, "data check on reads," "data check on writes" or both. Data checking increases disk I/O by causing read-after-write operations and, optionally, read-after-read to verify data integrity. If you have data checking enabled and you do not really need the extra level of safety it affords, disable data checking with the following DCL command:

```
$ SET VOLUME /DATA_CHECK=(NOREAD,NOWRITE) diskname
```

This is the default condition for a newly initialized disk.

Turn Off Erase On Delete

Use the DCL command SHOW DEVICES /FULL to find whether a disk has *erase on delete* enabled. If it does, you will see in the SHOW DEVICES display footing the words, "erase on delete". *Erase on delete* increases disk I/O by causing a system-specified pattern to be written into a file area when the file is deleted. The pattern makes it harder to figure out what was in the file before it was deleted. Some sites, particularly in the defense industry, require this for security purposes. If you have *erase on delete* enabled and you do not really need the security it affords, disable it with the following DCL command:

```
$ SET VOLUME /NOERASE_ON_DELETE diskname
```

Increase Extend Quantities

Use the DCL command SHOW RMS_DEFAULT to find out what the RMS[60] extend quantity is. The RMS extend quantity determines how many blocks are allocated each time a file is extended. This should be raised to a large value, such as 100. If a file, such as a log file, is extended many times, and the extend quantity is small, the file is likely to become extremely fragmented because the (small) extents are created in different places on the disk. If the extend quantity were large, the file would be less fragmented because the pieces of the file would be larger. There is little adverse impact to this action, as excess allocation is truncated when the file is closed. Use this DCL command to set the RMS extend quantity:

```
$ SET RMS_DEFAULT /SYSTEM /EXTEND=100
```

Note that changing the volume extension quantity with the DCL command SET VOLUME /EXTENSION=100 is overridden by the RMS_DEFAULT value.

Other Hints

With all these preventive measures, it is important to bear in mind that *the whole purpose for defragmenting is to speed system performance and responsiveness.* While fragmentation is guaranteed to ruin system performance, it is not the only thing that causes performance problems. If one of the things covered in the two sections above is out, the performance degradation that results may be as bad as fragmentation-induced problems or worse. Needless to say, if your purpose is to improve performance, these remedies should be used in addition to defragmenting to get all the gains you can get.

Unneeded data checking, for example, can *double* the number of I/O operations on a disk. If the extra safety of data checking is not needed on your system, enormous performance gains can be had by the one simple measure of disabling data checking.

Along these same lines, you should know that system disks are the worst place to store user files. System disks work pretty hard for OpenVMS and storing user files on the system disk causes excess disk I/O whenever a user is accessing those files. Worse, that user's disk I/O, since it is I/O to the system disk, affects the performance of the entire system. The situation is compounded for a common system disk,[61] as two or more OpenVMS systems are working from the same system disk. Give yourself a big performance boost by moving all user files off the system disk.

One last recommendation I have is that you reduce subdirectory[62] levels. Each time a file is accessed, the file itself is not the only disk access required. The Master File Directory

---

[60] **RMS:** *R*ecord *M*anagement *S*ervices. An OpenVMS facility to aid in storing and retrieving file data.

[61] **common system disk:** A system (OpenVMS-resident) disk that is used by more than one VAX (or Alpha AXP) simultaneously as the system disk for that VAX. Two comparable VAXes using one common system disk doubles the I/O to that disk. Three VAXes would triple the I/O, and so on.

[62] **subdirectory:** A directory within a directory. Seven levels of subdirectories are allowed in OpenVMS.

must be accessed, the main-level directory file, and any subdirectory files as well. Each access requires a disk read, unless the directory is already in the directory cache. Fortunately, directories are usually in the cache (often 90% of the time), so this is a minor problem. Nonetheless, a definite performance improvement can be obtained by reducing the number of subdirectory levels on a disk.

When Would You *Not* Want to Defragment a Disk?

The simple answer to this question is that the only time you would ever want to *not* defragment a disk is when it is already defragmented. It is hard to imagine a circumstance when you would want to leave a disk fragmented. But I'll do my best. . . .

The INDEXF.SYS file, as noted earlier, is deliberately fragmented into four pieces. Leave it that way if you want your disk to be accessible after the next reboot. If the index file is fragmented into more than four pieces, however, you can improve free space consolidation quite a bit by defragmenting it. The only way this can be done is by BACKUP and RESTORE, but when you reinitialize the disk between BACKUP and RESTORE, you must pre-allocate sufficient file headers (see page 74, the section on pre-allocating file headers).

OpenVMS contains support for locking a file at a specific LBN. Such a file is called a *placed file*. Theoretically, in a realtime environment, you could lay out a disk with files placed at specific, known points around the surface of the disk and thus guarantee the fastest possible transition of the disk head from one file to the next. I say *theoretically* because I have never heard of anyone actually doing this and it certainly would be a meaningless exercise for a disk in an on-line, interactive user environment. The random motions of the head seeking data for multiple user applications would defeat utterly any pre-planned movement of the head amongst placed files.

Finally, I return to the same old argument: you would not want to defragment a disk when the cost of doing so exceeds the return you would get in terms of performance. So after each defragmentation pass, some little time must pass and some amount of performance degradation must occur for the cost of the next defragmentation pass to be justified. Let me tell you, we are really getting down to the picky details now. All I am saying is that you would not want to attempt to defragment a disk immediately after you had just defragmented it.

The Cost of Fragmentation

To determine whether a defragmentation pass is worth it or even whether the purchase of a defragmenter is worthwhile, you need to know the cost of fragmentation. There is no flat answer to this. It is different for every system. A little-used system in a non-critical environment has a lower cost for performance losses than one in a round-the-clock, mission critical application.

To sort this out for *your* system, this book includes an appendix (Appendix B) devoted to a step-by-step calculation of the costs of fragmentation and justification of the cost of handling it.

Conclusion

The conclusion is, inescapably, that while you can do something to prevent fragmentation, the prevention is incomplete and temporary. And, while there are solutions built in to OpenVMS, these solutions are incomplete and tedious in the extreme. A defragmenter is the only solution that directly addresses and is specifically designed to solve the fragmentation problem. Accordingly, the next chapter is devoted to a detailed discussion of defragmentation by means of a defragmenter.

CHAPTER 6

GETTING THE COMPUTER TO CLEAN UP AFTER ITSELF

This chapter is devoted entirely to the defragmenter as a solution to the fragmentation problem.

History

Defragmenters are not new, as things go in the computer industry. The first one became available for VAX/VMS in 1986. The concept was a simple one: get the computer to clean up after itself, saving the System Manager from the drudgery of doing it himself. I hasten to point out that this simplicity and clarity of purpose was not as obvious at first as it seems in looking back. In fact, the first defragmenter for VAX/VMS took longer to run and had a higher risk of data corruption than backing up the entire disk to tape and restoring it. It had the sole distinction of being the first software product designed specifically for defragmenting disks and disk files. It achieved this distinction by virtue of being a conversion of a defragmenter from another computer and operating system to VAX/VMS. To be first, it paid the price of insufferably slow performance and severe risk of data loss. Needless to say, this product and the company that produced it have long since vanished from the market.

Nevertheless, it was a start, and a crack in the walls of Digital Equipment Corporation's system software[63] fortress. Before 1986, Digital had a virtual monopoly on system software for the VAX. But, when it came to defragmentation, Digital's official view was that on-line defragmentation was "not an easy problem."

Each year, a large group of Digital's customers, members of the Digital Equipment Computer Users Society (DECUS), surveys its members to determine the things that most need improvement in the OpenVMS operating system. This survey is called the System Improvement Request (SIR) ballot. In the 1985 SIR ballots, on-line disk compression (another word for defragmentation) placed first in the survey by a large margin in the United States and second in Europe. Digital customarily responds to the top ten items on the SIR ballot. In Europe, Digital's response took the form of a talk by Andy Goldstein, a top guru for Digital's revered VMS Central Engineering group, in which he said:

> We agree that's a fine idea. . . We certainly intend to take a good hard look at this problem. I have some experience with it. I actually worked for RSX[64] back in the old days when we had a gadget called DCU[65] which some of you may

[63] **system software:** That software which is intended solely for the benefit of the computer system, including its environment and operational management. It is differentiated from *application software,* which has the purpose of providing a specific service or result to *users* of the computer system.
[64] **RSX:** *R*esource *S*haring e*X*ecutive. The name of an earlier operating system for Digital's PDP-11 model computer.
[65] **DCU:** *D*isk *C*ompression *U*tility. An off-line style defragmenter for RSX systems.

> remember. I think DCU was a very good demonstration to us all that this is not an easy problem. One of the interesting problems, other than simply interpreting the file structure correctly, is coordinating the compression with ongoing file activity, and of course clusters add a unique twist to that. Also, the performance problem is quite difficult because in-place disk compression is to the best of my understanding an n-squared problem[66] and so with some very large disks you run into some very serious performance problems. Obviously you can do intelligent things to make it run faster, and we are going to have to spend some considerable time and attention in getting reasonable performance out of it.[67]

In the U.S., Digital's official response appeared in the February 1986 DECUS newsletter:

> While the importance of on-line compression is obvious in retrospect, this is a new request for us in that it has never appeared so prominently in past SIR ballots. We do not have any current plans to build such a facility. However, we understand its importance and we understand that it will increase as time goes on.
>
> There are a number of difficult problems to deal with, including coordinating ongoing file activity with the compression process, and solving the performance problem on large disks (since disk reorganization is inherently an n-squared order problem).
>
> We will investigate this for future VMS development.[68]

These statements by Digital were alarming. Here we had a very large group of customers on two continents declaring this to be their single biggest problem with Digital's flagship product and Digital's official response was that they had no current plans to deal with it!

It would appear that the roadblock in Digital's path was the fixed idea that on-line defragmentation was an "n-squared order problem." This idea is basically a declaration of the impossibility of solving the problem in an acceptable way. Fortunately for the customers, there is nothing like a public declaration of impossibility from an expert to prompt entrepreneurs into action.

The second quote, in fact, was a driving factor in convincing more than one software company to throw its hat into the defragmenter ring. It seemed to be assurance that Digital would not be coming along anytime soon to steamroller the market with its own solution in the form of an "official" Digital defragmenter, even in the face of huge customer demand. True enough, it was not until more than five years later, on December 9, 1991, that Digital announced a disk defragmentation product. During those five years, Digital repeatedly declared its policy on the subject of defragmenters to be that the

---

66 An **n-squared order problem** is one that squares in difficulty for each increment in size of the problem. For example, a problem of size 2 has a difficulty of 2 x 2 = 4, while a problem of size 3 has a difficulty of 3 x 3 = 9. As the numbers grow large, the difficulty of the problem snowballs. A problem of size 20, though only ten times as large as the 2 problem, has a difficulty of 20 x 20 = 400, or 100 times the difficulty of the 2 problem.

67 VAX Special Interest Group Question and Answer session held at the DECUS European Symposium at Cannes, France. September 1985.

68 *PAGESWAPPER* (newsletter of the VAX Special Interest Group within the Digital Equipment Computer Users Society), February 1986.

possibility of obtaining performance gains by use of a disk defragmenting utility was a "misconception." The official Digital solution was:

> Digital recommends that disk volumes be saved and restored on a regular basis, using the VMS Backup Utility. When the volume is restored, all the files will be allocated contiguously, and the free space on the disk will be collapsed into one area. Plus, a backup copy of the disk will exist.[69]

The policy statement went on to speculate on the horrors that might befall a defragmenter user if something went wrong.

This policy was based on unsound advice. The policy statement ignores the risk inherent in backup and restore: that of unreadable tape. This is not an insignificant risk. What happens if you backup a disk to tape, reinitialize it and then find that the tape is unreadable? You're up the river without a paddle, as they say. That data is gone and it's gone for good. Not so obvious, but a serious concern is that the backup and restore process is so tedious and so time-consuming[70] that one-quarter of the System Managers surveyed recently said *they have never bothered to do it*. How good can a solution be if it is never used at all?

On top of that, Digital's policy statement lacked any serious testing to determine whether the facts on which it was based were true. I know, because *I did serious testing*. The best that could be said for Digital would be that Digital had lumped all defragmenters together and assumed that what is true for one must be true for the rest. Don't get the idea that I think badly of Digital. I admire the company in many ways. But Digital has over 95,000 employees and sometimes some of these employees don't communicate very well with each other.

So, first Digital said it couldn't be done. Then, when it was done by others, Digital said its usefulness was a misconception. Now Digital is fielding its own defragmenter product. You draw your own conclusion.

In any event, in 1986 the defragmenter happened. Now there was a tool for the specific purpose of defragmenting disks. Best of all, an on-line variety of defragmenter was developed and did everything itself, automatically.

An On-Line Defragmenter

Laying aside the off-line variety as an unsatisfactory solution, let's take a look at what an on-line defragmenter is, exactly, and how it works.

---

69 *VMS Systems Dispatch,* August 1989, Digital Equipment Corporation.

70 By forcing a disk out of service, the backup-and-restore process can also present a serious financial hardship to the organization that depends on the data on that disk for its operations.

An on-line defragmenter is distinguished from an off-line defragmenter by the fact that you do not have to shut down the system, kick the users off or take a disk out of service to use the defragmenter. An automatic on-line defragmenter goes a step further and includes a mechanism for determining when to defragment. The non-automatic version is manual in this regard – it requires the System Manager to decide when to defragment. The automatic on-line defragmenter has some mechanism for determining when to defragment – whether by sensing the state of fragmentation or by measuring the degree of fragmentation between defragmentation passes or just by waiting a certain time and then cleaning things up again.

Ideally, the on-line defragmenter keeps a record of how badly fragmented the disk is every time it makes a defragmentation run and, based on that information, increases or decreases the time intervals between runs.

This is not a simple problem. Perhaps the single greatest contributing factor to the problem is the fact that OpenVMS includes no mechanism for determining how often a particular file is accessed.[71] If you could find out how often a file is accessed, you would know how critical that file is to system performance and thus how much attention the defragmenter should give to keeping that particular file contiguous. Another important factor is the lack of any mechanism to determine whether a file has been accessed at all.[72] Without either mechanism, we are reduced to looking mostly at indirect measures of the impact of fragmentation on the system. These measures are described in Chapter 3.

What's Wrong With Fragmentation?

Once it has been determined, by whatever mechanism, that it is time to defragment a disk, the defragmenter has to determine whether defragmentation can be done safely at that time or whether it should wait for a better time to do it. It also has to determine whether the defragmentation activity would degrade system performance unacceptably at that time. It even has to check whether defragmentation will do any good; maybe the disk is in such good shape that defragmentation would be a waste of resources. In this case it would just wait for a while longer and check again later on.

When the defragmenter has determined that the time is right, the next question is, "What files should be defragmented?" On even the most badly fragmented disk, some files are contiguous. Attempting to defragment these would be a waste of time and resources, so some means is needed of detecting them and causing the defragmenter to skip processing those files – all with a minimum of overhead, of course. Other files (such as INDEXF.SYS) must not be defragmented because to do so would interfere with the proper operation of the operating system.

---

[71] OpenVMS does keep a revision date for files, but this tells you only when the file was last written. No information is kept about *reads* of files.

[72] There is an archiving mechanism used for determining when a disk volume or the files on it should be archived, but this mechanism does not properly serve our purpose and, worse, imposes a high amount of overhead.

Then, amongst the files that *should* be defragmented, some determination must be made as to which should go first. Should the files be processed in order of appearance in their directory files? Should the most fragmented files be processed first? Or is some other order best? Does it matter at all?

When a file is selected for defragmenting, the defragmenter has to determine where on the disk to put the newly-created defragmented file. The wrong location might do nothing to improve the condition of free space fragmentation or might even make it worse. Some intelligence is required to choose the best place on the disk for the defragmented file, keeping in mind the gaps that will be created when the fragmented version is deleted.

Then there is the question of what if no single place on the disk is suitable? Could the file be split into two or more pieces and still be better off than in its present fragmented state? Maybe. Maybe not.

Suppose the disk is so messed up that it is going to take two or more defragmentation passes to get the disk into good shape. How does this affect decisions on where to put a defragmented file? Could it profitably be put into a *worse* position on the first pass, anticipating movement to its ideal position in a subsequent pass?

When a new location is selected, how exactly should the copying be done? Should the file be copied directly into the new location or should it be copied first into a temporary location and then moved to its final destination? And how do you deal with user attempts to access that file while it is in the middle of being relocated? What if someone attempts to modify the original file after the copy has been made, but before the new file formally takes the place of the old one? And, not the least of our worries, what if the system goes down right in the middle of all this?

An automatic on-line defragmenter also has a quality control problem. How can it be sure the file was copied correctly and users can now access every bit of the new file exactly as they did the old?

These are the obvious problems in the simple case. No mention has been made of problems unique to multi-header files, files that span disk volumes, or files that are held open by the system on a complete bypass of the usual procedures so there is no way to tell whether a file is in use or not.

OK, gentle reader, the scary part is over. I hope you are still reading so you can receive the news that there are solutions to all these problems. My purpose in rattling off these problems is to show you that defragmentation is a complicated undertaking, that it has been thought through and we defragmenter vendors are not playing around with your irreplaceable data with our heads stuck in the sand. The important thing to know is that the computer system itself has the answers to these questions within it or, at least, it has the data from which answers can be formulated.

An automatic on-line defragmenter then, is one which uses the data already available within the computer, without the need for operator intervention, to determine when to defragment disks and disk files, what files to defragment, the order in which to defragment them, where to put the new, contiguous files, whether to completely or only partially defragment a particular file, to do all this without interfering with user access to the disk and disk files and to do so with absolute 100% guaranteed data integrity. Yes, this can be done and, at this writing, is being done on tens of thousands of OpenVMS systems around the world.

Done right, this solution to fragmentation requires no attention from the System Manager or operations staff at all. It is a complete elimination of fragmentation as a problem for that OpenVMS system. Such an automatic solution to a problem inherent in the operating system is called an *operating system enhancement,* as opposed to the manual, tool-variety solution, which is called a *utility*.

Safety

A good on-line defragmenter does not just provide a means for recovery of user data in the event of a system crash during the defragmentation process; it actually processes files in such a way that no data can be lost. It is possible and practical to create the new, defragmented version of the file, verify its accuracy and replace the old version with the new in between user accesses to the file, all the while guaranteeing that directory and INDEXF.SYS file information refers to a flawless copy of the file. With such a method, there is no window for error in which a file of user data can be lost, even when the system crashes at the worst possible moment.

Apparently, it was concern about this potential window for error and uncertainty about its handling that kept Digital out of the defragmenter business until 1991. In that year Digital incorporated a mechanism into OpenVMS version 5.5 to relocate a file without any window for error. The mechanism adopted by Digital, called MOVEFILE, is similar to the mechanism a leading defragmenter had been using since 1986. When MOVEFILE appeared, Digital's public concerns about the safety of on-line defragmenters ceased, at least for those defragmenters that used the official Digital mechanism for moving files!

The solution is easily explained. Relocating a file on the disk for purposes of defragmenting is a multi-step process. Doing some of the steps without doing the rest can result in a file that is confused, damaged or even lost. The solution is to isolate *the critical steps that must be all completely done or none done at all* and treat these as a single step. Such a group of steps treated as a unit is called a *primitive*. In version 5.5 of OpenVMS, this operation is called the *movefile primitive*. It moves a file from one location on a disk to another, guaranteeing that all the steps necessary to move the file will be fully complete, or none of the steps will be done at all. Thus, you can be sure that the file is either fully moved intact or remains fully intact at its old location. No in-between state can exist.

Therefore, even if the system crashes, you can be confident that all your data still exists without corruption of any kind.

Unmovable Files

Some files are unmovable, either because the OpenVMS operating system depends upon the file being at a fixed location or because an application program has fixed the file at a certain location and requires it to remain there. The defragmenter must take care to detect such files and leave them where they are. It is worth noting, however, that programmer errors in applications and even in certain OpenVMS utilities, such as the MAIL facility, sometimes result in a file having the "fixed placement" attribute when there is no reason or intention for that file to remain fixed in place. So how do you know whether a file is supposed to be placed or not? The rule I use as a System Manager is that no one has any business fixing files in place except the System Manager; at least not without his or her knowledge and permission. So, if the file is not an OpenVMS system file and you, as the System Manager, did not put it there, the file is erroneously marked "placed" and you can feel free to move it.

This is not a very safe rule for a defragmenter, however, and any defragmenter should honor file placement control just in case someone really does need that file to be in that exact place.

System Disks and Common System Disks

System disks present special problems for a defragmenter and common system disks are even harder to deal with. Until recently, there were exactly nine files on an OpenVMS system disk that could never be defragmented while the system was up. Now there are many more, though the number varies from system to system. The only ways to process these untouchable files are to shut down the system and use Stand-Alone Backup to backup and restore the system disk, or to arrange for the system disk to be accessible from a VAX or Alpha AXP as a user disk and defragment the disk off-line.

These are not usually viable options, so system disks were originally excluded from processing by defragmenters. Some defragmenters skirted the issue by excluding all files in a system root directory,[73] processing only files that reside on the system disk outside those directories reserved for the OpenVMS operating system. The remarkable aspect of this is that user files residing on the system disk probably cost more performance than moderate levels of fragmentation. The System Manager could get a bigger performance boost by *moving those files off the system disk* than by defragmenting them, bigger perhaps than defragmenting all the fragmented user files on user disks.

A good defragmenter knows exactly which files can be moved and which cannot, so it can defragment a system disk just as freely as any user disk without risk to the system. The

---

[73] **system root directory:** A top-level directory that contains system files and subdirectories. All files used by the operating system are in this directory or subdirectories under it. System root directories are named SYS0, SYS1, SYS2, and so on.

same is true for a common system disk, where the system files of two or more different systems reside, though extra care must be taken by the defragmenter to ensure that another system's unmovable files are left in place even though they will not appear unmovable to the system on which the defragmenter is running.

Quorum Disks

A quorum disk is one which substitutes for a VAX or Alpha AXP computer, acting as a node in a cluster. The reasons for this are complex and not important to defragmentation. The important thing is that, as on a system disk, certain files on a quorum disk must not be moved. The defragmenter has to take this into account.

Performance

The main reason, if not the only reason, for defragmenting a disk is performance. If you know nothing of fragmentation, you can become quite perplexed watching a system's performance become worse and worse, week after week, month after month, with exactly the same hardware configuration, the same software applications and the same user load. It's almost as if the machine left the factory with planned obsolescence built into it. How can the performance of the exact same system be so much worse if nothing has changed? Well something did change: the files and disk free space fragmented with use. The proof? Defragment the disks, and the system performs like new.

The sinister side of this is that fragmentation occurs so gradually that you might not notice the creeping degradation. If system response worsens by only a fraction of a second each day, no one is likely to notice from one day to the next. Then, weeks or months later, you realize that system response is intolerable. What happened? Your system has caught the fragmentation disease.

Disk Access

The first rule of performance management is that *the cure must not be worse than the disease*. This is the rule that killed off-line defragmenters. Here's how it works.

Let's say, for the sake of argument, that your system is losing 10% of its performance to fragmentation. That is to say, jobs take 10% longer to run than they should or, put another way, only 90% of a day's work can get done in a day. Ten percent of a 24-hour day is 2.4 hours. The solution to your fragmentation problem has to consume less than 2.4 hours per day or it just isn't worth it.

Seems simple, doesn't it? Well, shutting down the system or taking a disk out of service to defragment it is a 100% degradation of performance. Performance just doesn't get any worse than "the system is down." So an off-line defragmenter that costs you three or four hours of computer time a day is more costly than the losses to fragmentation. The cure is worse than the disease.

The computer resources consumed by a defragmenter must be less, *much less,* than the performance losses due to fragmentation. The best way to violate this rule is to defragment using a method that requires taking the disk out of service. So a good defragmenter works on a disk while the system is up and while the disk being defragmented is being accessed by user applications. After safety, this is the most important feature of a defragmenter.

File Availability

A secondary aspect of this same disk access feature is that the files on the disk must be available to user applications. It is not enough to allow access only to the free space on the disk for the creation of new files. User applications must be able to access existing files as well. And while the defragmenter may be accessing only a single file out of perhaps 10,000 on a disk, guess which file some user's application is most likely to want to read? Yes, it is the one file that just happens to be being defragmented at that moment. Murphy's law[74] strikes again.

So an on-line defragmenter must assume that there will be contention for access to the files being defragmented. Other programs will want to get at those files and will want to get at them at the same time as the defragmenter. The defragmenter, therefore, must have some means of detecting such an access conflict and responding in such a way that user access is not denied. The defragmenter has to give way. Technologically, this is tricky, but it can be done and is done by a good defragmenter.

Locating Files

Another aspect of defragmenter performance is the amount of time and resources consumed in finding a file to defragment. Scanning through some 10,000 files by looking up file names in directories and subdirectories is out of the question. The time it takes to do this is a blatant violation of Rule One – it outweighs the performance gains likely to be obtained by defragmenting.

A much better way to rapidly find files for defragmenting is by reading the INDEXF.SYS file directly. The index file contains the file headers for all the files on the disk and within each file header is contained all the information a defragmenter needs to know about the state of fragmentation of a file. Specifically, the header tells how many fragments there are, where each is located on the disk and how big each one is. So a defragmenter can zip through the index file, picking out those files that need defragmenting, consuming typically only one disk access per file checked. Better yet, by reading several headers at once, *multiple* files can be checked for fragmentation with each disk access. A good defragmenter uses the index file to find files to process.

---

[74] **Murphy's Law:** "If anything can go wrong, it will."

The Defragmentation Process

After a file has been selected for defragmentation, the overhead involved in the defragmentation process itself can be significant. If the file is large, it can be *very* significant. After all, it is usually necessary to copy the file in its entirety to make it contiguous. As many as 200 disk accesses may be required to copy a 100-block file (100 reads and 100 writes). These two hundred disk accesses at 25 milliseconds apiece would consume 2.5 seconds. With this kind of overhead, processing even a fraction of 10,000 files on a disk holding hundreds of megabytes can be a time-consuming activity. Fortunately, the OpenVMS file system is more efficient than these figures would imply. Only the smallest disks, for example, have a cluster size of 1, so disk reads and writes generally move 2 or 3 or more blocks at once. Further, regular defragmentation holds down the amount of activity required. It is worth noting that performance worsens geometrically as the degree of fragmentation increases, so catching fragmentation early and defragmenting often requires less resources overall than occasional massive defragmentation.

The defragmenter itself can do a lot to lessen the impact of defragmentation overhead. A throttling mechanism, for example, can reduce defragmentation I/O during times of intense disk activity and increase it during slack times. This mechanism gives the appearance of greatly reduced overhead by scheduling the overhead at a time when the resource is not needed anyway. Using idle time in this way can make the defragmenter invisible to users of the system.

Perhaps the worst source of excess overhead for a disk defragmenter is the attempt to analyze an entire disk before defragmenting and plan a "perfect" defragmentation pass based on the results of this analysis. The idea is that a defragmenter can calculate the ideal position for each file, then move each file to the best position on the disk. This is a holdover from the off-line defragmenter days and, besides carrying the risks described in Chapter 5, it is enormously expensive in terms of overhead. Such an analysis requires examining literally every file on the disk. On top of that, the analysis becomes obsolete instantly if there is any activity on the disk other than the defragmenter.

A good defragmenter, then, should approach the process one file at a time and not require the overhead of analyzing every file on a disk in order to defragment only a few files.

Basic Functionality

After safety and performance, you should look for basic functionality in a defragmenter.

The most basic functionality is the decision of what to defragment and what to leave alone. Not in all cases is it desirable to defragment *everything*. Some selectivity is required.

A defragmenter has to exclude from its processing certain system files, like INDEXF.SYS. It should be wary of placed files and files that have allocation errors.[75] It should also have the capability of excluding a list of files provided by the System Manager. You might also look for the ability to *include* certain files in processing (or exclude "all files except ______") and possibly the ability to force immediate defragmentation of a particular file or group of files.

Disk Integrity Checks

Perhaps the most important basic functionality of a defragmenter is determining whether a disk is safe to defragment or not. It is possible, even commonplace, for a disk to get into a state where the data on the disk is not exactly where the file headers in the index file indicate it should be. When this occurs, it is extremely important for the matter to be corrected before any file involved is deleted, as deleting a file (using the erroneous information in the header from the index file) might cause the wrong data on the disk to be deleted! A good defragmenter must detect this condition and alert the System Manager to it so it can be corrected before defragmentation begins.

It is also possible for a good defragmenter to detect and isolate certain types of problems on a disk and avoid those areas while continuing to safely defragment the rest of the disk.

Frequency

How often should you defragment a disk? "Often enough so performance does not suffer noticeably," is the simple answer. Of course, by the time your system's performance is suffering "noticeably," it's too late, so this is not a workable answer.

To answer this question with a numeric quantity, like "every week" or "every two weeks," you have to know how long it takes for fragmentation to build up to a level where performance suffers noticeably. You can use a disk analysis utility or a performance monitor to measure the level of fragmentation on your system periodically, perhaps daily. Then, when performance begins to suffer noticeably, you can take note of what level of fragmentation you have. Let's say this happens when fragmentation reaches an average of

[75] It sometimes occurs that a file will contain a disk block that is supposed to be a part of some other file. Such a block might even appear to be in *both* files. This type of error is referred to as an **allocation error** and opens the door to further data corruption when the file is deleted, such as after being copied to a new location by a defragmenter.

1.1 fragments per file (10% fragmentation). Thereafter, you can periodically measure fragmentation and when it gets to, say, 1.05, defragment the disk.

An automatic on-line defragmenter includes a mechanism to measure fragmentation and schedule defragmentation passes accordingly. The ideal automatic on-line defragmenter would detect performance drains attributable to fragmentation and eliminate the causes before the drains became noticeable.

Full Disks

It is one thing to ramble on about the workings of a defragmenter in an ideal, laboratory environment, but it is quite another thing to see one working in the real world. One of the tricks played on us System Managers in the real world is full disks. Somehow, despite our best efforts, disks that really ought to remain 80% full or less drift up to 98%, 99% or even 100% full. Sure, you can spot this and take appropriate steps to handle it, but what happens to your defragmenter during that critical window of time between the disk going 100% full and your clearing off some space? Look for a defragmenter that survives this circumstance intact *and* leaves every bit of your user data equally intact. A defragmenter can't do much in the way of defragmenting with zero free space on the disk. The point is, if it can't defragment, it shouldn't consume overhead either. So a good defragmenter should do nothing at all when there is nothing useful it can do.

Large Files

Another side of the same coin is the fragmented file that is larger than the largest free space on the disk. Suppose, for example, you have 10,000 blocks of free space, all in one place, but there is a 12,000 block fragmented file. How does the defragmenter deal with that?

Older defragmenters used to rely on scratch space on a second disk to handle this problem, but that proved so unreliable that it has disappeared as a practice. Some defragmenters don't deal with the problem at all; they just ignore the file. A good defragmenter will *partially* defragment the file, giving you the best result it can within the constraints of space available, and then return to the file later for complete defragmenting when sufficient space has been freed up.

Always-Open Files

Another one of those real world tricks that doesn't show up in the test lab is the file that is held open *all* the time, leaving no "downtime" for that file in which to defragment it. Database files are prime candidates for this trick, particularly *large* database files. And why not? That big database probably contains most of the data that justifies the computer's existence. It *ought* to be in use around the clock. A defragmenter needs to take such files into account and provide a means of dealing with them safely.

Besides the always-open file, there is also the one file that a user application happens to need at the instant the defragmenter is working on it. What happens in that case? Does the defragmenter give way? Does it even notice? Or does the application program trip, fail and abort with a file access error?

The minimum proper action is for the defragmenter to 1) notice that an attempt is being made to access the file, 2) abort its own operation safely and quickly, and 3) try again later. The ideal defragmenter would process files in such a way that no user application could ever falter from or even detect an access conflict. In other words, the defragmenter should have enough control over system operation to move the file at a time when no user is attempting access and in such a way that no attempted access by an application would ever fail.

File Creation and Modification Dates

Another simple but important piece of basic functionality is the preservation of file creation and modification dates. You can defragment a file quite easily by simply using the DCL command COPY /CONTIGUOUS. If there is a free space of sufficient size available, DCL will make a contiguous copy of the file for you. The problem with this method is that it gives the copy a new file creation date. You might not care whether the date is changed or not, but the OpenVMS BACKUP utility will. The next time you do an incremental backup,[76] the copied file will be saved even though it was saved on an earlier backup. The reason is the new date given to the file by the COPY command. For a single file, this may be no big deal, but clearly a defragmenter cannot go around changing file creation dates wholesale. Nor can the file's modification date or date of last backup be changed. Either action would cause your incremental backups to explode from relatively small savesets[77] to ones rivaling full backups in size.

A good defragmenter should not change file creation dates, file modification dates, file backup dates or *any* other information in the file header except the size and location of the extents (fragments) that make up the file.[78]

Directory Files

Directory files never become fragmented, but they are otherwise just like any other file. Directory files do fragment the disk's free space, however. Directory files present a special problem for a defragmenter in that while a defragmenter has a directory file locked or held open for relocation, not only is that directory file inaccessible to users, so is every

---

[76] **incremental backup:** A backup in which the only files saved are those which have been created or modified since the last backup. The OpenVMS BACKUP utility optionally records the backup date in the header of each file saved. This gives a later incremental backup the ability to determine whether or not a file needs to be saved to have a complete copy of all files without having to save copies of the same file repeatedly.

[77] **saveset:** A container file holding the data saved during backup.

[78] Changing the extent size and location data in the header requires changing two additional pieces of administrative information. The header contains a count of the number of map area words and this must be changed when a defragmenter reduces the number of extents. There is also a special number used for data integrity purposes and this must be updated whenever there is any change to the header.

file in that directory and every file in every subdirectory below it. To access a file by name, a user application must go through the directory or directories containing that file's name. If the directory is locked, the user application gets an access conflict error. If the user application is not expecting an access conflict error or is not designed to deal with such errors, the application may abort.

A good defragmenter is designed with this problem in mind and moves directory files without any restrictions whatsoever on user access to files in that directory or its subdirectories. It is no solution to just ignore directory files, as this leaves your free space badly fragmented.

Red Herrings

"Optimization" by File Placement

"Optimization" of disk access by deliberate placement of files in certain locations is a red herring – an attempt to draw your attention away from the real issues of defragmentation and onto something else entirely.

First of all, optimization has nothing to do with defragmentation. Defragmentation is the solution to the problem created by fragmented files and disk free space. Your system is slow. The real reason it is slow is that files and disk free space are fragmented. The solution is to make the files contiguous (not fragmented) and group the free space together. That's it.

Where does optimization come in? Well, this is a different subject altogether. The concept of disk optimization supposedly accelerates file access even when all the files are contiguous and all the free space is grouped together. Disk optimization is an attempt to speed up file access by forcing certain files to be permanently located in certain positions on the disk. The theory goes that if you put the INDEXF.SYS file in the middle of the disk and group the most frequently accessed files around it, the disk heads will generally have to travel a shorter distance than if these files were located randomly around the disk.

There are some major holes in this theory. In fact, the holes are so major that I think the "optimization" proponents either don't fully understand the OpenVMS system or are just using optimization as a marketing gimmick. There are too many holes in the theory.

Hole number one: There is no standard, supported way on an OpenVMS system to tell which files are most frequently accessed. In fact, there is no way to tell which files are frequently accessed or even which files have *ever* been accessed. You can tell which files have been written and when they were last written, but not when they were read. The only thing that comes close to providing this information is the enabling of volume retention[79] dates, but enabling this feature consumes more overhead than you are likely to get back by "optimizing" file placement. The cure is worse than the disease.

Hole number two: Extensive analysis of real-world computer sites shows that it is not commonplace for entire files to be accessed all at once. It is far more common for only a few blocks of a file to be accessed at a time. Consider a database application, for example. User applications rarely, if ever, search or update the entire database. They access only the particular records desired. Thus locating the entire database in the middle of a disk is wasteful at best and possibly destructive as far as performance is concerned.

Hole number three: File placement capability in OpenVMS was designed for the realtime laboratory environment in which a single process has continuous control of the computer system. In such a system, the time consumed by head movement from one particular file to another particular file can be critical to the success of the process. The system designer can minimize that critical time lag by calculating the ideal location for the second file in relation to the first and forcing the two files to exact locations. Then, when the process has completed reading the first file, access to the second is effected with minimal delay.

By comparison, consider the typical interactive user environment. Dozens or even hundreds of interactive users might be logged on and active at any moment, running who knows what applications, accessing innumerable files willy-nilly in every conceivable part of a disk. How can one even hope to guess where the disk's read-write head might be at any given time? With this extremely random mode of operation, how can a disk optimizer state flatly that positioning such-and-such a file at such-and-such an exact location will reduce disk access times? It seems to me that such a statement is foolish and such file positioning is equally as likely to *worsen* system performance as to improve it. Even if the two conditions balance out at zero, the overhead involved gives you a net loss.

Hole number four: When you force a file to a specific position on the disk by specifying exact LBNs, how do you know where it really is? You have to take into account the difference between *logical* block numbers (LBNs) and *physical* block numbers (PBNs). These two are not the same thing. LBNs are assigned to PBNs by the disk's controller. Disks supplied by Digital Equipment Corporation often have as many as 10% more physical blocks than logical blocks. The LBNs are assigned to most of the physical blocks and the remainder are used as spares and for maintenance purposes. You see, magnetic disks are far from perfect and blocks sometimes "go bad." In fact, it is a rarity for a magnetic disk to leave the manufacturer without *some* bad blocks. When the disk is formatted by Digital or by the customer, the bad blocks are detected and "revectored" to spares. *Revectored* means that the LBN assigned to that physical block is reassigned to some other physical block. This revectoring can also be done on the fly while your disk is

---

[79] **Volume retention dates** are used by OpenVMS to determine when a file on the volume "expires." When a file is created, its expiration date is set to the current date and time plus the specified maximum retention time. Each time the file is accessed, the current time is added to the minimum time. If the sum is greater than the expiration date, the expiration date is recomputed. This allows the System Manager to determine which files are not being used and so might be candidates for archiving.

in use. The new block after revectoring might be on the same track and physically close to the original, but then again it might not. Thus, all LBNs do not correspond to the physical block of the same number and two consecutive LBNs may actually be widely separated on the disk.

So I ask again, "When you force a file to a specific position on the disk, how do you know where it really is?" You may be playing probabilities and perhaps you should think twice before gambling with user data and system performance.

Hole number five: Where is the "middle" of a disk? Obviously, no one is suggesting that the geometric center of the round disk platter, like the hole in a phonograph record, is the "middle." Of course not. We are talking about data storage. The middle is the point halfway between LBN zero (the "beginning" of the disk) and the highest LBN on that disk volume (the "end" of the disk). Right?

Well, maybe not. We have already seen that LBNs do not necessarily correspond to the physical disk block of the same number. But what about a multi-spindle disk (one with two or more sets of platters rotating on separate spindles)? There are several different types of multi-spindle disks. Besides the common volume sets and stripesets, there are also disks that use multiple spindles for speed and reliability yet appear to OpenVMS as a single disk drive. Where is the "middle" of such a disk? I think you will agree that, while the location of the apparent middle can be calculated, the point accessed in the shortest average time is certainly not the point halfway between LBN zero and the last LBN. This halfway point would be on the outermost track of one platter or on the innermost track of another – not on the middle track of either one. Such disk volumes actually have several "middles" when speaking in terms of access times.

There are even disks that have no performance middle at all. I am thinking of electronic (semiconductor) disks, which have no heads and thus no head movement. With an electronic disk, all overhead associated with "optimizing" file placement is wasted time and lost performance.[80]

Hole number six: With regular defragmentation, a defragmenter needs to relocate only a tiny percentage of the files on a disk; perhaps even less than one percent. "Optimization" requires moving virtually all the files on the disk, every time you optimize. Moving 100 times as many files gives you 100 times the opportunity for error and 100 times the overhead. Is the result worth the risk and the cost?

Hole number seven: What exactly is the cost of optimizing a disk and what do you get for it? The costs of fragmentation are enormous. A file fragmented into two pieces can take twice as long to access as a contiguous file. A three-piece file can take three times as long, and so on. Some files fragment into hundreds of pieces in a few days' use. Imagine

---

[80] Lest anyone complain that electronic disks are so fast that any argument about optimization or defragmentation is moot, let me point out that "fast" is a relative concept. I know of at least one application that requires a large array of electronic disks with striping, data caching and defragmentation to achieve the necessary performance. File placement adds absolutely nothing to the speed of this application.

the performance cost of 100 disk accesses where only one would do! Defragmentation can return a very substantial portion of your system to productive use.

Now consider optimization. Suppose, for the sake of argument, that disk data block sequencing really did correspond to physical block locations and you really could determine which files are accessed most frequently and you really knew the exact sequence of head movement from file to file. By carefully analyzing the entire disk and rearranging all the files on the disk, you could theoretically reduce the head travel time. The theoretical maximum reduction in average travel time is one-quarter the average head movement time, after subtracting the time it takes to start and stop the head. If the average access time is 32 milliseconds (for an RA82 model disk) and 24 milliseconds of this is head travel time, the best you can hope for is a 6 millisecond reduction for each file that is optimized. On a faster disk, such as the RA71 (12.5 milliseconds), the potential for reduction is proportionately less – about 2 milliseconds. Taking rotational latency into account, your savings may be even less.

Each defragmented file, on the other hand, saves potentially one disk access (32 milliseconds) per fragment. That's over *five times* the optimization savings, even with the bare minimum level of fragmentation. With badly fragmented files, the difference is astounding.

On top of all that, what do you suppose it costs your system to analyze and reposition every file on your disk? When you subtract that from the theoretical optimization savings, it is probably *costing* you performance to "optimize" the files.

The fact is that it takes only a tiny amount of fragmentation, perhaps only one day's normal use of your system, to undo the theoretical benefits of optimizing file locations. While "optimization" is an elegant concept to the uninitiated, it is no substitute for defragmentation, it is unlikely to improve the performance of your system at all, and it is more than likely to actually worsen performance in a large number of cases.

In summary, file placement for purposes of optimizing disk performance is a red herring. It is not technologically difficult to do. It is just a waste of time.

The "Perfect" Disk

What should the end result of defragmentation be? What, exactly, is the product of a defragmenter's efforts?

How about a *perfect* disk? Wouldn't that be reassuring, to know that your disks are "perfect"?

A perfect disk, in terms of fragmentation, is a thing of beauty. It is a disk which has each and every file in a perfectly contiguous state, with every bit of free space all collected together in one spot, preferably at the beginning (near LBN 0) of the physical disk.

This seems straightforward and well-grounded in sensible reasoning, yet there is quite a controversy over the matter. Why?

Well, there are other factors that need to be taken into consideration.

Some say that free space on the disk should not be organized at the beginning of the disk; that putting the free space there does no good because new files are allocated from blocks pointed to by the extent cache (blocks recently freed up by file deletions) instead of from repeated scanning of the storage bitmap.

This may be true, but it is also true that the extent cache is loaded first from the storage bitmap and then added to as files are deleted. It is also true that the location of blocks freed up by deletions is relatively random across the disk. A defragmentation strategy that groups files near the beginning will merely reinforce the random nature of the extent cache because holes caused by deletions will appear near the beginning (as well as everywhere else) and the extent cache will be loaded with lots of little pieces. On the other hand, if the defragmentation strategy grouped free space near the beginning, the extent cache would be loaded initially with a large amount of contiguous free space. This would then result in newly created files being more likely to be created contiguously in the first place and reduce the need for defragmentation. In other words, performance would degrade less (remain high) through prevention.

I must admit that when we are talking about *where* to consolidate free space, we are splitting hairs. The performance to be gained from consolidating free space in a particular area of the disk is slight, even under the best of circumstances. Moreover, consolidation of free space is overrated. While *badly* fragmented free space is likely to cause performance problems indirectly by forcing new files to be created in a fragmented state, *slightly* fragmented free space does not affect performance at all. In the absence of an absolute requirement for large contiguous files, there is no performance benefit whatsoever to a single large contiguous free space over as many as a few hundred smaller free spaces. Any resources expended consolidating a few free spaces into one large one are likely to be wasted. The important number to look at is the percentage of free space that is consolidated into a few large spaces.

Some say that free space on a disk should be grouped around the index file in the middle of the disk. Their argument is that, by placing free space near the index file, the disk head will have less distance to travel to and from the INDEXF.SYS file when creating new files. By keeping the head near the middle tracks of the disk, the greatest overhead factor in disk performance, head movement, is reduced.

This is certainly true under certain specific circumstances, but it is decidedly *not* true under others. For example, while this technique is sensible for creating new files, what about accessing the *existing* files? By relegating these files to the outside edges of the disk (the lowest and highest LBNs), the distance the head must travel to access these files is *increased*. Should we assume that any file created before the defragmentation will never be accessed again? Or that such "old" files are not accessed often enough to matter? Surely *somebody* accesses data files that are more than a day or two old. Under a scheme such as this, those data file accesses are going to be slowed, not speeded.

There is also the question of where *is* the INDEXF.SYS file located? This scheme assumes that it is located in the middle of the disk. But OpenVMS allows for the INDEXF.SYS file to be located at the beginning, at the end, or at any specific block location the System Manager might choose. What happens to your system's performance if the INDEXF.SYS file is positioned at the beginning of the disk and the defragmenter groups all the free space in the middle? Performance gets clobbered, that's what happens.

The problem with schemes like this is that they are based on theoretical assumptions rather than on real-world observation of disks in use on live computer systems. The worst assumption of all is that disks have a "beginning," an "end" and a "middle." As noted earlier, we talk of disk locations in terms of LBNs, or *Logical Block Numbers*. While a logical block ordinarily corresponds to a physical block, this is not always so. The OpenVMS disk architecture allows for *logical* block numbers to be reassigned, if necessary, to any *physical* disk block at all. This allows a disk to continue to be used even though one or more physical disk blocks are unusable. The corresponding LBNs are merely reassigned to other physical blocks. It also allows for widely varying physical disk architectures that can be treated identically by the I/O subsystem of OpenVMS.

Take a multi-spindle disk as an example. A disk with a single platter on a single spindle, with only one side used, is easy to discuss in terms of "beginning," "middle" and "end." Here is a diagram showing such a disk:

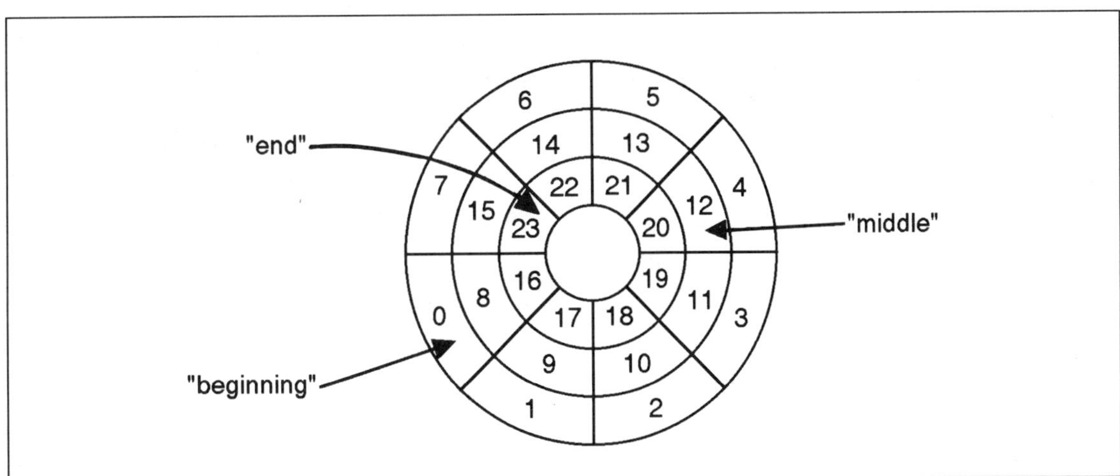

Figure 6-1 Single Disk

Now here is a diagram of a two-spindle disk with LBN numbers and arrows indicating the "beginning," "middle" and "end."

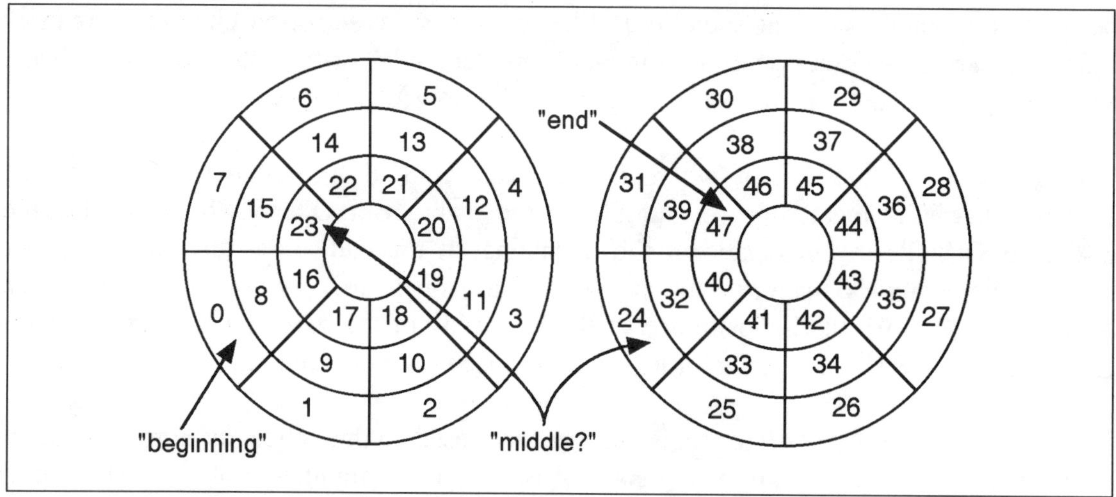

Figure 6-2 Two-Spindle Disk

Note that the "middle" of this disk spans the innermost tracks of one platter and the outermost tracks of the other. What will happen to head movement if the INDEXF.SYS file is placed at the "middle" of this multi-spindle disk and the free space is all grouped on either side of it? It will be a disaster performance-wise.

Your disk might not look like this. But it also might not look like the idealized conceptual scheme used by designers of such a system. The point is that, to be useful, the design of a defragmentation strategy must be based on the *logical* architecture of the disk and must work well regardless of different *physical* structures. A strategy that assumes one particular physical architecture may be devastating for other types of disks.

Grouping free space near the *logical* beginning of a disk (LBN 0) is guaranteed to reduce time spent scanning the storage bitmap for free clusters. It is also guaranteed to maximize the probability that newly created files will be created contiguously or, at least, minimize the number of fragments in newly created files, *regardless of the physical architecture of the disk involved.*

The final and worst problem with a "perfect" disk is that its perfection doesn't last. Moments after achieving that exalted state, some user application has created, deleted or extended a file and the perfection is history. You now have an imperfect disk that is well on its way to becoming less and less perfect. So just how valuable is that fleeting moment of "perfection"?

The True Goal Of Defragmentation

I submit that a perfect disk is the wrong goal. Elegance, beauty and perfection in disk file arrangement are not the ideals to which a System Manager aspires. You cannot take them to management and show them off as a demonstration of your value to the organization. You cannot even use them to keep yourself employed. How many System Manager resumés include a section for "beauty, elegance and perfection" of disk file arrangement? None.

The true goal, of course, is *performance.* Now there's something you can take to the bank. A system that is so slow you can't log on this week is a system that will get you fired. A system that performs even better than the expectations of users and management might just get you a raise or a promotion or both. So let's talk about *better performance of the system.*

The mistake made by the "perfect disk" advocates is that of viewing a disk and even a VAX (or Alpha AXP) computer system as a static, unchanging thing. Static, unchanging VAX systems don't need defragmenters. They need a lift to the nearest scrap yard.

A real VAX or Alpha AXP system is dynamic, in motion, changing continuously – almost *alive* with activity. Real perfection, in my mind, would be having all this activity streamlined for efficiency and directed at the specific production goals of the organization and the individuals who make it up. Let's see a computer system that can be pointed at a computational problem and *vaporize* that problem in a flash. The culprit we are targeting is slowness, sluggishness, the can't-help-you-now-I'm-too-busy-doing-something-else of a mismanaged computer system. The ideal defragmenter would vaporize that problem and give you the laser-fast precision instrument you expect.

Let us take a careful look, then, at exactly what factors are important to deliver this capability. What really counts when it comes to defragmentation *results?*

Factor Number One: Safety

Your defragmenter must be safe. Above all other requirements, features and benefits, safety of user data is the most important. One trashed disk of user data, one crashed system, even one lost user file can outweigh all the performance benefits in the world. What good does it do to talk of performance increases when the system is down and user data forever lost?

There must be no compromises with safety, either. "99% safe" is not a feature. "Able to recover most lost data" does not go over too well with users and management. What you want is absolute, 100% guaranteed safety; no chance whatsoever of any user data being lost *at all.*

Even the ability to recover lost data in the event of a catastrophe is dicey. The minute you hear that data is lost, even temporarily, your confidence is weakened. The thread of recovery is too tenuous for you to sit back, relax and coolly await the recovery of the lost data by the very tool that trashed it moments ago. OK, maybe it's better than a poke in the eye with a sharp stick, but it's still not a very comforting situation.

Factor Number Two: Low Overhead

Earlier, we covered the troublesome defragmentation techniques that consumed more system resources than they gave back – the "cure" that is worse than the disease. We answered the question, "How long should a defragmenter take to do its job?" with "Less than the time and resources being lost to fragmentation."

While it is a definite improvement for a defragmenter to spend 19% of the system's resources to get a 20% improvement in performance, it is a much *better* improvement for a defragmenter to spend only 2% of the system's resources to get a 20% improvement in performance. As a rule of thumb, your defragmenter should consume not more than two percent (2%) of the system. You can measure this by using the DCL command SHOW PROCESS or looking in ACCOUNTING records, then dividing the resources consumed (CPU time, for example) by the total resources available during the same time period. For example, if the defragmenter consumed two hours of CPU time out of every 100, that would be 2 divided by 100, or 2% of the available CPU time.

The ideal defragmenter would not only consume less than 2% of the system resources, it would take its 2% from resources that are otherwise idle, such as CPU idle time and unused disk I/O bandwidth.

Factor Number Three: Worst Problems Handled First

Sometimes, in a highly technical subject, it is easy to get so caught up in the details that one overlooks things of major importance. Like the disk that is 99% full. Defragmenting such a disk is a complete waste of time. Except in extreme cases, the performance benefits you might get from defragmenting such a disk are insignificant when compared to the performance benefits available from simply clearing off 10% or 20% of the disk. When a disk is very nearly full, OpenVMS spends so much time looking for free space, waiting for the disk to spin around to bring a tiny free space under the head, and allocating files in lots of little pieces all over the place, it is a wonder that any useful work gets done at all.

Similarly, as mentioned earlier, the defragmenter that works hard to consolidate every bit of free space into a single contiguous area is wasting its time. Rigorous testing shows clearly that an OpenVMS disk with up to 63 free spaces performs just as well as a disk with one large free space. So all the overhead expended by the defragmenter consolidating free space into less than 63 areas is wasted. And it is *your* computer resources that are being wasted.

A defragmenter should address itself to *real* problems instead of theoretical ones and deliver immediate, real solutions to them. The single most important piece of advice I can give on the subject of defragmenters is to distinguish between the idealized results obtained in a perfect laboratory environment and what can be expected in *your* system under real-world conditions.

Who Buys a Defragmenter?

According to Computer Intelligence Corporation, a respected source of information about the VAX market, only 1% of all VAX sites had a defragmenter installed in October 1987. By October 1988, the number had grown to 4%. By October 1989, it had shot to 11%. The survey was not done in 1990, but in October 1991, market research showed 18% of all sites running a disk defragmenter.

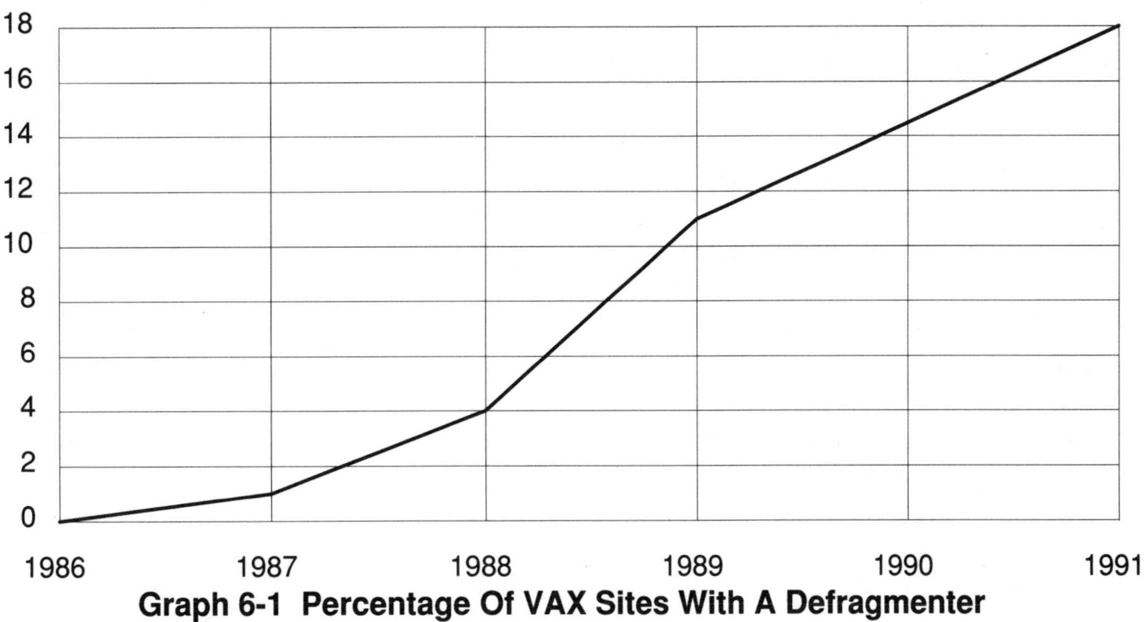

Graph 6-1 Percentage Of VAX Sites With A Defragmenter

For comparison, the next graph shows the increase in disk capacity over the same time period (these figures are also from Computer Intelligence):

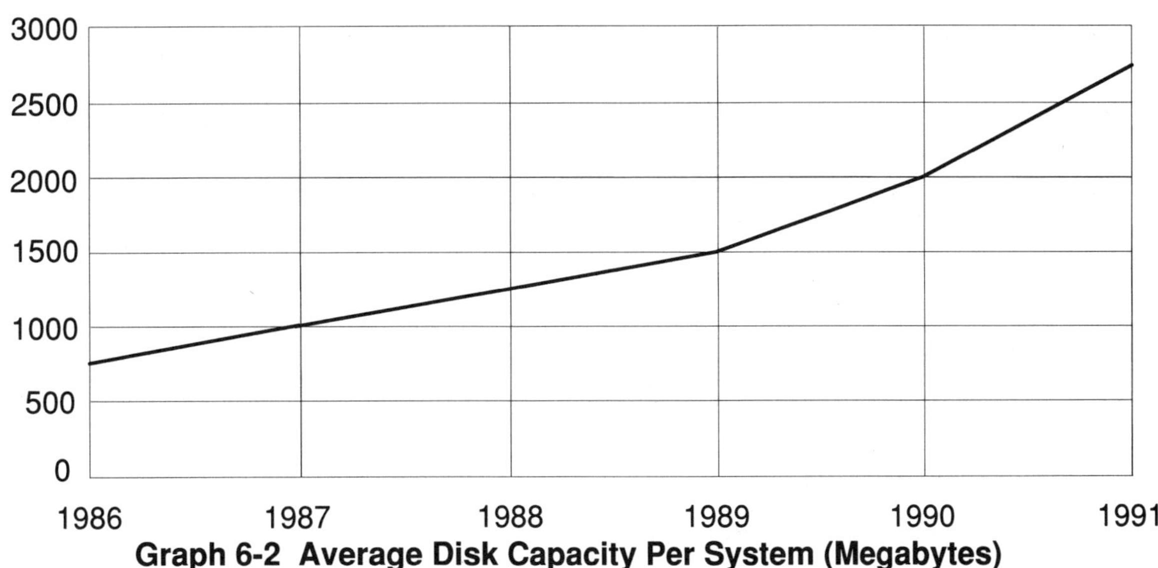

Graph 6-2 Average Disk Capacity Per System (Megabytes)

Experienced System Managers: The average System Manager has three years experience. Fully two-thirds of the defragmenters in existence are in the hands of the more experienced half of the System Managers. A much higher percentage of System Managers with eight or more years of experience use a defragmenter than System Managers with less experience.

Sites with many users: The average VAX site has 102 users. Two-thirds of all defragmenters are installed at sites with 50 or more users. Twenty-six percent of sites with 200 or more users have a defragmenter. That's substantially more than the 18% of all sites that have a defragmenter.

Sites with many disks: The average VAX site has 7.5 disks. (Don't you love statistics that imply that someone has half a disk?) Sixty percent of all defragmenters are installed at sites with six or more disks. Twenty-four percent of sites with 10 or more disks use a defragmenter. Again, substantially more than average.

One more interesting statistic is that 62.5% of System Managers who have attended training classes at Digital Equipment Corporation use defragmenters.

In looking at the distribution of defragmenters amongst VAX sites, it can be seen that defragmenters are not distributed evenly across all sites. More sites than you would expect from an even distribution have a defragmenter when:

- They have a VAX 6000, 8000 or 9000 series computer (the larger VAXes);
- They have over 500 users (the sites with heaviest usage);
- They have three or more VAXes (the larger sites); and
- They have six or more disks (the larger sites).

Specifically, survey results from Computer Intelligence show that the sites running the big VAXes have 26% to 33% more defragmenters than a random distribution would predict; sites with 500 or more users are 36% more likely to have a defragmenter, and sites with three or more VAXes are 131% more likely to be running a defragmenter.

Also, as you might expect, the survey results show that System Managers with the most experience and training are substantially more likely to use a defragmenter than inexperienced, untrained System Managers.

The conclusion is plain: the people who buy defragmenters are the more experienced and trained System Managers, the ones with many users, many disks and many VAXes, and particularly those with the big machines.

In surveying defragmenter buyers as to why they made the purchase, the overwhelming response is that they had to handle the fragmentation problem, but backing up to tape and restoring each disk was far too tedious and time-consuming. The defragmenter frees the System Manager from this unpleasant chore and saves time so he or she can get more done.

Finally, it should be noted that ninety percent of defragmenter buyers place the safety of the product above performance in importance, but three-quarters of them expect a performance improvement as a result of defragmenting.

Who Does Not Buy a Defragmenter?

The people who don't buy defragmenters are the sites that have more disk space, by far, than they really need. Files tend to be created contiguously in the first place, as there is plenty of free space to do so. By keeping lots of free disk space available, these sites suffer very little from fragmentation.

Naturally, these tend to be very small sites. At a larger site, the cost of a defragmenter is a very small portion of the computer budget.

As we have seen from the Computer Intelligence data, inexperienced System Managers don't buy defragmenters. These folks either don't understand the cause of their system's slower and slower performance or they lack the expertise to demonstrate the problem and the need for a solution to those who hold the purse strings. This book is the answer to both problems, the former in the main body of the book and the latter in the appendices.

What Does the Future Hold for Defragmentation?

We have seen, much earlier in this book, that fragmentation did not just happen. Rather, it was deliberately introduced as a solution to an earlier problem. The file structure for the OpenVMS operating system and its predecessor, RSX-11, was purposefully designed to allow fragmentation so users would not have the more serious problem of running out of file space prematurely. Then, as disk capacities grew to proportions previously unimagined, fragmentation came to be a problem in its own right.

Reverting to a file system that allows only contiguous files is no solution for the nineties. The automatic on-line defragmenter is the ideal solution for now. But what does the future hold? Can we envision what disks might be like ten years from now? What new and even more capacious forms of storage might come along and how would these impact the problem of fragmentation and its defragmenter solution?

We have already seen the introduction of another deliberate form of fragmentation: disk striping. With striping, files are deliberately fragmented across two or more disks in "stripes" of data that can be retrieved from the multiple disks much faster than they could be retrieved from any one disk. Extensions of this technology to large arrays of disks could dramatically counter the fragmentation problem.

Electronic "disks" have made their debut and, with falling prices for semiconductor memory chips, could become a viable form of mass storage. Even before seeing electronic storage broadly in use, however, we will see more of the hybrids, which combine electronic storage with magnetic. All that is needed is some mechanism for sorting out the performance-critical data from the non-critical and this system becomes very cost effective. We are seeing this type of system now with data caching, particularly as caches are built into disk controllers to provide better performance.

This path can be extrapolated to intelligent disk subsystems that determine for themselves where best to store data and have the data all ready to return promptly when needed.

We can also envision a new file allocation strategy that is not sensitive to fragmentation. Thinking of files as "flat" one- or two-dimensional objects leads us to think of the parts of files as being "close together" or "separate." A collection of data can also be thought of as a three- or more-dimensional pile of associated records that can be accessed in any old way. More elaborate indexing methods give us faster access to the data. Larger and faster storage devices allow for more elaborate indexing methods.

This all culminates in a vision of data storage as a completely automatic mechanism without any files at all. You put *data* in and you get *information* out. Don't ask me how it works, but that's where I think we are headed. Naturally, without files, there can be no file fragmentation, so the problem is gone altogether, no doubt to be replaced by some new, even more perplexing problem that will keep us system programmers in business for a long time to come.

Conclusion

It should be clear by now that fragmentation is well understood and a good solution is available in the form of an automatic on-line disk defragmenter. It should also be clear that a defragmenter designed for a static laboratory environment won't cut the mustard in the real world where things are changing continuously. It is vital both for performance and for the safety of your data that the defragmenter be able to deal with a disk that is organized differently from defragmentation pass to defragmentation pass, with files that appear and disappear and with heavy user loads at unexpected times. In choosing a defragmenter, look for one that addresses known, demonstrable performance issues and not just theoretical problems demonstrable only in a laboratory environment. I have taken a great deal of time in this chapter to explain the ins and outs of defragmentation so that you will be well-informed and better able to judge your needs and the best solution for you. I believe that the more you know about fragmentation and defragmentation, the easier your job will be. How much do you need to know? Enough to handle the problem once and for all and get on with more important and interesting things.

CHAPTER 7

THE ULTIMATE SOLUTION TO THE FRAGMENTATION PROBLEM

Disclaimer: This chapter is an unabashed advertisement for DISKEEPER, the defragmenter sold by Executive Software. Rick Cadruvi and I conceived of, designed and developed DISKEEPER together in 1986. We took great pains to create exactly what System Managers wanted. We were both performing VAX management functions at the time and had years of experience managing VAXes. More importantly, we did a lot of research to find out what System Managers thought about fragmentation, how they dealt with it and how they wanted to deal with it. We designed our product to be exactly what they wanted.

Through Executive Software, I have continued to stay closely in touch with System Managers – tens of thousands of them. Therefore, I believe what I say to you now and I have good reason to believe it. If you are offended by the fact that I own the company that sells the product I recommend in this chapter, please don't read it. If possible, I request that you take note of my relationship to the company and to the product, accept my offer to help and read on.

As noted at the beginning of the previous chapter, the first defragmenter became available for VMS in 1986. Within a year, there were seven on the market. During the next few years, defragmenter competition and a skeptical marketplace weeded out the weakest of the products and one defragmenter, DISKEEPER, from Executive Software, rose to dominate the field, achieving an installed base roughly double that of all others combined. Obviously, this defragmenter had something going for it.

I believe that the reason for the success of DISKEEPER is that careful market research was done to find out what System Managers needed and wanted most in a defragmenter, careful technical research was done to determine whether that could be provided, and we then delivered to the System Managers all they had asked for and more. Since that time, we have always tried to outdo ourselves, enhancing the product to fit customer needs and take advantage of new technology, always striving for the seemingly unobtainable goal of the utter elimination of fragmentation as a System Manager headache.

We have come very close, and we are not finished yet.

I have nothing to say about other defragmenters. Most of them have disappeared from the market, for a variety of reasons. The ones that remain are offered by well-intentioned people who really believe their product is the best for you. I know that it is the customer who decides and, in a free market, he who serves the customer best wins. I want to win, but only if you win, too. By giving you everything you want and more, at a fair price, with first-class service, we all win.

Design Goals

The driving requirement for DISKEEPER was that it run automatically, in the background, safely reorganizing files as needed to keep a disk performing optimally, while users continued accessing files on the same disk.

DISKEEPER was designed with the following goals in mind:

1. The product must be *completely safe to use.*

2. It must *make OpenVMS operate more efficiently.*

3. It should *process any OpenVMS supported ODS-2 disk.*

4. It should *process live disks without interfering with user access to files on that disk.*

5. It should *operate while OpenVMS is running without affecting performance.*

6. It should *process system disks as well as user disks.*

7. It should *run without operator intervention.*

The implementation of each of these design goals is discussed in detail below.

Goal 1: Safe to Use

The foremost design goal was to make sure that no data is ever lost – neither user data nor OpenVMS internal information. To accomplish this, the DISKEEPER proprietary method for relocating files was developed. It uses the following criteria for accessing files:

- The contents of data files are never modified under any circumstances.

- Only one file is processed at a time, not the whole disk.

- Each processing pass is independent of the other passes.

- No information is stored on any other device or in a "scratch space."

- A file currently in use is not processed.

- DISKEEPER accesses a file in such a way that no user access can conflict with DISKEEPER during the critical portion of the relocation process.

- Read and write checks are used in all I/O to verify that the relocated file is a bit-for-bit duplicate of the original.

- File relocation is aborted if any error is encountered, leaving the file in its original state.

- File structure integrity is verified before any files are processed.

The program was designed to err on the side of caution. In other words, the program only moves file information on the disk when it is absolutely certain that no data will be lost, including file attributes. The only change to file attribute information is the physical location of the file on the disk. None of the file dates are changed and no reserved fields in the header are used to store DISKEEPER information. Placement control is not changed unless DISKEEPER is explicitly instructed to do so by the System Manager.

If your system crashes while DISKEEPER is running, or if DISKEEPER aborts abnormally, the worst that can happen is that some empty disk blocks may end up marked allocated when they are not part of any file. DISKEEPER properly deallocates any such blocks resulting from DISKEEPER interruption.

With OpenVMS V5.5, Digital introduced a mechanism for moving files that is guaranteed safe by Digital. This mechanism, called the MOVEFILE primitive, only moves a file if the following conditions are met:

- The program has write access to the file.

- The file is closed.

- MOVEFILE operations are not disabled for the file by the DCL command SET FILE /NOMOVE.

- The operation is not interrupted.

- The source and target locations are on the same disk.

When DISKEEPER is run on OpenVMS V5.5 or higher, you may select either of these methods of relocating files – proprietary or MOVEFILE.

Goal 2: Make OpenVMS More Efficient

When a file is moved by DISKEEPER, it is made contiguous or, at the very least, less fragmented. If it is already contiguous, the file is not moved unless moving it would markedly improve the arrangement of free space on the disk.

With plenty of contiguous free space, file creations are faster and new files tend to be created contiguously, or nearly so. To demonstrate this, try copying a large file on a non-DISKEEPER disk (use the DCL COPY command), then do the same on a disk processed by DISKEEPER (or run DISKEEPER on the same disk and COPY the same file). Use the DCL DUMP /HEADER command to examine the file headers of the copied files. You should see fewer map pointers for the file created on the DISKEEPER disk than on the other.

All this adds up to better performance because files are created faster and files can be accessed more quickly because they are contiguous.

Note that the goal was not "to make every file contiguous" or "to combine all free spaces into one large contiguous free space." Disk perfection is not a requirement to get better performance from OpenVMS. In fact, a perfect disk will perform no better than a nearly perfect disk. While a single giant contiguous free space will allow the creation of a single giant contiguous file, it does no more for performance than a small number of relatively large contiguous free spaces. It is not the difference between one 100,000 block space and four 25,000 block spaces that makes a difference in performance; it is the 30,000 three-block spaces that really hurt.

Nonetheless, DISKEEPER will do an excellent job of consolidating free space on your disks. But do not use this as a yardstick for measuring defragmentation benefits; it is the number of fragments into which your files are broken that really impacts disk I/O performance.

How much better will performance be? That depends on your particular circumstances. If your system is not I/O bound, the gains may be slight. If it is, the gains should be dramatic. It is not unreasonable to expect a 20% improvement in CPU utilization and disk I/O from even a well-managed system. Some sites may achieve a much greater improvement.

Goal 3: Process any OpenVMS ODS-2 Disk

This design goal was accomplished by using OpenVMS itself to do the "diskeeping" wherever possible.

DISKEEPER supports the entire range of OpenVMS ODS-2 disk types: system disks, common system disks, quorum disks, user disks, volume sets, stripesets and shadow sets. DISKEEPER supports fixed, removable, and floppy disks. It works in clusters whether the disk is on a local controller, an HSC,[81] MSCP[82] served, or LAVC-style[83] MSCP served. It can deal with empty or full disks and anything in between.

DISKEEPER works with all Digital and third-party disk controllers.

---

[81] **HSC:** *H*ierarchical *S*torage *C*ontroller. A disk and tape management facility physically separate from the computer(s) it serves.

[82] **MSCP:** *M*ass *S*torage *C*ontrol *P*rotocol. A software system that allows computers to access disks on other nodes in a VAXcluster.

[83] **LAVC:** *L*ocal *A*rea *VAXc*luster. A VAXcluster that communicates over Ethernet rather than specialized VAXcluster hardware.

DISKEEPER is designed for any Digital-supported configuration.

Note that system disks and common system disks really are processed. DISKEEPER does not merely exclude all files in system-rooted directories. DISKEEPER actually processes all files on a system disk except open files and a few reserved files that cannot be moved while OpenVMS is running from that disk. The same applies to common system disks.

Goal 4: Process Live Disks Without Interfering With User Access To Files

As covered earlier, it is not acceptable to force users off the disk while defragmenting it. To do so would be a case of the cure being worse than the disease. Access to fragmented files is better than no access at all.

The only acceptable solution is to defragment on-line with users active on the same disk. DISKEEPER was designed with this in mind, and accomplishes the task without compromise, primarily due to the following features:

No File Access Conflict

During most of the time DISKEEPER is processing a file, it shares the file with any other users that may access the same file. The last step of processing the file, however, involves locking the file for a very brief period, the duration of two QIO operations, a matter of milliseconds. If another user requests a file that DISKEEPER has locked, that request is suspended for the brief period until DISKEEPER releases the file. Then the request is serviced. There is never an interruption of either process as a result of this delay.

I/O Throttling

DISKEEPER limits its own I/O to the equivalent of disk I/O "idle time." This feature, especially important for the MicroVAX *RQDXn* disk controller, makes the impact of DISKEEPER on the load of your VAX or Alpha AXP virtually unnoticeable, even during peak levels of activity. This feature is particularly important on any system where I/O to the disks is usually at or close to the maximum possible throughput. Suspending defragmentation activity when users most need access to their data assures maximum system performance.

Exclusion List

DISKEEPER gives the System Manager the option of excluding certain files from processing. The Exclusion List is evaluated at the start of each set of multiple passes and the files specified (in the list) are skipped over by DISKEEPER.

On-Line Directory Moves

DISKEEPER moves directory files, provided the directory is not open. This allows larger contiguous free spaces to be made which, in turn, allows larger files to be defragmented by DISKEEPER, or created contiguously by the user.

Caches Updated

DISKEEPER does take into account the file header cache, and makes sure that the file headers are correctly updated so that no data is lost. The extent cache is not changed.

Open Files Ignored

Files that are always held open are not processed by DISKEEPER. These files can be made contiguous safely only by DCL COPY /CONTIGUOUS, by backup and restore, or by closing the files so DISKEEPER can process them. As long as the files remain open, they will be untouched by DISKEEPER.

Goal 5: Operate While OpenVMS Is Running Without Affecting Performance

Three steps were taken to assure that DISKEEPER overhead had the lowest possible impact on system performance:

First, DISKEEPER is designed to be run as a detached process running at priority 2. With the typical OpenVMS system running user jobs at priority 4 and batch jobs at priority 3, DISKEEPER will use only CPU time that would otherwise be idle. Priority 1 remains available for even lower priority jobs that you do not want to interfere with DISKEEPER.

Second, advanced system programming techniques were used to write DISKEEPER, to assure the highest possible performance. It uses QIOs[84] for I/O instead of high-overhead RMS services, and it copies a file only once – directly from its original location to the new location. No intermediate copies are made, so no scratch space or second device is required.

Third, DISKEEPER includes a built-in I/O throttling capability. DISKEEPER monitors I/O on the disk being processed and adjusts its own I/O accordingly. If the I/O rate increases, DISKEEPER reduces its own I/O. If the I/O rate decreases, DISKEEPER raises its I/O level. This mechanism effectively limits DISKEEPER I/O to the equivalent of disk "idle time."

As proof of its efficiency, DISKEEPER typically requires only a few minutes of CPU time per day to keep an active 456MB RA81 disk defragmented. This constitutes overhead of a small fraction of 1%.

---

[84] See Chapter 1, **HOW A DISK WORKS** for an explanation of QIO.

Goal 6: Process System Disks As Well As User Disks

A system disk by itself has little need for defragmentation because few files are ever created on the system disk. The only files ordinarily created on the system disk are log files. These do not particularly affect performance because they are rarely, if ever, read. Some sites, however, put user files on the system disk, and small systems such as MicroVAXes sometimes have only one disk for both system and user files. DISKEEPER can be run on such a shared system/data disk without having to shut the system down and without making the system unusable during the processing.

DISKEEPER processes are automatically prevented from moving all system files that OpenVMS will be expecting to find in a particular location on the disk. There are three different ways in which this is done.

First, any file that is currently open is not moved. In addition to open user files, this includes INDEXF.SYS on every disk and such files as PAGEFILE.SYS and all SYS$MANAGER:*.LOG files currently in use on a system disk. This includes installed images[85] that are installed with the /OPEN qualifier, such as License Management, Cluster Server, Audit Server, Logical Name Server, and many other operating system components.

Finally, some files are excluded from DISKEEPER processing by file specification. Wild card file specifications are used to look up and identify the specific files on each disk to be excluded in this manner.

One system file is too critical to trust to exclusion by file specification. That is the boot image, VMB.EXE. Because it is possible for the boot image to have a different file name, DISKEEPER identifies the file by way of the boot block in the INDEXF.SYS file, rather than by file name, then excludes that file from DISKEEPER processing. This assures that the boot image is 100% safe, regardless of its file name.

DISKEEPER, running on any CPU in a cluster with separate or common system disks, can process all disks accessible by that node, including system disks.

Goal 7: Run Without Operator Intervention

Regardless of how much a defragmenter increases system performance, the System Manager has no need or desire for the added problem of figuring out how to run the defragmenter and taking the time to baby-sit it. System Managers need *less* work, not more. Accordingly, one of the primary design goals of DISKEEPER was for it to do its job with little or no intervention by a human operator.

---

85 **installed image:** An executable program that is kept in an "always ready" state. Part of the program is kept in memory and the program image file is kept open so the program can be started faster than it could be otherwise.

We accomplished that in our design so well that a System Manager can literally install the software, start it up and just forget about fragmentation (and DISKEEPER) thereafter. DISKEEPER cleans up the existing fragmentation and then prevents it from returning.

I remember calling up one of our customers to see how he liked the product. I was calling specifically to find out how his life had changed now that he had had DISKEEPER on his three VAXes for six months. I was particularly interested in this fellow because he was the System Manager for a Computer Aided Design facility that depended so heavily on contiguous files that he had to backup his disks to tape and restore them *every night.* I thought, if anyone would love my product, this would be the guy.

When I asked him about DISKEEPER, he at first didn't know what I was talking about! Then he remembered and burst out laughing. "You know," he said, "I haven't spent even *one evening* in the office since DISKEEPER took over the defragmentation chores." DISKEEPER is so automatic, he had forgotten it was there.

How does DISKEEPER determine when to defragment a disk? It uses a heuristic formula, which means a formula based on feedback from the real world. Each time DISKEEPER defragments a disk, it waits a while and runs again. It compares the two passes and determines whether it had to work harder or not as hard the second time. If it had to work harder the second time, then clearly it waited too long, so it adjusts itself to wait a little less and work a little more often. If it had less work to do the second time, it adjusts itself to wait a little longer between passes. The waiting between passes saves DISKEEPER from incurring unnecessary overhead. This automatic mechanism keeps DISKEEPER running at just the right frequency to keep your disks optimally defragmented all the time with the smallest amount of system overhead.

Special File Handling

Certain file types are processed by DISKEEPER differently from others. These include partial files, multi-header files, multi-volume files, placed files, directory files, INDEXF.SYS, page files and swap files. The differences are explained below.

Partial Files

If a fragmented file cannot be made contiguous, DISKEEPER can make the file less fragmented by partially defragmenting it. It uses the largest free spaces on the disk and moves successive file fragments into these spaces. This feature allows DISKEEPER to process a file even when the file is bigger than the largest free space on the disk. DISKEEPER uses this mechanism to process a file to obtain the minimum number of fragments that can be achieved within free space constraints.

Multi-Header Files

Sometimes file fragmentation can become so bad that all the pointers to the pieces of a badly fragmented file will not fit in a single Files-11 file header. When this occurs, OpenVMS allocates a second file header for the same file and the file becomes known as a *multi-header file*.

When DISKEEPER encounters a multi-header file, it defragments the file segments that are associated with each of the file's headers. Having done that, it cannot accomplish further defragmentation of a multi-header file because it cannot safely consolidate the segments of the file mapped to different file headers. To consolidate two or more file headers would mean having to do multiple I/Os to the disk to complete the header consolidation. DISKEEPER accomplishes all defragmentation using only atomic (uninterruptable, indivisible) operations for critical actions such as updating file headers. This is not possible with a multi-header file.

There are two manual methods by which you can consolidate multi-header files. The file can be copied with either the COPY command or the BACKUP utility. Among the drawbacks of these two approaches are:

- A new version of the file is created and mapped to another file header. This changes the File ID, creation date and other identifying attributes of the file. This could also cause interference with OpenVMS batch and print queues because they reference files by File ID.
- The disk must have enough contiguous free space for an extra copy of the file, at least temporarily.
- Either of these approaches may be very time-consuming, especially for large files.

DISKEEPER includes a Multi-Header Consolidate Utility (MHC). With MHC, the System Manager has a third and better method available for consolidating multiple header files. MHC protects the files from the risks of automatic consolidation in the following ways:

- The temporary situation of blocks multiply allocated to two file headers is very brief, and under the direct observation of the System Manager. Under normal circumstances, it is eliminated as MHC successfully completes consolidation of the file. In the rare instance where MHC is interrupted while this condition exists, the System Manager knows about it and has the means to correct it easily.
- Files that use Access Control Lists (ACLs) are safeguarded. On VMS versions prior to V5.2 such files are not consolidated by MHC, so their contents and controls are never jeopardized.

MHC allows the System Manager to consolidate all eligible multi-header files on a disk, one by one, without the drawbacks of using COPY or BACKUP. This is true because:

- No new version of the file is created. All of the file's identifying attributes, including File ID and creation date, remain unchanged. There is no risk of interference with OpenVMS queues.

- No disk free space is used by this operation, because the data in the file is never copied or relocated by MHC.

- MHC handles each file in a fraction of the time of COPY or BACKUP. This is most noticeable with large files.

- Access Control Lists are not jeopardized.

Multi-Volume Files

DISKEEPER does not process a volume set as a set. Each disk in the volume set is processed separately and defragmented as an individual disk. Files are not relocated from one volume in the set to another.

A single file that spans two or more disk drives in a volume set, however, presents a particularly delicate problem for relocation. Often, the spanning is deliberately planned because of the unusually large size of the file. In this case, relocating the entire file to one disk may actually worsen performance. For this reason, DISKEEPER compresses each component of the multi-volume file separately and retains the component on its original disk volume. In other words, a multi-volume file remains a multi-volume file after processing by DISKEEPER, but the portion of the file on each volume is normally made contiguous.

Placed Files

Placed files are files that are deliberately located at a particular place on the disk by the System Manager. Usually, this is only done in a real time environment where file placement is critical for maximum speed. On an interactive OpenVMS system, placement control is not beneficial and can even worsen performance.

DISKEEPER leaves placed files where they are unless it is told to move them. Its Disk Analysis Utility can be used to list the placed files on your disk, if any exist. Then DISKEEPER can be used to remove the placement control from the files and relocate them as needed.

Directory Files

DISKEEPER moves directory files, unless forbidden by an override. As with any other files, directory files are moved only if moving them would improve the arrangement of free space on the disk.

Some people believe that placing directory files near the physical middle of a disk enhances performance. While this is true for some other operating systems, OpenVMS caches directories. If properly tuned, the directory cache hit rate should be at least 90%, meaning that directories are accessed from memory, not from disk. Therefore, the physical location of directory files on the disk is irrelevant for optimizing directory lookup time.

If directory files are not moved, it is more difficult for DISKEEPER to make a large contiguous free space. The free space tends to be broken up by immovable directory files.

INDEXF.SYS

INDEXF.SYS is used by OpenVMS not only for file headers but also as a container file for the OpenVMS home blocks.[86] These blocks are scattered in physically distant locations to maximize the probability that one of them will be intact following a physical failure of the disk. Accordingly, it is neither possible nor desirable to make the INDEXF.SYS file contiguous and DISKEEPER does not do so, nor does any other means of defragmentation, such as backup and restore.[87]

DISKEEPER holds INDEXF.SYS open for the duration of each defragmentation pass.

Page Files and Swap Files

PAGEFILE.SYS and SWAPFILE.SYS are not defragmented when DISKEEPER is run on-line. These two files and their alternates[88] should be created contiguously initially and should remain so.

Alternate page and swap files can be processed by DISKEEPER when they are not installed.[89] When they are installed, DISKEEPER detects them as unprocessable and skips over them, whether they are on the system disk or any other disk.

---

[86] The **home block** contains the disk volume label, protection information about the volume and the location of the INDEXF.SYS file. There are several copies of the home block in addition to the original.

[87] It is worth noting that the file INDEXF.SYS is created by the DCL INITIALIZE command with a default size of 16 blocks, then extended a few blocks at a time as needed, even when INDEXF.SYS is created by OpenVMS BACKUP. It is highly likely that these numerous small extensions will cause the file to be badly fragmented, ruining free space consolidation on your disk. I recommend that you initialize your disks using the /HEADERS=*n* qualifier and specifying a value for *n* that is a bit higher than the total number of files you expect to store on that disk. A recent full backup log will tell you how many files are on the disk now.

[88] An **alternate** page file is a second or third file that can be used for paging. Swap files can have alternates as well.

[89] Page and swap files are installed using the OpenVMS SYSGEN utility. See the OpenVMS documentation set for further information.

Note: Fragmentation of PAGEFILE.SYS should not be confused with fragmentation of the record space within that file. This latter form of fragmentation is reported by OpenVMS with the message *PAGEFRAG, pagefile badly fragmented, system continuing.* The condition warned about by this message cannot be resolved by defragmenting the page file, as it indicates that the page file is probably too small. The condition can be temporarily alleviated merely by rebooting the system, which causes the page file to be flushed and reloaded. To correct the condition permanently, it is necessary to extend the page file or create a new one with sufficient space. DISKEEPER can be used effectively to create a contiguous free space large enough for a page file of sufficient size.

The Impact of Moving Files

When DISKEEPER relocates a file on a disk, only the mapping pointers in the file header are changed. The mapping pointers tell OpenVMS where the file is located on the disk. The file ID is not changed; the creation, modification, expiration and backup dates are not changed; and no data in the file is ever changed.

No reserved fields in the file header are used by DISKEEPER. The file in its new location is bit-for-bit the same as before the move. No change is made to the file's allocation, either. Even if excess blocks are allocated to the file, DISKEEPER leaves the allocation the same.

Only with this hands-off approach can you be confident that your data is safe.

What Makes DISKEEPER Unique?

DISKEEPER is rich with features, but lives up to its reputation for being "elegant in its simplicity." By using a simple approach, useful features are incorporated, yet system overhead is kept to a minimum. Nearly twice as many VAXes are defragmented with DISKEEPER than all other defragmenters combined.

DISKEEPER was designed with the basic assumption that the files on a disk are constantly changing. In a typical OpenVMS timesharing environment, new files are being created, and existing files are being accessed, updated, and extended by a large number of diversified users. DISKEEPER was designed to operate under these conditions, without adversely affecting performance of the applications on the system.

DISKEEPER is designed to run as a detached process, alternating between brief periods of defragmenting the disk and long periods of inactivity. It automatically determines the frequency of defragmentation periods, based on the file activity experienced on each disk.

DISKEEPER can keep a reasonably active 456MB RA81 disk, for example, defragmented in just a few minutes of CPU time per day. If it took an hour of CPU time to defragment a disk, that hour might be more than the performance benefits of defragmenting, so the cure would be worse than the disease.

DISKEEPER does not waste valuable system resources by attempting to "optimize" a disk.

DISKEEPER adjusts the level of its own direct I/O to assure that it does not interfere with the I/O requirements of application processes on the system. It typically runs as a detached process at priority 2, so it uses what would otherwise be CPU "idle" time.

DISKEEPER defragments one file at a time, choosing a new location for the file that best defragments disk free space, also. In the course of defragmenting that file, it is never in an unsafe state. The data in the file is accessible from application programs, without risk, at all times.

DISKEEPER has a unique method for checking the integrity of data blocks on a disk. This feature provides the System Manager with an early warning system for detecting potential problems. It does this by indicating to the System Manager the presence of invalid data blocks on a disk. The DISKEEPER validation procedure checks for:

1. Multiply allocated blocks. These are blocks allocated to more than one file at the same time.

2. Blocks that are allocated to a file but appear to be free according to the storage bitmap.

Based on the information it finds in the validation procedure, DISKEEPER decides whether or not to run, and lets the System Manager know exactly where the problem blocks are located and in which files, so that the System Manager can take steps to handle the situation.

DISKEEPER includes an interactive utility for safely consolidating multiple header files on a disk, without risk to file attributes or Access Control List (ACL) data.

DISKEEPER includes a 100% full satisfaction money-back guarantee.

DISKEEPER technical support is available 24 hours a day, 7 days a week.

DISKEEPER is the ultimate answer to your fragmentation problem. From the day you install it, you will never have to concern yourself with fragmentation again.

Unless you already have DISKEEPER installed and running on your OpenVMS disks, fragmentation is costing you time, money and performance every day. If you follow the advice in Appendix B on the cost of fragmentation, you will see that the cost is substantial – certainly more so than the price of DISKEEPER.

System Managers sometimes see clearly the need for and benefits of DISKEEPER, but they have a hard time communicating these effectively to management. It seems like others view this important product as a nice-to-have. If this sounds familiar to you, see Appendix C on justifying the purchase of a defragmenter to management.

Conclusion

In this book, I have explained the ins and outs and the terminology of disks. I have explained fragmentation in considerable detail. I have shown you how to detect fragmentation and explained what is wrong with it. I've shown you what you can do about it and how to get the computer to clean up after itself. I have even included methods for calculating the cost of fragmentation and justifying the cost to management. In short, I have told you just about everything I know about fragmentation and defragmentation.

I have done what I can do. The rest is up to you.

My purpose in doing this has been to educate. I believe that the more you know about fragmentation, about defragmentation and about System Management, the better off you will be.

If I have missed something, if you have any questions, or if you just want to communicate, write to me at:

Executive Software
701 North Brand Boulevard, 6th Floor
P.O Box 29077
Glendale, California 91209-9077

APPENDICES

APPENDIX A

What Is A Computer?

COMPUTER – An electronic machine for making calculations, storing and analyzing information fed into it, and controlling machinery automatically. (*Oxford American Dictionary*)

That, simply stated, is what a computer is.

A computer is capable of feats just so long as one does not make the mistake that it is thinking. It isn't thinking. But it can sure be made to look like something that thinks. In actual fact, the ones doing the thinking are the computer system designer, the programmer and the user.

I should mention that what I mean by "user" is not a typist or someone who simply feeds in data. The user is somebody who knows how to get data into the computer and out of it. He knows that the computer can be *made to do work,* and he is running that computer for blood.

Operating a computer is not operating a calculator. A computer is not something which "eases the work" or "saves time" or "permits staff to do other things." That comes under the heading of wasting a computer. Used right, they can dig up and generate income by the steam shovel-full, and boost efficiency and production to the sky. They are a tool with mammoth capabilities. The state of mind to assume in using a computer is "Now how can I use this thing to enormously increase the production and income of an area?"

What's happened on this planet, obviously, is that they think the computer will think – when it can't – and so they don't do enough thinking for the computer in terms of developing uses for it and putting these into action.

One point should be mentioned which is very valuable: and that is the speed of operation which can be attained using a computer. The computer can contribute enormously to operational speed in its ability to rapidly relay information over long distances, its ability to keep constant and accurate track of thousands of individual data and actions, and its capacity for rapid data collection and evaluation for action.

The datum here is that power is proportional to the speed of particle flow.

This is the real secret behind the prosperity which can arise in connection with a computer operation.

Given good ideas, a good heart, a worthwhile project and the addition of near instantaneous computer particle flow, the power of an organization becomes almost unlimited.

L. RON HUBBARD

APPENDIX B

File Fragmentation Cost Analysis

Fragmentation is a costly affair. Fragmentation can slow a computer down within a week. The speed with which performance degrades is dependent upon the number of users, the type of applications being run and the frequency of adding, changing and deleting files. Typically, a system experiences a noticeable slow-down in performance within the first week of normal operation after a complete backup and restore or other defragmentation. This performance drain averages 10% to 15%.

How much does this performance drain cost? There are no set figures for all sites, obviously, so you have to calculate the cost of fragmentation based on conditions at your own site. The following worksheet is designed to give you a good ballpark estimate of the cost of fragmentation on your system.

The figures I have given in this worksheet are typical, based on normal industry practice. If you know what your figures are and they differ from mine, by all means use yours.

Worksheet

SECTION A: FRAGMENTATION DRAIN ON YOUR SYSTEM

Below is a series of questions designed to gauge the percentage of performance drain on your system due to fragmentation. Please fill out each question, then total the point value for all the questions and fill in the total at the end of this section. From the total you will be able to get a good idea of the degree of performance drain you are experiencing from fragmentation on your system. This will not give you an exact answer. By answering these questions you will get an approximate figure you can use to find out approximately how much fragmentation is costing you, in dollars and cents.

1. If your disks are:	Below 79% full	fill in 1 point
	80-89% full	fill in 4 points
	90-95% full	fill in 7 points
	over 95% full	fill in 10 points______________

2. How much idle time does your system have? To find out, at a peak period of the day, and if on a cluster, on your busiest node, type this command:

$ **MONITOR MODES**

Observe the bottom line of the graph. Which range does it mostly fluctuate in?

75-100%	fill in 1 point
50-75%	fill in 3 points
25-50%	fill in 6 points
0-25%;	fill in 10 points______________

3. What is your split transfer rate (split I/Os)? To find out, at a peak period of the day, and if on a cluster, on your busiest node, type this command:

$ **MONITOR IO**

The fourth line gives you the split transfer rate. Use the figure from the "AVE" column.

0.50 or below	fill in 1 point
0.50 to 2.00	fill in 5 points
2.00 to 10.00	fill in 8 points
over 10.00	fill in 10 points______________

4. Is your computer used primarily for:

a. Furniture	fill in 1 point	
b. Research & Development	fill in 4 points	
c. Real time Data Collection	fill in 7 points	
d. Multi-User Applications	fill in 10 points	______________

5. Types of applications you are running: Please check all that apply. If you check more than one, take the full value of the highest one, then half value for all others.

a. Backup or redundant system	fill in 1 point	______________
b. System used for R&D only	fill in 3 points	______________
c. Running inventory control production control	fill in 4 points	______________
d. Running word processing/text editing/electronic mail	fill in 5 points	______________
e. Running databases that use pre-allocated disk space	fill in 5 points	______________
f. Running CAD/CAM	fill in 7 points	______________
g. Compiling/executing FORTRAN/ Ada/BASIC/Other languages	fill in 7 points	______________
h. Running databases that do not use pre-allocated disk space	fill in 10 points	______________
	TOTAL	______________

6. How many hours per day is your computer being used with users logged in?

a. less than 8	fill in 2 points	
b. 8-12 hours/day	fill in 4 points	
c. 12-16 hours/day	fill in 7 points	
d. 16-24 hours/day	fill in 10 points	______________

7. Is your system part of a computer cluster?

a. No	fill in 1 point	
b. Yes; 2-4 nodes	fill in 4 points	
c. Yes; 5-8 nodes	fill in 7 points	
d. Yes; 9 or more nodes	fill in 10 points	______________

SECTION A: TOTAL:

8. Total of your answers to questions 1-7 above: ___________

If your total is:
- 8-21 your estimated percentage of performance drain is 5%
- 22-36 your estimated percentage of performance drain is 10%
- 37-62 your estimated percentage of performance drain is 15%
- 63-80 your estimated percentage of performance drain is 20%

9. YOUR PERCENTAGE OF PERFORMANCE DRAIN FROM FRAGMENTATION (from table above) __________%

SECTION B: COST OF SYSTEM

1. Cost of computer system ___________

Cost of the computer system, both hardware and software; if you do not know, estimate it as one of the following: $20,000; $50,000; $100,000; $200,000; $500,000; $1,000,000.

2. Payback period

The payback period is the time within which your organization expects the computer system to have paid for itself. Typically this is 15 months, although some use 12 months, 18 months or some other period (if you don't know the payback period used at your site, use 15 months).

Take the length, in months, of the payback period, and use the information below to convert this figure into hours. Fill in the payback period months and number of hours on the lines below.

12 month payback period:
One 8-hour shift = 2,000 hrs, Two 8-hour shifts = 4,000 hrs,
Three 8-hour shifts = 6,000 hrs

15 month payback period:
One 8-hour shift = 2,500 hrs, Two 8-hour shifts = 5,000 hrs,
Three 8-hour shifts = 7,500 hrs

18 month payback period:
One 8-hour shift = 3,000 hrs, Two 8-hour shifts = 6,000 hrs,
Three 8-hour shifts = 9,000 hrs

Payback period months ____________ Total Hours ________________

3. Hourly cost of computer
(Cost from line 1 above divided by total hours in payback period from line 2 above) ___________

4. Weekly cost of computer
(Cost from line 3 above times work hours per week – 40, 80, 120, etc) ___________

5. Monthly cost of computer
(Weekly cost from line 4 above times 4.35) ___________

6. Monthly cost of hardware maintenance and software update service ___________

7. Total monthly cost of computer
(Add lines 5 and 6) ___________

8. Percentage of performance drain due to fragmentation
(percentage from Section A line 9) ___________

9. MONTHLY SYSTEM COSTS LOST DUE TO FRAGMENTATION
(line 7 times line 8 above) ___________

SECTION C: VALUE OF COMPUTER SYSTEM OPERATIONS PERSONNEL LOST DUE TO FRAGMENTATION DRAIN

Computer Operations personnel are paid to make the computer perform. All maintenance, entry, programming and management jobs are wasted if the computer is down and being used as furniture. In such an instance 100% of these salaries would be wasted.

But a computer with 10% of its resources needlessly devoted to retrieving file fragments is wasting 10% of the Computer Operations personnel time and salaries. They cannot produce their service 100% of the time.

Record the approximate weekly salaries of computer system operations personnel (computer operators, system managers, database administrators and so on). If you don't know the weekly salaries, you can use these figures as a rough guide:

System Managers	$800 - 1500	Average: $1150
Programmers	$800 - 1800	Average: $1300
MIS Directors	$1200 - 2000	Average: $1600

1. Weekly salary of person #1 (or hourly rate times hours per week) ___________

2. Weekly salary of person #2 (or hourly rate times hours per week) ___________

3. Weekly salary of person #3 (or hourly rate times hours per week) ___________

4. Weekly salary of person #4 (or hourly rate times hours per week) ___________

5. Weekly salary of person #5 (or hourly rate times hours per week) ___________

6. Weekly salary of person #6 (or hourly rate times hours per week) ___________

7. Weekly salary of person #7 (or hourly rate times hours per week) ___________

8. Weekly salary of person #8 (or hourly rate times hours per week) ___________

(Use more paper if needed for additional personnel)

9. Total weekly salary of all personnel (sum of lines #1 - 8 above) ___________

10. Monthly computer personnel salaries (weekly salaries from line #9 times 4.35) ___________

11. Percentage of performance drain due to fragmentation (percentage from Section A line 9) ___________

12. MONTHLY COMPUTER PERSONNEL SALARY WASTED DUE TO FRAGMENTATION (line 10 above times line 11 above) ___________

SECTION D: VALUE OF USERS LOST DUE TO FRAGMENTATION DRAIN

The computer has users. These users produce something, and this something has a value. Management has already assigned a dollar amount to the minimum value of what they produce – which is their salaries.

If users have to spend time waiting for the computer to perform various functions because it has been slowed down due to fragmentation, then the amount of time, added up, gives one a wasted expense. The users were paid to sit there and wait, whereas they could have been getting more work done. So a computer that is being slowed down 10% due to fragmentation is wasting 10% of the salaries of those working on it who have to wait for it to do their work. Users may not even notice this time after a while because they are used to it. But if the loss were not there, they could be accomplishing 10% more useful work.

Typically, there are two types of users: 1) full time computer users who use the computer all day every day and who depend upon it to do their jobs; and 2) part time computer users, who use the computer occasionally and who get a productivity boost out of using it.

Here are some typical salary ranges and averages to use. If you know your figures and they are different from these, then by all means use your figures.

Clerical workers	$400 - 600	Average: $500
Sales	$600 - 1600	Average: $1100
Management	$600 - 1500	Average: $1050
Research/Scientific	$1000 - 2000	Average: $1500

FULL TIME USERS

	# of Users	Category		Avg. Salary		Total Salaries
1.	___________	Clerical	X	____________	=	_______________
2.	___________	Sales	X	____________	=	_______________
3.	___________	Management	X	____________	=	_______________
4.	___________	Research/Scientific	X	____________	=	_______________

5. Total salaries from full time users _______________

PART TIME USERS

	# of Users	Category		Avg. Salary		Total Salaries
6.	___________	Clerical	X	____________	=	_______________
7.	___________	Sales	X	____________	=	_______________
8.	___________	Research/Scientific	X	____________	=	_______________
9.	___________	Management	X	____________	=	_______________

10. Total salaries from part time users _______________

11. Total part time salaries from line 10 above divided by 4
(to account for only part time use of the computer) ___________

12. Total weekly cost of all users
(sum of line 5 and line 11 above) ___________

13. Monthly cost of all users ___________
(weekly cost from line 12 above, times 4.35)

14. Percentage performance drain due to fragmentation
(percentage from Section A line 9) ___________

15. MONTHLY USER SALARY WASTED DUE TO FRAGMENTATION (multiply line 13 times the percentage from line 14) ___________

SECTION E: TOTAL FRAGMENTATION COSTS

Now add up all the fragmentation-related costs and losses (from the previous sections):

1. MONTHLY SYSTEM COSTS LOST DUE TO FRAGMENTATION (from Section B line 10) ___________

2. MONTHLY COMPUTER PERSONNEL SALARY COSTS WASTED DUE TO FRAGMENTATION (from Section C line 12) ___________

3. MONTHLY USER SALARY LOST DUE TO FRAGMENTATION (from Section D line 15) ___________

4. TOTAL MONTHLY FRAGMENTATION-RELATED COSTS AND LOSSES (sum of lines 1-3 above) THIS IS THE AMOUNT DISKEEPER WILL SAVE YOU MONTHLY, ONCE PURCHASED ___________

5. ANNUAL COST (line 4 above times 12). THIS IS THE AMOUNT DISKEEPER WILL SAVE YOU YEARLY ___________

SECTION F: COST JUSTIFYING DISKEEPER

As you can see, the costs of fragmentation are quite high, even if it is causing only a 5% drain on system performance. Remember, too, these estimates are conservative because without regular defragmentation, the performance drain due to fragmentation is compounded weekly.

Now let's do the final figures to see how fast DISKEEPER will pay for itself at your site.

1. YOUR QUOTE FOR BUYING DISKEEPER on your system. ___________

2. If your quote (line 1) is higher than the monthly cost of fragmentation from Section E line 4, divide line 1 above by the number from Section E line 4. This is the number of months it will take DISKEEPER to pay for itself. ___________

If Section E line 4 (monthly cost of fragmentation) is higher than your quote (from line 1), then DISKEEPER will pay for itself in less than one month, by speeding up system performance, allowing for more useful work to be done, and for better utilization of personnel. In such a case, fragmentation is costing your organization a great deal of money, and buying DISKEEPER now will start saving you money within one month.

APPENDIX C

How To Get a Company to Spend Money for Something You Need and Want

Many System Managers are in the awkward position of having a great deal of responsibility for one of their company's most valuable assets – its information – yet having very little authority to act to preserve that information or care for it, particularly when it comes to purchasing authority. The reason for this is entirely within your control as the System Manager.

Get the idea that there are two hats you wear as System Manager: One is the responsibility for ensuring that the computer system produces the products and services required of it for the company. The other is the responsibility to act in the best interests of the company in all things. The first is the *System Manager* hat and the second is the *staff member* hat. Doing what is best for the system and its users is the System Manager hat. Doing what is best for the company is the staff member hat.

These two hats are usually in sync; what is best for one is best for the other. But there are occasions when the two seem to conflict. Nowhere is this more evident than in purchasing. For example, the CPU is saturated and really needs to be upgraded. Clearly, a bigger CPU is in the best interests of the computer and its users. But how does the (substantial) *cost* of that CPU affect the company's interests?

If the CPU upgrade costs $100,000, you may find considerable resistance to your spending that much money, particularly if your spending authorization limit is $500. No one doubts that you know what is best for the computer and its users. What they are concerned about is that you do not know what is best for the company. Perhaps that $100,000 could be spent much more profitably elsewhere in the company. How would a System Manager know? He knows nothing of profit and loss, return on investment, or tax and balance sheets, right? Wrong. You know all you need to know of these things already. I'll show you.

If you have read Appendices A and B, in this book, and worked through the worksheet in Appendix B, then you already have a clear idea of the terrific value of a computer system to the company. You know that it can enormously increase the production and income of an area. You know that it can be a great burden financially if it is not cared for and managed properly. And, with the data from your Appendix B worksheet, you even have the dollar figures to quantify the importance of the computer system in terms that can be well understood by management: money.

All you need now is a foolproof means of communicating your information to management. To do this, you need to be able to adopt the management viewpoint, the *investment* viewpoint.

Most people understand investing. You put money into a savings account and a year later you can take that money out with a little extra added to it in the form of interest. That interest is the *return* on your investment. It is what comes back to you (returns) at the end of the investment cycle. This is perhaps the simplest way there is to make a profit. The only problem is that the profit is so small.

Most people understand that companies run on profits. When they make a profit they survive. When they don't, they don't. But few people realize that a company, any company, must make a very dramatic return on their investment to survive. Our stock market mentality has people thinking of companies as commodities that are bought and sold like pork bellies. This viewpoint is OK for capitalists, stock brokers and hostile takeover artists, but it is *not* the viewpoint of management. To management, a company is an *income producing machine*. Management has to make a company produce income. If they can do that well, they survive and earn bonuses. If they can't, they are replaced.

For you to communicate with management, you have to be able to adopt their viewpoint. Try it. What do you think management wants to hear from you about your proposed CPU upgrade? They want to know how much *income* it will produce, how much *profit* it will generate, how much *return* they will get on their $100,000 investment.

Now this is really important: Management is not anti-spending. They are not dead set against spending anything at all. Just look at how much your company spends every week; they spend virtually all that they make. The trick is not to avoid spending. The trick is to spend well.

Your job, from your hat as a staff member, is to communicate to management how your proposed $100,000 expenditure is in the best interests of the company because it will result in *more than $100,000* in income. Of course, you also have to show that it will do so quickly.

How quickly? *Very* quickly.

With a savings account, you can put some money into the account one year and take it out the next, with interest. All during that year, your money is right there in the account, safe and sound *and* earning interest. You can get it back any time.

With a business, each week you spend your money. *All of it,* or very nearly. When you spend it, it's gone. It's not there any more. It's not sitting in a "safe" savings account where you can get it back. It has been spent on such things as rent, payroll (*your* pay, for example) and equipment (a CPU upgrade, for example).

So the money the company made that week is gone. Yet the company has to bring in more money the next week to be able to cover the next week's rent, payroll and equipment, and so on, week after week. Where does the next week's income come from? It comes from the paid staff using the purchased equipment in the rented space, who create products or services that are exchanged with customers for income.

Are you with me so far? If not, read over the previous few paragraphs until it is clear.

Here is the heart of managing a company: each week, the production of the staff and equipment has to produce enough to exchange for the income needed to pay the staff, buy the equipment and rent the space, plus a little extra. And it has to do so in time to make the next round of payments. Every week, the company is reinvesting virtually everything it has to raise the money to make it through another week. If your $100,000 expense will derail that plan, you won't get the money. If your $100,000 expense won't derail the plan but might erase all the profits, you probably won't get the money, either. *But,* if your $100,000 expense will bring in $100,000 in income, *plus* a tidy profit, your expense stands a very good chance of getting approved.

The worksheet in Appendix B shows you how to calculate the value of a defragmenter to your company. Collect up the data you need to fill out the worksheet, do the calculations, and then write a memo to accompany your purchase request. Lay out the memo in three sections:[90]

First Section: The exact situation your purchase is intended to handle. The situation, in this case, is the horrid expense fragmentation is incurring for the company. (To you, it's a performance problem; to management, it's an expense. Get the idea?)

Second Section: All the data needed to demonstrate the truth of your assertions about this horrid expense, and to support your proposal that purchasing a defragmenter will resolve the whole matter *and* pay for itself *and* bring in a tidy profit to boot. Hint: If the data is lengthy, put it in attachments, keeping the cover memo to one or two pages.

Third Section: The solution, which should be entirely self-evident at this point, which is to approve your purchase.

Do this, and you will get your truly needful purchases approved every time.

---

[90] The idea for this memo layout is taken from the essay *Completed Staff Work (CSW) – How to Get Approval of Actions and Projects,* by L. Ron Hubbard.

GLOSSARY OF TERMS

Access: To store on and retrieve data from a *disk* or other *peripheral device*. The term *access* is used as a verb in the *computer* world, and it means to retrieve a *file* or part of a file from *disk* so that the data (in the file) can be looked at, modified, and so on. Users access files constantly.

Access Control List (ACL): In *OpenVMS*, a list that defines the kinds of *access* to be granted or denied to users of *objects* such as *files*, *devices* and *mailboxes*. Each access control list consists of one or more entries known as "access control list entries."

Address: The location on *disk* or in *memory* where information is stored. Just as addresses are used to distinguish houses on a street, the *computer* uses addresses to distinguish the exact locations of all the pieces of information stored either in memory or on the disk.

Allocate: To reserve a resource such as *memory* or *disk*.

Allocated: Reserved for use. Before data can be stored on the *disk*, space for the data must be allocated from whatever remains available. One *cluster* is the minimum amount that can be allocated.

Application: A *computer program* which controls the computer system to perform some useful work for the user.

Architecture: The basic design of something, the way in which it is built; e.g., *disk* architecture, software architecture.

Arm: *Disk* heads are mounted on arms that hold the *head*s close to the *platter* surface at precisely the right point to read or write data. There may be one arm for each head, but on multiple-platter disks a single arm may support two heads; one for the platter above the arm and one for the platter below.

Average Access Time: This is not exactly equal to half the sum of the rotational latency plus the seek time, as the rotation and the seek occur at the same time. The average access time, therefore, is somewhat less than half the total.

Bandwidth: The measurement of the transmission capacity of a communication channel, usually a set of wires within a *cable*. The higher the bandwidth, the more information can be transmitted on these wires. The bandwidth is measured in *bits* per second. The more bits (of information) per second that can be transmitted, the better, as this speeds up the flow of communication between *computer*s in a network, for example.

Batch: 1. Group, or collection, of items. 2. A method of scheduling and executing programs in which the programs run with no programmer interaction. (*The Digital Dictionary*)

Binary: *Binary* means "having two and only two possible states" such as *on* or *off, true* or *false,* and so on. Taken from the Latin "bini," meaning two by two and "ary," meaning of, or pertaining to. Therefore, binary describes a numbering system for counting, where only two digits (0 and 1) are used.

Bit: *BI*nary digi*T*. The smallest part of information in a *computer*. Groups of bits make up storage units in the computer. For example, it takes eight bits to make up a *byte*, which is equivalent to one character, whether it be a number, letter, punctuation mark, or even a space. In written communication, bits are represented as zeros and ones.

Bit Map, Bitmap: A *binary* representation (literally, a *map*) in which each *bit* or set of bits corresponds to a particular condition (such as "empty," "not empty") or *object* (such as a type of font or an *image).* A bitmap is a table or series of bits which indicate whether something is, or is not in a certain condition. An example would be a table of ones and zeros, pre-determined to mean "yes" and "no," representing the ratio of girls to boys sitting in a classroom, where "yes" meant "girls," and "no" meant "boys." By looking at the bitmap, you could tell where the girls were sitting in relation to the boys. In the context of *VAX computer*s, a bitmap is located at the beginning of the *disk*, and is a set of bits, one for each *cluster* (of *blocks*) on a disk, indicating whether or not those blocks are available for use.

Block: In *OpenVMS*, a block is a collection of 512 *byte*s. OpenVMS *disk*s are *formatted* into blocks of 512 bytes each. A block is a unit of data storage space on a disk that equals approximately one third of a page of text. A block is 512 *contiguous* bytes of information (or empty disk space), and is the smallest *address*able unit of data that can be transferred in an I/O operation on a *VAX* computer. A block of space on a disk is equivalent to a *page* of space in *memory*.

Boot: Refers to causing the *computer* to start executing instructions. The term comes from *bootstrap*, since bootstraps help you get your boots on, booting the computer helps it get its first instructions.

Boot Image: The *program* that *boot*s the system. The instructions that tell the *computer* how to start itself up. See *boot* and *image*, definition 2.

Bottleneck: A slow down due to too much activity being requested when inadequate facilities for the requests exist. In relation to a *computer* system, this refers to a situation that occurs when many *process*es are slowed down because there are too many *I/O*s waiting to be handled by the disk.

Bucket: A storage structure of 1 to 32 *disk block*s that is used to store and transfer data in *file*s. Unlike a block, a bucket can contain only entire *record*s.

Bug: Programming error occurring in software. The term was coined in the 1940's when a moth was found inside an early computer prototype, shorting its circuits.

Byte: When eight *bit*s are considered together, they are referred to as a *byte*. A single eight-bit byte is the amount of *computer* storage typically used to store a single letter of the alphabet or other symbol of human communication. The word "animal" could thus be stored in six bytes of computer storage.

Cable: The *electronics* in the *disk drive* are connected to circuitry in the *computer* by means of cables, which are no more than wires with a certain type of connector on each end. Often, the individual wires are color-coded for clarity.

Cache: 1. Dramatic performance improvements can be gained by placing a significant amount of *memory* inside the *disk controller*. This *local memory* is called a *cache* and is used to store data recently retrieved from the disk by the *computer*. Then, if the computer should happen to request exactly the same data again, the controller can service the request from the *local* cache at memory speed (*microseconds*) instead of at *disk* speed (*milliseconds*). 2. A very fast memory that can be used in combination with slower, large capacity memories, such as disks.

Cache Hit Rate: The rate at which I/Os are satisfied from the *cache*, rather than from *disk*. Each time an *I/O* is satisfied from the cache, it is referred to as a *hit*.

CD-ROM: *C*ompact *D*isc *R*ead-*O*nly *M*emory. A compact disc format used to hold text, graphics, and high-fidelity stereo sound. As suggested by its name, the end user cannot write data to a CD-ROM, but can only read what is already on the CD.

Chip: A very small component that contains a large amount of electronic circuitry. Chips are the building blocks of a *computer* and perform various functions, such as serving the computer's *memory* or controlling other chips.

Chunk: Due to the way *OpenVMS* disks are structured, disks in a stripeset are divided into "chunks" rather than clusters, chunks consisting (usually) of more blocks than clusters.

Cluster: 1. *Disk block*s are grouped into clusters, which are groups of blocks read and written as a unit. In other words, a cluster is the minimum allocation quantity for a disk. The cluster size, in terms of number of blocks per cluster, can be varied only by reinitializing the disk. 2. See *VAXcluster*.

Common System Disk: A *system disk* is the disk which holds the *operating system* and all the *file*s necessary to start the *computer*. A *common* system disk is the system disk in the *VAXcluster* from which all the other nodes in the *cluster boot*.

Compatibility Mode: Some *VAX*es have the ability to run *PDP-11* programs as if the VAX were a PDP-11 computer running the *RSX-11*M operating system. When operating in this way, the VAX is said to be in *compatibility mode*.

Computer: The simple definition of *computer* is: An electronic machine for making calculations, storing and analyzing information fed into it, and controlling machinery automatically.

Contiguous: Adjacent; placed one after the other.

Controller: Sometimes referred to as an *interface,* or *storage controller.* The controller, which is attached to the computer, decodes instructions from the computer and issues instructions to the *disk drive* to do what the computer has instructed. The controller also receives data and status information from the disk drive, which it passes on to the computer in a form the computer can understand. A single controller may service more than one disk drive. See also *HSC.*

CPU: *C*entral *P*rocessing *U*nit. The computing part of the *computer.* In general use, the term *CPU* implies *memory* as well, since data must be stored in memory in order to be processed.

Cylinder: The tracks at the same radius on each *platter*, taken together, are referred to as a *cylinder.* If you visualized these tracks without any other part of the *disk*, they would form the shape of a hollow cylinder.

Data Structure: A design for the way data is laid out in a file for access by a *program.* Not unlike the concept of basic building blocks, there are several different standard data structure designs which apply to different uses. Word processing documents, spreadsheets and database *file*s are all examples of *data structures.*

DAU: *D*isk *A*nalysis *U*tility. The DAU can provide anything from a quick summary to a very detailed analysis of the condition of a disk. It can be run at any time on any *Digital*-supported disk and it is not necessary to *allocate* the disk, dismount it, or stop users from *access*ing it.

DCU: *D*isk *C*ompression *U*tility. DCU was an *off-line* style defragmenter for *RSX systems.*

DECUS: The *D*igital *E*quipment *C*omputer *U*sers *S*ociety. A world-wide organization of users of *Digital* products, including thousands of System Managers. Provides technical information exchange among its members.

Delete: To remove an item of data from a *file* or to remove a file from the *disk.*

Desktop Workstation: A high-performance, single user microcomputer or minicomputer.

Detached Process: A *process* which runs without further intervention from the user. The user can set it up, and then the process will go ahead and run without the user having to give it any more instructions.

Digital: The preferred name (by Digital) for *Digital Equipment Corporation.* Also known as DEC.

Direct I/O: An *I/O* that goes to *disk* to read or write data without going through a *cache* first.

Directory: A *directory* is "a *file* that briefly catalogs a set of files stored on a *disk* . . . " (*The Digital Dictionary*) From the user's point of view, a directory is a catalog of the names of files that are grouped in a particular way.

Disk: A thin, round plate with a *magnetic* surface coating on which data can be stored by magnetic recording. (*The Digital Dictionary*)

Disk Cartridge: A removable *disk* unit which consists of a case containing a *hard disk* or a *floppy disk.*

Disk Compression: Another word for defragmentation.

Disk Device Designation: In *OpenVMS*, a *disk* is referred to by a unique code consisting of letters and numbers that indicate exactly which disk is meant. In the example *DUA0*, "D" means it is a disk device, "U" indicates the type of disk, "A" indicates that it is the first controller for disks of that type on this computer (the second would be "B", the third "C" and so on), and "1" indicates that it is the second disk drive associated with that controller (the first would be "0").

Disk Drive: The combination of one or more *spindle*s, *arm*s, *head*s, *platter*s and *electronics* into a single physical device for storing and retrieving data is known as a *disk drive.* The term *drive* is often used to refer to the disk drive.

Disk File Structure: The standard form used for arranging *file*s on a *disk.*

Disk I/O Bandwidth: The *bandwidth* is the transmission capacity of a *computer* channel or communications line of any kind. In this case, the *disk I/O bandwidth* refers to the amount of disk I/Os that can be transmitted; i.e., the number of I/Os that can be transferred to and from the disk.

Disk Structure: The way data is organized on a *disk.*

Drive: See *disk drive.*

Driver: The set of instructions used to manipulate a *controller* is known as a *driver.* The driver resides at the lowest levels of a *computer*'s *operating system*, where it can interact directly with the hardware. The driver interprets instruction codes of the *disk* controller into standardized instructions recognizable and usable by the more generalized parts of the computer system, and vice versa. The driver enables an *application program* to issue a generic "get data" instruction, for example, to the disk without having to concern itself with the peculiarities of that particular disk (the number of *tracks*, *platters*, and so on). A single disk driver may service more than one disk controller.

Dump: (Noun) A printable *file* showing the contents of *memory*, *disk* or tape, often occurring in response to an error condition. Often preceded by the word "crash" (as in *crash dump*). Useful for the analysis of what was taking place when a *computer* system crashes, for example. The computer literally "dumps" the data onto paper.

Dump /Header Command: A command used to analyze the contents of a *file header* with the *OpenVMS* Dump Analysis Utility, which, as the name suggests, is a utility used for analyzing *dumps*.

Electronics: Electronic circuitry is required to sense and record the magnetism on the surface of the *platters* and to move the *heads*. This circuitry is commonly referred to as the *electronics* of the *disk*. The electronics communicate data between the *physical disk* and the *computer*.

Electronic "Disk": Another name for "Solid State" or "Semiconductor" *disks*. *Memory chips* (in a separate box) set up to emulate a *hard disk*.

.EXE: A *file* extension commonly used to show that the file is an *executable* file.

Executable: A *program file* in a language which the *computer* can understand that is ready to run. Any commands contained in that file can be executed by the computer. A non-*executable* file is a file that holds data, such as a user data file.

Extent: When *OpenVMS* allocates space on a *disk* for a *file*, it is not always possible to allocate all the needed space *contiguously* on the disk. Sometimes it is necessary to allocate part of a file in one place and the remainder in another. Files have been known to be allocated in dozens and even hundreds of pieces scattered around the disk. Each piece of a file so allocated is called an *extent*.

Extent Cache: A portion of the system's *memory* set aside solely for the use of the *OpenVMS* file allocation mechanism. The extent cache stores the *addresses* of deallocated (i.e. *free*) *block clusters*, making it fast for OpenVMS to find free *disk* space by reusing these same clusters. This saves the *overhead* of scanning the *storage bitmap* of a disk to find free space.

Extent Header: A *header* that contains the additional *map area pointers* of a *file*. A *file header* contains (in addition to other data) map area pointers and it can hold only so many of these. As a file becomes more and more fragmented it has to have more and more map area pointers in order for all the fragments of the file to be located. Therefore, at a certain point an extra file header must be created to hold these, hence the term (*extent* header).

FCP: *F*ile *C*ontrol *P*rimitive. The FCP is the set of instructions that are used to control files.

Field: An area reserved for data. The smallest unit normally manipulated by a database management system. For example, in a personnel *file* the person's age might be one field and their zip code another.

File: Information stored on a *disk* is ordinarily stored in a file. In fact, for any *OpenVMS* disk using the *ODS-2* structure, no information can be retrieved from a disk unless it is contained in a file. A file is "a collection of related *records* treated as a unit and usually referenced by a . . . name." (*The Digital Dictionary*)

File Fragmentation: *File fragmentation* refers to *computer disk* files that are not whole but rather are broken into scattered parts, while *free space fragmentation* means that the empty space on a disk is broken into scattered parts rather than being collected all in one big empty space.

File Header: "A *block* in the *index file* that describes a file on a . . . *disk.* Every file residing on the disk has at least one header, which provides the location of the file's *extents*." (*The Digital Dictionary*). All the information necessary to identify, secure, and *access* a file is contained in the header. The header is NOT stored as part of that file; it is stored, along with all other headers, in a special file on each disk, called *INDEXF.SYS.*

Filespec: *File* Specification. Reference to the location of a file on a *disk*, which includes *disk drive*, *directory* name, filename, and file type (or extension).

Files-11: The name of the *disk structure* used by the *OpenVMS operating system.*

File System: A method of recording, cataloging, and *access*ing *file*s on a *disk.*

Fixed Disk: See *hard disk.*

Floppy Disk: A removable storage medium. It consists of a single, round *disk* of flexible, tape-like material housed in a square envelope or cartridge.

Formatted: The term *formatted* is used to mean that the *disk* has certain marks that trigger reading and writing of data in particular spots, allowing storage and retrieval of data in groups of a particular size. In the case of a *Files-11* disk, the size of the data groups is 512-*byte block*s.

Fragmentation: The word *fragmentation* means "the state of being fragmented." The word *fragment,* means "a detached, isolated or incomplete part." It is derived from the Latin *fragmentum,* which in turn is derived from *frangere,* meaning "break." So *fragmentation* means that something is broken into parts that are detached, isolated or incomplete.

Free: Not *allocated.*

Free Space Fragmentation: The condition in which *free* space on a *disk* is broken up into small pieces or areas and scattered around the disk.

Goes Down: *Computer* industry slang for "stops running."

Hard Disk: A metal *disk* covered with a *magnetic* recording material. It comes in removable and fixed varieties that hold from five to several thousands of *megabytes* of information.

Head: A tiny *magnetic* device capable of reading or writing magnetic *bit*s of information on the *disk* surface. The *platter* spins near the head(s), so that a single *track* of recorded information is continuously passing under the head, available for reading or writing. The head never touches the surface. Rather, it floats on a cushion of air so thin that a human hair or even a particle of cigarette smoke cannot pass between the head and the surface. As foreign particles that small would cause the disk to fail, such disks are sealed in air-tight containers.

Header: See *file header.*

Hit: When an *I/O* request is satisfied from the *cache*, it is referred to as a *hit.*

Home Block: The *block* contained in the *INDEXF.SYS file* on a *disk* or tape that contains information such as what type of disk or tape it is, and establishes the characteristics of that storage medium.

HSC: *H*ierarchical *S*torage *C*ontroller. A *controller* which controls, organizes, and prioritizes the activities of the storage devices connected to the system.

Image: 1. Duplicate information or data copied from one medium to another. 2. A *program file* of which an image (or copy) is made and placed in *memory* to run.

Incremental Backup: Backing up only *file*s that have been changed since the last backup, rather than backing up everything.

Index File: *The Digital Dictionary* defines *index file* as "The file on a . . . *volume* that contains the *access* information for all files on the volume and enables the *operating system* to identify and access the volume." The index file is a catalog of all the files on a particular *disk*. In fact, the *header* of a file resides within the index file. All the information needed to access a file is contained here.

Indexed Files: Indexed *file*s have an index that contains pointers to organized data records elsewhere in the file. In such a file, variable length data records are stored in *buckets* of a certain number of *block*s each.

INDEXF.SYS: This is the name of the *file* which contains the *header*s for all the files on that *disk*. It also contains certain information critical to the system's ability to *access* data on that *disk volume*, like the location of the INDEXF.SYS file itself. *INDEXF* stands for *index file*. The file type, *.SYS*, indicates that this is a system file, reserved for use by the *OpenVMS operating system*. In a *volume set*, there is an INDEXF.SYS file on each disk in the set.

Initialize: The *process* by which the *computer* prepares a *disk* for handling user information. This process erases any information that was on the disk.

I/O (Input/Output): Refers to the transfer of data between the *CPU* and a *peripheral device*, such as a *disk drive*, or a printer. An I/O is a read or write transaction. A user or *application* either needs to read data *from* the disk (*output*) or write data *to* the disk (*input*).

I/O Bound: A condition in which it takes an excessive amount of time to get data in and out of the *computer*, as compared to the time it takes to *process* the data. This condition adversely affects the performance of the computer by slowing it down.

Input/Output (I/O) Request Queue: A *driver* has associated with it a *queue* for holding *I/O* requests. This queue is merely a *data structure* enabling the *computer* to store an I/O request while it carries on with its work without it having to wait for the I/O processing to complete.

Install: To place software in a *computer* and get it up and running.

Installed Image: An *executable program* that is kept in an "always ready" state. Part of the program is kept in *memory* and the *program image file* is kept open in order that the program can be started faster than it could be otherwise.

Intelligent Disk Subsystems: A *disk* subsystem which handles some of the work involved in *access*ing and managing *file*s which would otherwise be done in the *CPU*. An intelligent disk subsystem is created by moving some of these functions (such as determining file placement on the disk) from the software into the disk *controller*.

Interrupt Stack: When an external event must be serviced by the *computer operating system*, an "interrupt" occurs. During this time, all *process*es are temporarily halted, while the operating system works to service the event. Then all the processes resume their operations. During the interruption, process information is stored on the "interrupt stack."

I/O Bottleneck: Refers to a situation that occurs when many *process*es are slowed down because there are too many *I/O*s waiting to be handled by the *disk*.

I/O Routine: A set of instructions that perform tasks related to *I/O*.

I/O Subsystem: See *I/O* and *subsystem*.

I/O Throttling: Refers to the act of evaluating the amount of *CPU* idle time and reducing the number of *I/O*s to the *disk*.

I/O Transfer: The actual carrying out of an *I/O* request.

Kernel Mode: Kernel mode is the deepest operating mode in a *computer* system. So called because it is the central part, or core, of the computer. Device *driver*s operate at this level.

LAVC: *L*ocal *A*rea *V*AX*c*luster. A VAXcluster is a group of *OpenVMS computer* systems which can share *disk*-related resources. The computers also share certain other resources which ease the task of managing users and their system usage.

LBN: *L*ogical *B*lock *N*umber. When the *block*s on a *disk* are considered from a programming point of view, they are viewed as *logical blocks*. The *address* of a logical block on a disk is its Logical Block Number (LBN). LBN 0 (zero) is the first LBN on a disk. Logical blocks correspond one-for-one to *physical blocks*, but the logical block number might not correspond directly to the same physical block numbers.

Local: Directly connected to, as in *local disk* or *local node*.

Local Memory: *Memory* used by a single *CPU*, or *allocated* to one single *program* function.

Logical: In *computer* terms, *logical* means "conceptual." For example, a disk may be given a logical name, such as USERDISK, so that users do not need to know the hardware (or physical) name.

Logical Block Number: See *LBN*.

Machine: A slang term for *computer*.

Magnetic: When something is said to be *magnetic,* it means that it is capable of storing a small amount of magnetism.

Mainframe: A large *computer*.

Map: 1. (Noun) A picture (or list of *address*es) of the location of data or objects. 2. (Verb) To *map* an object (such as a *file*, for example) is to locate it physically on the *disk* by indicating the individual *blocks* in which it is stored. When an *LBN* is mapped to a *PBN*, the *LBN* can be located and any data stored on it can be retrieved.

Megabyte: One million *bytes*.

Memory: The *computer*'s working storage that is physically a collection of chips. All *program* and data *processing* takes place in *memory*. The program instructions are copied into memory from a *disk* or tape. Memory can be viewed as an electronic checker board with each square on the board holding one *byte* of data or instruction.

Memory Chip: A *chip* that holds *programs* and data either temporarily or permanently.

Microsecond: One one-millionth of a second.

Millisecond: One one-thousandth of a second.

Monitor: A high-resolution display screen for output from a *computer*, camera, VCR, etc.

MOVEFILE Primitive: Relocating a *file* on the *disk* for purposes of defragmenting is a multi-step *process*. Doing some of the steps without doing the rest can result in a file that is confused, damaged or even lost. The solution is to isolate *the critical steps that must be all completely done or none done at all* and treat these as a single step. Such a group of steps treated as a unit is called a *primitive*. Beginning with version 5.5 of *OpenVMS*, this operation is called the *MOVEFILE primitive*.

MSCP: *M*ass *S*torage *C*ontrol *P*rotocol. A software program which acts as a *server* to make all locally connected *disks* available to all nodes in the *cluster*.

Multi-Header File: As its name implies, this is a *file* with more than one *header* or, to be more precise, with a header containing so many *retrieval pointers* they won't fit into a single one-*block* header. *OpenVMS*, therefore, *allocates* a second (or third or fourth) block in the *INDEXF.SYS* file to accommodate storage of the extra *retrieval pointers*.

Multiprogramming: The capability of running two or more *programs* at the same time without interference.

Node: A single *computer* in a network or *cluster* of computers.

"(An) n-squared order problem": A problem that squares in difficulty for each increment in size of the problem. For example, a problem of size 2 has a difficulty of 2 x 2 = 4, while a problem of size 3 has a difficulty of 3 x 3 = 9. As the numbers grow large, the difficulty of the problem snowballs. A problem of size 20, though only ten times as large as the 2 problem, has a difficulty of 20 x 20 = 400, or 100 times the difficulty of the 2 problem.

ODS-2: *O*n-*D*isk *S*tructure Level *2*. The second generation *disk file* structure supported by *OpenVMS*.

Off-line: Not connected to or not *install*ed in the *computer*. If a terminal, printer, or other device is physically connected to the computer, but is not turned on or in ready mode, it is still considered off-line.

On-line: 1. A *peripheral device* (terminal, printer, etc.) that is ready to operate. 2. An *on-line computer* system refers to a system with terminals and users.

OpenVMS: An *operating system* used on *VAX* and Alpha AXP *computer* systems. The *VMS* stands for *V*irtual *M*emory *S*ystem. *Open* was added to the original VMS name in 1993 to illustrate the fact that VMS now runs on more that one type of computer.

OpenVMS Home Block: A *block* in the *index file* on a *disk* that contains information about the *disk* as a whole.

Operating System: A collection of *program*s that controls the execution of *computer programs* and performs system functions. It is the software which organizes a *CPU* and *peripheral devices* into an active unit for the development and execution of programs.

Overhead: Amount of *process*ing time used by *system software*, such as the *operating system*, or database manager.

Override: (Noun) One action which is set up to override (i.e. change, or prevent from occurring) another action.

Page: 1. (Noun) In *OpenVMS*, one page is 512 *byte*s, the same size as a *block*. In other systems, a page may be more or less than 512 *byte*s. A page is to *memory* as a block is to *disk*. 2. (Verb) The *process* of putting a page of memory on disk. See *pagefile*.

Page file, Pagefile: An area of a *disk* that is set aside to hold information intended to reside in the *computer*'s *memory*. The information can be brought into memory from this *file*, a few pages at a time, for use whenever needed. This mechanism requires a much smaller amount of physical memory than would be required if the entire program were to be loaded into memory at once.

PAGEFILE.SYS: The name of the *pagefile*. The extension *.SYS* indicates that this is a *system file*.

PBN: *P*hysical *B*lock *N*umber. The actual arrangement of information on the surface of a *disk platter* is referred to as a *physical block*. The physical *block* number (PBN) is an address used for identifying a particular block on the surface of the disk.

PDP-8: *P*rogrammable *D*ata *P*rocessor-*8*. A 12-*bit computer* preceding the *PDP-11*. The PDP-8 is widely regarded as the first minicomputer, which, at that time, was simply defined as a computer which cost less than $100,000. Considering inflation, the cost of such a computer would be closer to $1 million today.

PDP-11: *P*rogrammable *D*ata *P*rocessor-*11*. A 16-*bit computer* on which the *VAX* was based. The PDP-11 introduced *virtual memory* to the *Digital* world, although early versions of the PDP-11 lacked this capability.

Peripheral device: Any hardware device connected to a *computer*, such as a terminal, printer, *disk drive* etc.

Physical Block: The actual arrangement of information on the surface of a *disk platter* is referred to as a *physical block*. The physical *block* number (*PBN*) is an address used for identifying a particular block on the surface of the disk.

Physical Disk: The actual, real, touchable *disk*.

Platter: A *disk* may consist of one or more platters, each of which may be recorded on both sides. The platter spins like a phonograph record on a turntable.

Primitive: Relocating a *file* on the *disk* for purpose of defragmenting is a multi-step *process*. Doing some of the steps without doing the rest can result in a file that is confused, damaged or even lost. The solution is to isolate *the critical steps that must be all completely done or none done at all* and treat these as a single step. Such a group of steps treated as a unit is called a *primitive*.

Process: 1. (Verb) To manipulate data in the *computer*, regardless of what is being done, is referred to as *processing*. It could refer to updating data in a *file*, or displaying the data on the terminal screen. 2. (Noun) One individual complete manipulation of data, such as updating data in a file, logging on, etc. is referred to as a *process*.

Program: A collection of instructions that tell the computer what to do. Synonymous with "software."

Program Image File: See *image file*.

QIO: *Q*ueue *I*nput *O*utput. The *OpenVMS operating system* contains a mechanism for queuing (inserting) an *I/O request* to the *queue* of a *driver*. This mechanism is called the *$QIO system service*. The dollar sign indicates that this abbreviation is *Digital*'s. *QIO* stands for "Queue Input Output," where *queue* is used as a verb.

QIO Operation: A single act of *queuing* the *I/O requests*.

Queue: A sequence of items waiting for service, like people in line at the checkout counter in a store.

Quorum: A quorum *disk* is one which substitutes for a *VAX*, acting as a *node* in a *VAXcluster*.

RAM: *R*andom *A*ccess *M*emory. The *computer*'s primary working memory in which *program* instructions and data are stored so that they are accessible directly to the central processing unit *(CPU)*.

RA81 Disk: A type (or model) of *disk* made by *Digital*.

Random: In a random *access* or direct access *file*, every *record* is the same size. Because of this, records can be *delete*d and replaced with new ones easily. An example of a direct access file is a bookshelf full of books. You can go directly to any book desired and withdraw it from the shelf. *Fragmentation* of the contents of such a file causes virtually no performance problems, as the file is designed to be accessed in random order and any new *record* is guaranteed to fit precisely within any *free* space in the file.

Realtime: Immediate response. Processing time that corresponds to the real world. Realtime video transmission produces a live broadcast.

Reboot: To reload the *operating system* and restart the *computer*.

Record: A collection of related data items treated as a unit. A record contains one or more *field*s. (*The Digital Dictionary*)

Removable Disk: A type of *disk* that is inserted into a *disk drive* for reading and writing and removed when not in use. *Floppy disks* and *disk cartridges* are examples of removable disks.

Reserved Field: A *field* which is reserved by *Digital* for possible future development. A segment of a data *record* that is set aside for special functions and cannot be used for anything else.

Retrieval Pointers: Sometimes referred to as *Map Area Retrieval Pointers*, or *Map Pointers*. Within the *file header*, the information critical to a discussion of file *fragmentation* is the section headed *Retrieval Pointers*. These pointers indicate where the file's data is located on the *disk*. Each pointer consists of the *LBN* of the first data *block* and a count of how many successive *contiguous* blocks contain data for that file.

Revectored: *Revectored* means that the *LBN* assigned to that *physical block* is reassigned to some other physical block. This revectoring can also be done on the fly while your *disk* is in use. The new *block* after revectoring might be on the same *track* and physically close to the original, but then again it might not.

RISC: *R*educed *I*nstruction *S*et *C*omputer. By using simple sets of instructions, processing speed can be increased considerably. Digital's Alpha AXP computer uses RISC technology, as do other computers.

RK05: The RK05 *disk*, an older model disk, which held 2½ *megabytes* (5,000 blocks).

RMS: *Record M*anagement *S*ervices. The *VAX file* management system.

Rotational Latency: As a *disk platter* spins around the *spindle*, the *block*s in a single *track* of recorded data are brought near a disk *head.* The head can only read or write a block when that block is immediately under the head. Accordingly, the time to *access* a block of data on the disk varies. It is much quicker to access a block that is currently or about to be under the head than it is to access a block that has recently passed under the head and is moving away. The block that has just passed under the head has to wait nearly a full rotation of the disk for another access opportunity. This delay is known as *rotational latency.*

RPM*:* *R*evolutions *P*er *M*inute.

RQDXn Disk Controller: A type of *controller.*

RSX-11: *R*esource *S*haring e*X*ecutive-11. An *operating system* used with *PDP-11 computer*s which allowed several users to share the computer simultaneously.

RT-11: *R*eal *T*ime-11. An *operating system* used with *PDP-11 computer*s.

RZ23: A model of *disk drive* made by *Digital.* In size, it is about 2 inches by 4 inches by 6 inches, and it has a storage capacity of 104MB (mega*byte*s).

Saveset*:* A container *file* holding the data saved during a backup operation.

Sectors: The surface of a *disk* is sectioned into parts. This sectioning is not a physical marking on the surface, but rather it is just an idea that the disk is so divided. These sections are called *sectors* or *blocks.* The term *sector* is more common to personal computers and *VAX* and Alpha AXP hardware, while *block* is common *OpenVMS* terminology.

Seek: The movement of a *disk head* from one *track* to another is called a *seek.* The time it takes for a head to seek is one of the most critical factors in determining the speed of a disk.

Seek Ordering: By keeping track of the exact position of the *head*s at all times, the *controller* can determine which one of multiple requests from the *computer* can be serviced in the shortest time. Then, instead of servicing the computer's requests in the order received, the controller can service first the requests for data nearest the heads and then the requests for data farther away. This is called *seek ordering,* which simply means putting the *seek*s in a better order.

Seek Time: The time it takes for a *head* to *seek* is the most critical factor in determining the speed of a *disk.* This is known as the disk's *seek time.*

Semiconductor Disk: See *electronic disk.*

Sequential: In a sequential *file*, every *record* except the first falls immediately after the preceding record. There are no gaps. An example of a sequential file is a music cassette. You cannot get to any selection without searching through the tape. Accordingly, sequential files are not subject to internal *fragmentation.* The situation simply cannot exist.

Server: A specialized part of the *computer* system. It takes over one specific function of the computer to provide better service to the other parts of the system and to the people using it. For example, "Printserver" is a computer in a network that controls one or more printers. It stores the print *image* output from the users of the system and feeds it to the printer one job at a time. See *HSC* and *MSCP.*

Shadow Set: A group of two (or more) identical *disk*s combined so as to be treated by *OpenVMS* as a single disk equal in capacity to only one of the disks in the group. Each time a block is written to the shadow set, the same block is written to all the disks in the set.

SIR: *S*ystem *I*mprovement *R*equest. Each year, *DECUS* surveys its members to determine the things that most need improvement in the *OpenVMS operating system.* This survey is called the System Improvement Request (SIR) ballot.

Spindle: A *disk platter* is attached to a spindle around which it rotates like a wheel on the axle of a car. The spindle is at the exact center of the platter. The *arm* moves the *head* from the outer edge of the platter toward the spindle at the center and back out again.

Split Transfer, or Split I/Os: This refers to how many times the *VAX* is having to do two or more *I/O* transfers when one would serve. A split transfer is the result of *fragmentation.*

SPM: *S*oftware *P*erformance *M*onitor. A performance analysis tool from *Digital* Equipment Corporation. SPM provides limited fragmentation analysis capability.

SQUEEZE: Under the *RT-11 operating system*, the solution to the problem of not enough *contiguous free* space to create a *file* was the SQUEEZE command. SQUEEZE compacted the *disk*, rearranging the files so they were all together near the beginning (*LBN* 0) of the disk, leaving all the free space in one large, contiguous area at the end.

Stack: A reserved amount of *memory* used for arithmetic calculations for keeping track of internal operations. Called a *stack* because it handles things in a "first in, last out" sequence, like a stack of papers to be read, or plates to be washed.

Standalone: A single computer that is not part of a *VAXcluster*.

Stand-Alone Backup: A version of the *OpenVMS* BACKUP utility that runs by itself without OpenVMS running on the computer. Used to make backup copies of the *system disk*.

Storage Bitmap: Literally a *map* made up of *bits*, each of which represent an *object* or condition. In the case of a *storage bitmap*, the map would represent which *blocks* or *clusters* are *free*, and which are *allocated*.

Stripeset: Two or more *disks* can be combined into a stripeset. A stripeset is similar to *volume set* in that the full capacity of all the disks in the set is available for data storage, and in that the whole set is treated by *OpenVMS* as a single large disk. The main difference is that, while each *file extent* must reside entirely on a single disk in a volume set, in a stripeset each extent of the file is deliberately spread across multiple disks. One chunk resides on one disk, the next chunk in sequence resides on the next disk, the next chunk on the next disk, and so on, starting over at the first disk when the last disk in the set is reached.

Subdirectory: A directory within a directory. Seven levels of subdirectories are allowed in *OpenVMS*.

Subsystem: In *OpenVMS*, a set of instructions that implement a particular facility in the system such as the *file* subsystem, *batch* subsystem, *I/O* subsystem and so on.

SWAPFILE.SYS: The *file* that contains the data pertaining to files which have been written to *disk* to make extra room in *memory*.

SYS$MANAGER:*.LOG File: SYS$MANAGER: is a *directory* name. *.LOG refers to all the log *files* in that directory.

System Disk: The *disk* containing the *program images* and main *data structures* for the *OpenVMS operating system*, from which the operating system is loaded into *memory* at *boot* time.

System Root Directory: The top-level *directory* that contains system *files* and *subdirectories*. All files used by the *operating system* are in this directory or subdirectories under it. System root directories are named SYS0, SYS1, SYS2, etc. Those directories are reserved for the *OpenVMS* operating system.

System Software: *Programs* used to control the *computer* and run *application* programs.

Third-Party: Software products made by companies other than *Digital*, but whose products are compatible with Digital's.

32-bit Architecture: A *computer* system with the capability of *processing* 32 *bits* of information simultaneously in each cycle of the computer. Like a 32-lane highway, the path on which data flows through the computer carries 32 bits of data at once.

Throttling: Regulating the flow or speed (of *I/O*s, for example).

Throughput: Speed with which a *computer* processes data.

Track: A single track is one strip of *disk* space beginning at one point on the surface and continuing around in a circle ending at the same point. The tracks are concentric rings, not a spiral like the grooves on a phonograph record. Each surface has many tracks.

VAX: The brand name of a *computer* system made by *Digital* Equipment Corporation of Maynard, Massachusetts. VAX is a high-performance, *multiprogramming computer* system based on a *32-bit architecture*. VAX stands for *V*irtual *A*ddress e*X*tension. (*The Digital Dictionary*) The name indicates the ability of the hardware to give the user a limited amount computer *memory* to work with while simulating much more. See also *Virtual Memory*.

VAXcluster: A group of *OpenVMS computer* systems which can share resources such as *disk* and tape storage.

VMS: *V*irtual *M*emory *S*ystem. See *OpenVMS*.

Virtual Address: The *address* of a location in a conceptual *memory* space that may or may not correspond to a location in the *computer*'s physical memory, but which is translated by the computer in such a way as to make it appear that it does so correspond.

Virtual Memory: In the *OpenVMS operating system*, to give the appearance of having more *memory* than it does, the operating system *software* places some of the user's *program*s and data in peripheral storage (usually on a *disk*). When they are needed, the system "swaps" one or more *block*s of data from the disk with one or more *page*s of data from memory which are not currently in use. This gives the appearance of having much more memory than there is in actuality.

VMB.EXE: The main *boot program* for the *OpenVMS VAX operating system*.

Volume: In *OpenVMS*, the word *volume* refers to a structured (*initialize*d) *disk*. When considering a disk as a *logical* (conceptual) unit of storage, rather than a physical unit of storage, it is referred to as a *volume*.

Volume Retention Dates: Volume retention dates are used by *OpenVMS* to determine when a *file* on the *volume* "expires." When a file is created, its expiration date is set to the current date and time plus the specified maximum retention time. Each time the file is *access*ed, the current time is added to the minimum time. If the sum is greater than the expiration date, the expiration date is recomputed. This allows the System Manager to determine which files are not being used and so might be candidates for archiving.

Volume Set: *OpenVMS* has the capability of treating one or more *physical disk drive*s as one disk. This capability is implemented in software and does not involve any additional *electronics* or cabling. When two or more disks are so combined, the combination is referred to as a *volume set.* A volume set is a group of two or more disks combined so as to be treated by *OpenVMS* as a single disk equal in capacity to the total capacities of all the disks in the set.

VPA: *V*AX *P*erformance *A*dvisor. A performance analysis software tool from *Digital* Equipment Corporation. VPA provides limited *fragmentation* analysis capability.

Window: The term *window,* as it relates to this book, means the set of *retrieval pointers* the system keeps in *memory* to *access* the *file.* If the file is *contiguous*, only one pointer is needed to access the file. A window typically holds seven pointers.

Window Turn: The situation in which *OpenVMS* had to load new *retrieval pointers* from a *file*'s *header* to gain *access* to the desired portion of a file. If the file is *contiguous*, only one pointer is needed to access the file. A *window* typically holds seven pointers, so a file can be fragmented in up to seven pieces and still can be accessed with no further action on the part of the operating system. When there are eight or more pieces, however, one or more pointers have to be flushed out of the window and new pointers loaded to locate the later parts of the file. This is known as a *window turn.* If a file is fragmented into many pieces, window turns can become a major performance *bottleneck.*

Zero Length File: A *file* with no *block*s *allocate*d to it.

INDEX

If the Business Reply Cards have been removed from this book and you would like further information, please contact Executive Software at 800-829-HELP.

Please give any extra Business Reply Cards to associates who can use this information.

DO YOU WANT TO KNOW MORE?

Take this opportunity…

- ❐ to receive any future updates of this book
- ❐ to receive news of other books by Craig Jensen
- ❐ to receive a free copy of the Disk Analysis Utility
- ❐ to receive more information about DISKEEPER®

…by filling out this card*

(please include your phone number).

NAME ______ TITLE ______

COMPANY ______

PHONE ______ FAX ______

ADDRESS ______

CITY ______ STATE ______ ZIP ______

***Or Call Executive Software at 800-829-HELP**

DO YOU WANT TO KNOW MORE?

Take this opportunity…

- ❐ to receive any future updates of this book
- ❐ to receive news of other books by Craig Jensen
- ❐ to receive a free copy of the Disk Analysis Utility
- ❐ to receive more information about DISKEEPER®

…by filling out this card*

(please include your phone number).

NAME ______ TITLE ______

COMPANY ______

PHONE ______ FAX ______

ADDRESS ______

CITY ______ STATE ______ ZIP ______

***Or Call Executive Software at 800-829-HELP**

DO YOU WANT TO KNOW MORE?

Take this opportunity…

- ❐ to receive any future updates of this book
- ❐ to receive news of other books by Craig Jensen
- ❐ to receive a free copy of the Disk Analysis Utility
- ❐ to receive more information about DISKEEPER®

…by filling out this card*

(please include your phone number).

NAME ______ TITLE ______

COMPANY ______

PHONE ______ FAX ______

ADDRESS ______

CITY ______ STATE ______ ZIP ______

***Or Call Executive Software at 800-829-HELP**

NO POSTAGE
NECESSARY
IF MAILED
IN THE
UNITED STATES

BUSINESS REPLY MAIL

FIRST CLASS MAIL PERMIT NO. 25 GLENDALE, CA

POSTAGE WILL BE PAID BY ADDRESSEE

Executive Software

701 North Brand Blvd 6th Floor
Glendale CA 91203-9949

Copyright © 1994 Executive Software International, Inc. All rights reserved. DISKEEPER is a registered trademark of Executive Software, Int., Inc. Alpha AXP is a trademark of Digital Equipment Corporation.

NO POSTAGE
NECESSARY
IF MAILED
IN THE
UNITED STATES

BUSINESS REPLY MAIL

FIRST CLASS MAIL PERMIT NO. 25 GLENDALE, CA

POSTAGE WILL BE PAID BY ADDRESSEE

Executive Software

701 North Brand Blvd 6th Floor
Glendale CA 91203-9949

Copyright © 1994 Executive Software International, Inc. All rights reserved. DISKEEPER is a registered trademark of Executive Software, Int., Inc. Alpha AXP is a trademark of Digital Equipment Corporation.

NO POSTAGE
NECESSARY
IF MAILED
IN THE
UNITED STATES

BUSINESS REPLY MAIL

FIRST CLASS MAIL PERMIT NO. 25 GLENDALE, CA

POSTAGE WILL BE PAID BY ADDRESSEE

Executive Software

701 North Brand Blvd 6th Floor
Glendale CA 91203-9949